D0533044

THE **EASY DAY** WAS **YESTERDAY**

The **extreme** life of an **SAS soldier**

THE EASY DAY WAS
YESTERDAY

The **extreme** life of an **SAS soldier**

Paul Jordan

Cover illustration: Special forces soldiers in forest during patrol. © Teprzem, Dreamstime.com

First published 2012 by Big Sky Publishing Ltd
This edition first published in 2013 by Spellmount Publishing,
an imprint of The History Press

The History Press
The Mill, Brimscombe Port
Stroud, Gloucestershire, GL5 2QG
www.thehistorypress.co.uk

British Library Cataloguing in Publication Data.
A catalogue record for this book is available from the British Library.

ISBN 978 0 7524 9910 9

Typesetting by Think Productions
Cover design by The History Press
Printed in Great Britain

This book is dedicated to all my mates who are no longer with us and will not have the opportunity to take the piss out of me as they read my story.

CONTENTS

INTRODUCTION

This is not just another story about an SAS soldier and how tough they are — that's been done to death and, frankly, they all read the same.

This is a story about a life of struggle and adventure, about looking for the next challenge, about getting out of difficult situations and about making the best of the ordinary hand you're dealt. This is my life story and it's told simply and without exaggeration. This is me. I begin my story with my arrest in India for a simple, honest mistake. I only spent 24 days in that rat-infested toilet, but it was the hardest thing I've ever had to do (and I've been through a fair bit of shit in my time). During my stay in prison I had a lot of time to think about my life, what I'd done, what I'd seen and what I'd been through.

I was an SAS soldier — a warrior, the best of the best. While I was sitting in my cell I reflected on the SAS selection process, how I got there and how bloody tough it was. I thought about my childhood and how my father abandoned the family to a life of poverty and a daily struggle just to make ends meet. I thought about my brother's death when I was 11 and how that had an impact on the direction my life took. I thought about the jungles of Borneo and how hot it was. But it was hotter trying to sleep in the police station on the night I was arrested.

I went through the last war in Iraq with CNN. I prepared the humvee in Kuwait until the crew and I were embedded with an American cavalry unit. I drove through horrendous ambushes in Najaf, caught an artillery barrage in As' Samawah and got hammered on the freeway to Baghdad with a violent, brutal attack that never seemed to end.

INTRODUCTION

In Papua New Guinea I killed a criminal. In the Solomon Islands a rebel tried to kill me. In Rwanda I watched about 4,000 people being butchered in one day.

I wrote most of these stories as diaries and mainly for therapy. I have no experience of writing. This is my story and I've called it 'The Easy Day Was Yesterday'. The title comes from an old warrior who taught me a lot about the profession of soldiering and was responsible for selecting and moulding scores of SAS soldiers. ODC, as he is known, was as hard as nails and a great soldier. At the start of each day's training, ODC would say, 'Men, the easy day was yesterday.' With that, we'd all let out a silent sigh contemplating the tortures that lay ahead of us. I've carried that mantra through life. Those challenges and difficulties I faced in my childhood and as a young soldier set the bar high and, while I've certainly faced some challenges since then, they can't compare with those early years and so have proved far easier to negotiate. This, then, is my story.

1.

BREAKING POINT

July 2008. I am summoned to the Warden's office by a prison guard — the usual nightshift, Ugly Prick, who speaks to me in short grunts. It is late and almost time to be locked back in the cage for the night, so this is not the procedure I have grown used to. I slip on my flip flops and stagger across the prison yard with Ugly Prick in tow, carefully stepping over the piss drains, rubbish pits and where some bloke, clearly suffering from a nasty dose of bronchitis, has spat a horrible green blob into the dirt. In fact, if you look closely, the yard resembles an oyster farm with green, disgusting mounds everywhere — fucking pigs. I look but don't see. The crowd of prisoners parts and stares as I head towards the wooden door that separates the yard from the administration area. A guard stationed at the door pushes me aside and motions for me to get back to my cell. Well, at least that's what I am able to determine from his hand gestures and the sound, 'arrrrrrgggghhhhhyyy'. But another guard steps in and tells me to go to the Warden's office. The first guard decides I need help through the door and gives me a good shove. I want to turn and give the fucker a beating he will never forget. I want to give him one of those savage prison-type beatings you see in the movies where one bloke just keeps on throwing the hits until the other guy's just a bloody pulp. But then if I do that, I'll never get out of here. So I turn and say, 'Thanks for that, mate.' He grunts, spits and walks off. I shuffle past the two prison clerks sitting behind an old table stained with tobacco juice. They wear a look of concern and whisper, 'Mr Paul, there are doctors waiting to see you, be more sicker.'

'Okay, fellas, thanks,' I whisper back.

I enter the Warden's office and he tells me to sit down. The Sub-District Magistrate (my new friend, Bala) is there and he says 'hello' to me in his very proper accent. I sit in the plastic chair and try to control my breathing. The walk to the Warden's office is only 30 metres, but a diet of biscuits and water for 16 days and doing nothing but lying down all day is taking a surprising toll on my fitness. This, combined with the skin infections, ear infection, rat bites and flu, is really slowing me down. If a chance came to escape, I'd have to question whether I still had it in me.

Bala tells me I am going to court tomorrow. I nod. 'If you plead guilty, you will be given maybe a six-month sentence, but the maximum is five years, so maybe it will be more,' continues Bala as my heart skips a few beats. 'So, you must plead not guilty, okay?' I nod in agreement. Then he introduces me to the other two men in the room. These are the court-appointed doctors who start their medical examination of me while I try to pretend to be sicker than I really am. They take my pulse and blood pressure then examine my various ailments. One doctor uses a stethoscope to listen to my heart and, after a minute or so, declares all to be in order.

'That can't be right,' I protest, 'listen again.' I grab the end of the stethoscope and try to jam it into my left atrium. Again, the doctor says I am fine. Bugger, I thought. This isn't going well. Aside from those infections and some weight loss I was okay, but what I didn't know was that Bala had already made it clear to them that I was to be transferred to the hospital tomorrow regardless.

'Is everything okay, Paul? You don't look well tonight,' suggests Bala with a hint of concern. Oh no, I'm fucking great. There's nowhere I'd rather be on a Friday night than this filthy shit hole. Oh, life doesn't get much better than this, I thought.

'I'm not feeling 100 per cent today, Bala, just a bit tired, I think. This has dragged on longer than I ever thought it would.'

'Well, you should go back to your cell and get some rest, you have a big day tomorrow.'

'Thank you,' I said and, after weakly shaking hands with the less than helpful doctors, I leave the office.

When I get back to the prison yard, it's dark and all the other prisoners have been locked in for the night. I can hear their murmuring voices and see them peering through the bars as I wander back through the ambient light towards my cage. I mull over the proceedings with the doctors. Had I done enough to ensure I would be sent to hospital? Were they convinced I was on death's door? I didn't think so. So I pick the only relatively clean piece of ground in the yard — the concrete area immediately surrounding the old water pump where we all wash. I stagger towards this spot and collapse in a heap. It is a beautiful performance, really something to behold. I go down like a sack of shit; not too hard, though, as I don't want to hurt myself after all. The prisoners watching me erupt into screams. In fact, it sounds like every prisoner is watching and screaming. Roughly translated, they are probably yelling, 'That white bastard has gone down!'

Guards come running, as do some prisoners who haven't completed their daily duties and are yet to be locked up. As I lie there with people fussing about, I feel like a big girl. How has this become my life? I'm in prison, for fuck's sake. I'm in prison in the poorest state in India for something utterly ridiculous. I thought I was better than this. Man, I really fucked up. Big time.

2.
BUGGER

The rickshaw ride was massaging my tired bones and calming my overworked brain. Standing up for six days teaching Nepali journalists was good fun, but bloody tiring and I was relieved to have 24 hours off to catch my breath. The training had finished after lunch and we were flying to the new location late the next day. Before Nepal, I'd been doing the same in Japan for a week, so I was really looking forward to a day off when I could just mooch around, catch up on sleep and not talk to anyone.

Ujwal, my Nepali interpreter and general guide for the duration of the training, suggested we get out of the hotel and maybe take a rickshaw ride to look at the Indian border. Ujwal wanted to show me the border and do a little shopping for his wife. Frankly, I couldn't be arsed, and when I found myself still lying on my bed at 3.00 pm, I thought he'd forgotten about the whole idea. The border might have been interesting, but I just wanted to stay where I was and do nothing but catch up on sleep. A few years ago, I was in Lahore, Pakistan, and visited the border with India. There they have a parade on each side of the border where they open and close the border gates with real pomp and ceremony. The enormous soldiers from both countries try to outdo one another with their perfect drill. It's quite a spectacle, draws lots of tourist and they even have tiered seating to allow people to get a better view of the display. But today I really just felt like relaxing and then maybe taking a lazy walk around town after a nap. I went for a decent run the day before but, on the final 200 metres, I managed to pull a muscle in my calf. I had a little bruising and a limp, so I was using this rest time to get my leg up and onto a bag of ice the lads in the kitchen brought for me and, yes, I felt like an old man. Ten minutes later, Ujwal knocked on my door, poked his head around the edge and said, 'Shall we go?'

Ah bugger it, I thought. Perhaps a ride in a rickshaw might be interesting and at least I can say I've seen the Indian border from two different countries.

'Yep, I'll just grab my bag.'

I always carried my pack with me everywhere when travelling overseas, particularly in Nepal. The hotel we were staying in was the best in Biratnagar, but by normal standards it was very ordinary and the lock on the door wasn't the best. So I always carried my valuables and lifesaving kit with me. My rationale was that, if the hotel was destroyed in my absence, I could still survive. So I carried my passport, plane tickets and money. This would ensure I could at least leave the country if everything else was lost. I also carried some bottled water and my camera for happy snaps.

Ujwal managed to secure a couple of rickshaws for the princely sum of about two bucks each, so away we went, with Ujwal and his rickshaw leading the way. We'd only travelled about a kilometre when we left the built-up centre of Biratnagar and travelled through beautiful flat farmland. The paddocks were green and the grass about two feet deep. If they didn't worship cattle this would be great beef country. Not only was there plenty of grass, but there were waterholes every hundred metres or so. The cattle would thrive here; they'd be fat, lazy and happy. The cattle back in Australia have to walk all day for a reasonable feed and then all the way back again for a mouthful of water. This would be like a cattle version of a health spa for Australian cattle.

Water buffalos bathed in the muddy waterholes along the roadsides, farmers tended their rice fields and children played games on the verges. I managed to snap off a couple of shots of the scenery — it was unbelievably peaceful. Ujwal's rickshaw stopped and he took my camera, getting some shots of me travelling along in my tiny, uncomfortable rickshaw. After three or four kilometres we started to move into more civilised areas. The open spaces and farms gave way to sporadic food stalls and houses until the farms were totally gone and we were in a crowded market area. I felt totally relaxed and was enjoying the ride as we wove our way through the crowds of people in the market. I got some good photos for the collection and decided just to chill, forget about work and enjoy my day off. I even managed a quick call to Zac (my youngest son) and told him where I was and that I'd be home in about five days. The markets were alive with smells, colours and sounds — these are the things I love about the subcontinent and they reminded me of the extraordinary markets in Karachi.

Ujwal's rickshaw pulled up, so I directed my driver to pull up next to him. Ujwal was deep in conversation with his driver, so I sat there for a moment enjoying the hustle and bustle of the market. A frenzy of high-pitched chatter filled the air as 20 different people haggled for a better price with 20 different shopkeepers. I loved it and was glad I had got my lazy arse out of bed to have a look at this place. I was just thinking about doing some shopping for the kids when I heard Ujwal stop talking.

'Wow, this is a great place mate, what's the plan?'

'Ahhhhh, we are at the border,' Ujwal replied, his voice tinged with concern.

'Really, where is it?' I asked, looking south for something that would identify the place where the two countries met.

'Behind us,' Ujwal pointed to a boom gate with a raised arm, completely concealed by a massive mango tree.

'What! Are we across the border? Are we in India?' I blurted out in disbelief.

'Yes, the border is just there, we rode through no man's land. I didn't know.'

'Fuck me!' I spat. I got out of the rickshaw and took a pace back towards no man's land and Nepal.

A man yelled at me from a small concrete building about 25 metres away and further across the border into India, so I stopped and looked at him. Then I had second thoughts: nope, screw you buddy, I'm outta here. The noise of the market seemed to fade and die as people paused in the midst of their haggling to watch what was happening. Two policemen stepped into my path. I contemplated running straight through these two fat coppers, but felt that twinge in my calf. Fuck it.

The police directed me towards the angry man who was still yelling at me in Hindi. Again, I thought of running straight through the cops. Each brandished a very old .303 rifle and I was sure that, even if they took aim and fired, I'd still be safe at a distance of 10 metres. But then I reconsidered. I hadn't done anything wrong and, besides, Ujwal was still sitting in his rickshaw and would be caught and the cops would eventually find me in Nepal.

Apparently the Nepalese and Indians are allowed to cross into each other's countries freely, but the same laxity certainly doesn't apply to foreigners. I was probably the first white man ever to sit in this rickshaw, so the drivers would've had no idea that I couldn't cross the border. And where were the border guards and immigration? The seating and parade ground? Where was the fence or formidable barriers to indicate I was entering a different country? That old boom gate behind the tree surely couldn't be it!

I was now more than a little concerned and wanted to kill Ujwal and the rickshaw drivers although, really, this was my fault. I shouldn't have dropped my guard. I should have known exactly where we were. I should have briefed the rickshaw drivers and Ujwal so we all knew exactly what was going to happen this afternoon. I didn't do any of that. I simply placed my destiny in the hands of virtual strangers and that was a mistake and something I would never usually do. I had been complacent and my complacency had led to this trouble. Damn, what an idiot!

'No problems Paul, I'll pay them off and explain it was a mistake, we'll be okay,' said Ujjwal as we walked towards the angry man and what I thought must be the immigration office, with two large police in tow.

As we approached the office I assumed it would be quickly sorted with a few laughs and a 'fine', but I was still filthy for putting myself in this predicament. I mean, we had crossed about five metres into India and hadn't even got as far as the immigration office, so I was sure this wanker just wanted some money. Ujwal and I stepped into this small, dirty concrete building and were directed to two plastic chairs on one side of a tiny, filthy wooden desk. I took the seat next to the wall and Ujwal took the other. Then the angry guy just went off. He yelled all sorts of obscenities at us. He was a tall guy, maybe 185cm, in his late fifties, with thick grey hair combed back over his head. He had a wispy white beard that was well trimmed and obviously suffered from a terrible case of vitiligo that left his face marked with sporadic patches of uneven pigment. He spoke good English and spat words like 'criminal', 'terrorist' and 'spy' at me, all the while continuing to sell himself, and the very sheepish guy next to him, as immigration officers. Then he started on Ujwal, calling him a motherfucker and cunt and seemed poised to launch himself at Ujwal. The smaller, quiet guy next to him said nothing and seemed very embarrassed by everything, even trying to stop the abuse with calming hands. The angry man demanded my passport and, despite having it in my pack, I said I didn't have it on me as I had no intention of coming to India. I thought if I gave it to them I'd never see it again. On hearing the news that I had no passport, he reeled back as though he'd heard something just too offensive to imagine. He frantically rummaged through his bag, fumbling around in search of something. Finally, he produced a recording device, put it in front of me and asked me to say that again.

'Say what?' I asked. Ujwal also started to say that this was ridiculous. The angry man interrupted by calling Ujwal a sisterfucker and telling him to shut the fuck up if he knew what was good for him.

'Mister,' he began, 'am I threatening you?' He didn't wait for my answer. 'You must answer the question, do you have your fucking passport you terrorist cunt?'

'I'm not sure what you mean,' I replied, stalling for time to consider my position.

On hearing this, the angry man entered a new level of rage. His face turned from spotted white and brown to bright red. He started to froth at the corners of his mouth and appeared ready to boil over. Then he let out a high-pitched scream.

'I'M ASKING YOU IF YOU HAVE YOUR PASSPORT YOU FUCKING TERRORIST CUNT! DO YOU HAVE IT OR NOT?'

Ha, interrogation, I thought, is that the best you can do, you ugly old prick? I've been interrogated by much better people than you and managed to survive 72 hours, so good luck trying to break me, you old wanker.

'Sorry, what is it you want?'

3.

INTERROGATION

In 1988, having successfully completed the SAS selection course and the four-week jungle training course, we entered the resistance to interrogation phase. I thought I was prepared for it, but nothing can prepare you for interrogation. We had just arrived back in Perth after the arduous eight-hour flight from North Queensland and were instructed to 'get on the buses and make sure you have a seat to yourself'.

At around 10.00 pm the buses drove into the barracks at Northam and were ambushed by the Counter Terrorist Squadron. I watched as the driver was roughly manhandled from the bus and thrown to the ground. Two men dressed in black and wearing gas masks ran up the aisle of the bus yelling, 'Look down!' and 'Put your hands on your heads!' Anyone who was too slow to comply was belted over the head and persuaded into the required position pretty bloody quickly. I was seated up the back of the bus, so it was a few seconds before they got to me and gave my head a solid slapping for good measure.

Moments before the attack we had been sterilising our gear so we couldn't be identified or linked to certain patrols. Col (a mate of mine from the 1st Battalion) expressed concern about his name written under the epaulettes of his jumper. We agreed that this might be a problem, but then he decided we were all being too serious and commented that they'd probably never find his name. We were expecting this interrogation exercise as the final phase of the patrol course and another test to gain entry to the SAS, so we prepared ourselves as much as we could. This included jamming as much emergency chocolate down our throats as we could take.

The men yelled and screamed in the aisle of the bus. When they told Col to stand up (he was seated in front of me) I thought they were talking to me, so I stood up as well. So Col and I are standing up together, but they only wanted one and it wasn't me just yet, so they punched me in the head and screamed at me to sit down. I didn't need to be told twice, and the unexpected punch all but put me back in my seat anyway. Col was dragged off the bus and then they yelled at me to stand up. I didn't want to make the same mistake again so stayed where I was. This really pissed them off and they grabbed me and forced me to my feet using my hair as a handle. I felt a short jab in my left kidney as additional persuasion to behave. The bus was full of tear gas so I had tears in my eyes, snot ran from my nose and my airway was on fire when they finally dragged my pitiful arse off the bus blindfolded and handcuffed.

They half-marched, half-dragged me, steering me by the scruff of my neck into a building and threw me to the ground. I lay face down with my hands above my head. I thought I was on my own until I heard a guard say, 'Ah, Col.' I allowed myself a little laugh, as did a few others. Col hadn't lasted 10 minutes before they had found his name on his epaulettes. We all copped a solid kick in the guts for laughing.

After about four hours lying face down on the floor, I was hauled to my feet, shoved into a room and forced into a chair. A senior soldier was seated on the other side of the desk. He was very matter of fact and seemed only to want to process me. He asked for my personal details and I gave him the usual name, rank, serial number and date of birth. Okay, that seemed to be acceptable. He then asked for an emergency contact, my next of kin.

'I can't answer that question, Sir.'

'But surely you'd like us to tell a family member where you are?'

'I can't answer that question, Sir.'

'You should feel free to talk to me. I want to do all I can for you and I'd like to tell your mother where you are and that you're okay. So what's her name?'

'I can't answer that question, Sir.'

'Okay, suit yourself. You will be issued with clothing, so remove all your clothes and put them in this bag.'

I got out of my gear and stood naked in front of the desk, suddenly struck by how bloody cold it was.

'Okay, sign here. You are being issued with a shirt and pair of trousers,' he said as he slid the neatly folded garments across his desk.

'I cannot do that, Sir.'

'What can't you do? Sign this form? Surely your army is the same as mine and all items must be accounted for?' he asked incredulously.

'I can't answer that question, Sir.'

'You do realise that I can't let you have these warm clothes if you don't sign the form?'

'I can't answer that question, Sir.'

'So be it. Guard!'

The guard walked through the door. 'Yes, Sir?'

'Take this prisoner away.'

The guard grabbed my elbow and shoved my naked arse outside the room where I was cuffed and a pillowcase forced over my head.

The interrogation continued for three days. Once a day (and at different times to confuse us) we were fed a combination of whitebait, lemon grass and potatoes, all served in boiling hot water. We were marched out in small groups holding onto the shoulders of the person in front. We then had to kneel down and a guard lifted our masks just so we could see what we were eating. We were told that if we looked left or right, the food would be removed. We only had a brief period to eat, so it was a matter of shoving as much food into my mouth as quickly as possible, despite the boiling water. When we were finally released from the interrogation, the roof of my mouth and my tongue were burnt and blistered.

During one interrogation session I just about cracked. It was probably my fourth session and I hadn't signed anything or divulged any information. But this bastard got to me. As I sat there naked wearing only handcuffs, the interrogator sat alongside me and started to rub my nipples with a pencil describing how I could move to his room and keep his bed warm for him at night. Fuck this, I thought. So I grabbed his camouflage shirt by the scruff and pulled him towards me. I released him and tried to punch him with my

Chapter 3

handcuffed hands. I managed to connect, but it was a pretty ordinary hit and he would have barely felt it. So I grabbed him again and he started yelling, 'Lunatic! Lunatic!' Then the walls of the interrogation room erupted as men raced in and grabbed me in a choke hold until I let go. They dragged my naked, sorry arse outside and rushed me back to the holding area. I was only back there for a few minutes enjoying the euphoria of having won that little tussle; I could still hear that fool yelling 'Lunatic! Lunatic!' and I chuckled to myself, enjoying my victory. But the feeling was short-lived and naive. I realised that this was probably the end for me and that the last eight weeks of hell had been for nothing. Then two men grabbed me and dragged me backwards out the door and forced me into the boot of a car. No-one said a word and I was thrown around in the boot for about 10 minutes as the car seemed to drive some distance, but probably only did laps around the camp.

When the car stopped and the boot opened, I could sense the bright lights through the pillowcase over my head. I was dragged from the boot and someone told me that I'd committed a terrible offence punishable by death but, due to the commander's leniency and his dislike for homosexuals, I would only have to walk through the punishment chamber. I sensed that there were a few people around me — maybe six or seven. They put a lasso around my waist and told me to walk. I took very small steps and waited for the kicks and punches to rain down, but only got one kick right in the middle of my back which sent me crashing into a swimming pool. The pool had underwater lights and I could see my pillowcase floating around my head. I tried to surface but struggled to swim while my hands were still cuffed. When I finally managed to break the surface, the wet pillowcase suctioned to my face so I couldn't take a breath and then someone stood on my head to force me under. I sank back down a few feet and again watched the pillowcase floating around my head. I tried to reach up and pull the pillowcase off my head so I could get a breath, but the lasso around my waste pinioned my elbows to my sides. I grabbed the rope and tried to pull it into the water, but I couldn't get a proper grip and my tormentors had a good hold of it. I was hurting now and starting to get a little concerned. I hoped the blokes on the side of the pool weren't having an in-depth discussion and wouldn't forget that there was some loser at the bottom of the pool. This was getting serious. I thought I was fucked and rapidly ran out of air. My lungs started to heave and pulsate and tried to force me to open my mouth and take a breath of water. I opened my mouth and the water sat there just waiting for me. Just when I thought my lungs would win, I was pulled from the water by the lasso.

As I struggled for air beneath the pillowcase, I was dragged to my feet and forced to run. Again the wet pillowcase clung to my face and limited my air supply, so every 10 paces I just ran out of air and fainted. My escorts flapped the opening of my pillowcase until I came around, and then I ran 10 more paces before collapsing again. My feet ached. I'd been wearing boots almost continuously for the past four weeks so my feet were soft, and running blindly on gravel bloody hurt. I'm glad the interrogators didn't ask me any further questions at that time. I guess I would have hung on knowing that this was just an exercise, but I was a wreck. I also realised that fighting an interrogator was foolish and I'd probably be lucky if I passed this process.

Six hours later and I was back in the interrogator's chair. After the swim in the pool I was given a pair of very loose cotton pyjamas bottoms that had no elastic in the waist so I had to hold them up with my handcuffed hands. This interrogator was a woman and introduced herself as Comrade someone or rather. She was very official and barely looked up as the guards pushed me into the room.

'Lance Corporal Jordan, I'm going to ask you some questions and you will answer them.'

She looked up at me expectantly, but I said nothing.

'Is that clear?'

'Jordan, Lance Corporal, 25th of March 19…'

'Yes, yes, yes,' she said, cutting me off from giving the reply required under the Geneva Convention. She studied me for a few minutes while I watched her. She was quite a nice-looking woman and I wondered if that was part of this interrogation session.

Chapter 3

'What are you doing with your hands?' she asked, but didn't wait for my reply. 'Put your hands above your head.'

If I did that, my pants would fall down. So I spread my legs and raised my arms above my head. My spread legs secured my pyjamas.

'Put your feet together,' she ordered, continuing to study me. Damn. I put my feet together and tried to lock my pyjama bottoms by squeezing my legs together. They fell a little, but still concealed my kit.

'Jump up and down.'

I should have told her to get fucked, but this was a test, and I was probably on thin ice given my last effort, so I just did it and that was the end of my pyjamas. They went straight to my ankles. So there I am jumping up and down with all the kit bouncing around. I would also say in my defence that it was very cold this particular evening.

'Stop jumping. Are all Australians built like that?' Again, she didn't wait for answer, but shook her head. 'Right, you were captured at this location. What were you doing there?'

Away we went and I started my usual Geneva Convention reply while periodically being forced to jump up and down with the Comrade watching me. After an hour of this I was marched back to the waiting area and forced to kneel on my board.

My board was my home for the duration of the interrogation phase. It was where I spent my time between sessions. It was about 30 centimetres wide and 150 centimetres long. Under foot I could feel that it was made of two lengths of rough-cut timber nailed to two cross members underneath. I couldn't see the other guys but knew they were in the room with me and were also kneeling. Prior to my arrival in the holding room, the guard tapped the bell twice which meant we had to kneel.

A few hours later I was abruptly dragged from my board and frogmarched outside. I was keen to get outside as identifying the position of the sun in the sky would help me with direction and the time of day. It had been dark when the Comrade got a look at my kit and now the sun was high in the sky. I was forced to walk quickly over the rough road for about three or four minutes before suddenly being ordered to stop, with the added warning, 'Don't move!'

I heard something being shifted; it sounded like a steel lid being opened. Then they grabbed me and pushed me down until I fell into a hole and I heard the steel lid sound again. I was able to spin around and sit in a tight ball, but when I lifted my head, I hit the steel lid. As I raised my eyes, I could see the shadows of my guards looking down at me and the steel grate trapping me in this hole. Then someone called down to me, 'I want the names of the men in your patrol. You would be well advised to give them to me. When you do, I will let you out. Do you understand me?'

'Jordan, Lance Corporal ... ah fuck,' I mumbled as a torrent of water smashed into me. I must have been sitting under a hydrant or something, as the pressure was intense. I dropped my head and took the jet in the back of my neck. I concentrated on each breath, as the pillowcase quickly become drenched, making it difficult to breathe. Then I thought of that boiling hot meal I had a few hours ago and how I had wiped my hands on the pillowcase and it occurred to me that this water would wash away those stains. Bizarre, but this was enough to make me laugh. I thought this situation was pretty hilarious, but my laughing stopped when I noticed that the water was getting pretty bloody high now. The top of the water was touching my chin and I thought they'd have to turn it off soon. I looked up at them as my interrogator yelled, 'Well?' Give me the names, Jordan!'

I couldn't be arsed with the spiel, so I said nothing and the water kept coming. Now it was so high that I had to push my mouth up through the grate to get some air. Every part of me was under water except my pillowcase-covered mouth. I could see the silhouette of the interrogator looking down on me. He was probably yelling, but my ears were under water and the noise of the water jet smashing into my forehead ensured that I couldn't hear a thing. Just as my neck muscles started to protest at the strain, the hydrant was turned off and the water started to subside. The grate was removed and my trusty guards dragged me out so fast I nearly left my pyjama bottoms in the pit.

Eventually, after 72 hours, the same guys who took us hostage rescued us and it was all over. One person had failed this phase, but the rest of us passed and moved onto the next course in the selection

Chapter 3

process. The best thing about the interrogation process was that it set a new benchmark for doing it tough and, for the rest of my time in the SAS, it would remain an unbeatable benchmark. If I could survive the interrogation phase, I could pretty much do anything.

So now this ugly, old, angry prick is going to have to try harder if he thinks I'm going to play his game. Obviously he doesn't know that abuse is the easiest form of interrogation to reject. However, the previous stuff with the SAS was training and the reality was that they weren't going to kill me, although they seemed to want to at the time. But this was real and I needed to get my game head on and get out. I noted the sheepish man to the left of the angry man trying to calm him and wasn't happy when words like 'terrorist' and 'mother fucker' were used and he certainly didn't like it when I was called a 'cunt'.

Again the angry man pushed his recording device in my face and demanded to know if I had my passport on me. I turned my head and ignored him. He yelled something in Hindi and told me I'd committed a terrible criminal offence, and then they left the room to discuss the matter.

'Ujjwal, hide all your money,' I said as I fumbled through my pack to hide my passport and money.

'Paul, maybe we should run for it,' Uhwal suggested with a note of concern in his voice.

'There are too many cops around, mate. If one of us gets caught, we are both done. Besides, we haven't actually done anything wrong.'

Then a local man entered the room. He told Ujwal that this had happened before and he should just pay the immigration officer 500 rupees each and we'd both be released. I knew it. The yelling was designed to force the price up a bit, but I'd pay the 500 rupees and then kick myself in the arse later.

We waited a little while longer and the local came back again and told Ujwal not to make the payment as they were talking about taking us to the police station. The angry man came back into the room and had a photographer with him. He tried to take my photo, but I kept turning my head. The angry man yelled at me to turn and face the camera and, as I turned to refuse, the flash went off and they both retreated outside again. Excellent. Now the prick has a photo of me.

They came back after a few minutes and told us we were going to the police station. When we left the immigration office I again thought of running, but there were a couple of police too close to be certain of success and if they caught me I'd really be in trouble. We were both placed in separate rickshaws and travelled about two kilometres further into India to the police station. They made Ujwal pay for the rickshaws. I noted that the angry man hadn't come with us. The short, sheepish man had come and had been joined by another, stern-looking man who wore an expression of someone who had been insulted and was preparing for revenge.

We pulled up outside an old, dilapidated building. The only thing suggesting its role as a police station was the ancient World War II jeep parked out the front with a blue light bolted to the roof. We were ushered into the Police Station Commander's office where Sub-Inspector Jai Shankar was sitting behind his desk. He looked at me with some amusement as though he couldn't wait to hear the serious crime I'd committed. He was a well-presented man, immaculately dressed as if awaiting a uniform inspection. He had short, well-trimmed hair and a pencil-thin moustache. The sheepish immigration officer outlined very quietly what we'd done and then Ujwal told our side of the story. As Ujwal spoke, the Sub-Inspector glanced at me from time and then, when he was almost finished, the Sub-Inspector's face assumed an expression of disgust. His pencil-thin moustache started to curl with the shape of his upper lip and a light sheen of sweat appeared on his forehead. He turned to the sheepish immigration guy and the other guy with the pissed-off look on his face and let them have it with both barrels. He stood and screamed at them while poking his finger in their chests. They both shrank and, for a minute, I thought the Sub-Inspector was going to start beating them. The look on the face of the pissed-off guy quickly changed into one of pleading: 'Oh God, please don't hit me, master!' I reeled back and nearly fell off my chair wondering what the hell had just happened. 'Ujwal, what's going on?'

'He's yelling at them for bringing you here because now he must follow due process. He's saying that they should have just pushed you back over the border, but now they have caused you too many problems.'

Chapter 3

They both looked like scolded children as they agreed to their mistake. Bit bloody late, you pair of arseholes, I thought.

The Sub-Inspector picked up his vintage desktop dial phone and spoke to the Superintendant of Police (SP) Siddiqui and explained the situation. He told the SP that we were not carrying any illegal substances and had strayed by accident across the border into India. The SP insisted on due process being followed. At the same time, the angry man tried to enter the police station to speak to me, but was told by the local police to bugger off. I later learnt that he wasn't an immigration official after all, but an informer for the SP. Had this bastard not been around, the immigration officer would've taken the 500 rupees and I'd be back in my hotel room by now. Apparently the angry man wanted to see me to ask for money to get me out of this situation. So the prick got me in the shit and then was denied access to get me out of it. In hindsight I should have attempted to control things better and slowed the situation down so I could determine accurately who was who. Instead I tried to be a smart arse — but then there had been nothing to suggest that the guy wasn't an immigration officer.

I sent a text to Sallie Stone, my partner and General Manager of the company I worked for, and told her I'd been detained at Jogbani police station but that everything would probably be okay. She thought I was an idiot and had a chuckle about my stupidity. Fair enough, I deserved to have the piss pulled out of me.

I'd been at the police station now for two hours and was starting to get mildly concerned. I pretended to be sick, hoping this might push things along a little, but it didn't. Ujwal continued to work like a champion trying to get them to see sense, but something was holding the process back. Finally, the Sub-Inspector came to Ujwal and me and said that he was taking us back to my hotel in Nepal to check my passport and Nepali visa, and to confirm with the hotel staff that I really had been conducting journalist training in Nepal and that I actually wasn't a terrorist.

We got into the back of the old jeep parked out the front and headed back to Nepal. I sat in the back with the Sub-Inspector while Ujwal sat in the front with the elderly sergeant driver. Once we were on our way, the Sub-Inspector turned to me and said in a very serious manner, 'Mister, we will first visit the Nepal police out of courtesy, then go to your hotel to check your story. This is normal due process.' I nodded in agreement. He continued, 'When my investigation is complete, you must return with me to the border so I can inform the SP that all is in order, then you can go. Do you understand this requirement?'

'Yes.'

'Do not worry Mister, all will be okay,' he said, smiling at me.

I thought my concern must have been written all over my face, so I relaxed my facial muscles slightly and began a conversation about the police, his rank and his equivalent in Australia. As we crossed the border I asked the Sub-Inspector to show me where the border markers were. He pointed to a raised boom gate jammed up behind a building and a clump of mango trees and said that we were now in no man's land. I told him that the hidden boom gate had been impossible to see from the rickshaw which had approached from the other direction. He agreed.

Just over the border, the Sub-Inspector stopped at the Nepali police station and explained the situation. The Nepali Inspector looked at me as if I was a condemned criminal and agreed to follow us. By the time we arrived at the hotel I had an entourage of about 20 police from two different countries.

At the hotel, the staff went into meltdown at the sight of all these cops. They walked around me quietly and stared more than usual. I raced to my room to pretend to get the passport that I actually had with me. The Sub-Inspector examined my passport thoroughly and then asked for it to be photocopied. The hotel workers were interviewed and confirmed that I'd been living there while working for three days teaching journalists.

Ujwal asked the hotel manager to bring food and drinks for the police because I wasn't confident about the situation and wanted to soften the coppers up a bit by filling their (generally) fat guts with food and drink. Several of my former students arrived to offer support. They were great and all told me not to worry, that it would be sorted.

While all this eating, drinking and in-depth discussion was going on, I was up and down the stairs to my hotel room pretending to be suffering from chronic diarrhoea. While in my room I also took time to update Sallie. It was very early in the morning for Sallie, so I told her it was all sorted and she should get some rest. Ujwal appeared at my hotel room with some former students and said it was time to return to the border.

'I'm not going anywhere, I'm staying here,' I said. 'You guys can go back to the border, but I'm not.'

They all looked concerned and said it would be better for me to go back and show that I'm an honest person, and that if I didn't go back, the Nepali police would have to arrest me. I walked downstairs and the Sub-Inspector could see my reluctance and told me not to worry as all was in order. So back we went. Once again, I informed Sallie of my movements.

At the border, the Sub-Inspector used the phone at the immigration building to contact the SP, but seemed to be having problems getting through. I stood with Ujwal and the Nepali police who had become my number one supporters. They told me not to worry because the SP owed them a favour and they were calling it in. My Nepali journalist friends were putting some weight on the Nepali police, as they owed the journalists a few favours. I was fortunate that I had so many contacts who had contacts and most were calling in favours on my behalf. The Sub-Inspector approached our group and told Ujwal that he couldn't get through to the SP and that we'd have to go to the police station. This was not good news, so I told the Sub-Inspector that I'd wait here with the Nepali police. No, that wasn't happening and I had to go back to the bloody cop shop as well. I delayed and spoke to the Nepali police who said their SP was on the way to assist. But eventually I had to get into the police car and accompany the Sub-Inspector back to the police station.

At the police station we waited and waited. The Nepali Inspector and his boss in Nepal continually harassed the Indian SP to let us go, arguing that it was a minor issue and just a waste of everyone's time. The Sub-Inspector also told the SP that there was nothing in this and he should let me go. At this time I also had about 10 former students with me, and a few Indian journalists whom I'd never met, all trying to assist in some way. I was starting to become concerned, but continued to feel like a real dick. I hated that I had put myself in this position. Periodically I walked into the Sub-Inspector's office to ask when I could go back to my hotel. He'd tell me it would just take a little time; just a little more time.

At about 10.00 pm the Sub-Inspector called me into his office and asked me if I knew the phone number for the Australian High Commission in New Delhi. Oh shit, now this is big. I didn't know the High Commissioner in India but, having previously worked as the security adviser to the Australian High Commission in Islamabad, Pakistan, I did know the number for the High Commissioner there. I wasn't sure if she was still there, but I needed someone to call the Department of Foreign Affairs and Trade (DFAT) in Canberra and tell them that I needed a hand. I managed to get through to the High Commissioner in Pakistan who, despite being at an official function, took my call and agreed to call back very soon. She did and I explained the situation. The High Commissioner was true to her typically professional form. She was precise and direct in her response, agreeing to call the right people in Canberra. I felt bloody embarrassed having to call anyone for help because I'm normally the one being called, and I normally help people in situations like this — or at least teach them how to avoid situations like this. I decided that I might have to attend my own class!

I sent a text to Sallie telling her I was now being officially arrested. Sallie, being totally organised, had the DFAT contact details prepared and rang them straight away. I also sent a text to the Chief Operations Officer from my company, asking if he had any contacts in this part of the world. He wanted to know if this was a serious situation. I said it was now and he agreed to start contacting his network in India and seek their intervention. Five minutes later, I received a call from DFAT and the lady said both the High Commissioner in Pakistan and Sallie had contacted her.

Ten minutes later, a consular official named Craig from the Australian High Commission in India called. His advice, once I explained what had happened, was to try to get out of this as soon as possible, to do what needed to be done to resolve this situation because, in his experience, it could reach a point at which it would have gone too far to be easily resolved.

'Have you been charged yet?' Craig asked.

'Not that I'm aware of, but they've just told me that I will go to court tomorrow in Araria,' I replied.

'Okay, we will try to help with legal representation. Have you signed anything yet?'

'No, and I won't be at this stage, but could you send a letter to the Superintendent of Police in Bihar explaining that I am an Australian citizen and I have your support?'

I gave Craig the number for the SP and the Jogbani police station. Craig advised me, 'You need to be aware that the Australian Government will not interfere with the legal processes of any country, despite how ludicrous the situation or charge might be. All the government can do is see that you receive legal representation, let the local authorities know we are interested in this matter, and ensure you are treated fairly. This means that you must be treated no worse than any other person arrested.'

'That's great,' I said. It was nice to know I had the support of the Australian government when I needed it, I thought. 'Whatever you can do, Craig, will be appreciated.'

It was now well after 10.00 pm and my Nepali journalist friends and police had to leave so that they could get their vehicle back across the border. They promised to return in the morning. They told me that I would be fronting the court in the morning at Araria, some 90 minutes' drive south. Naively, I asked what time I'd be in court, as I still thought I'd be able to make the flight to the next training venue at 1.00 pm. 'You will be in court around 10.00 and we will leave here at 8.30,' the Nepali police inspector told me. They left, promising to return in the morning to accompany me to court.

Ujjwal remained behind with another Nepali journalist to keep me company. I told them it wasn't necessary and that they should go to the hotel and get a good night's sleep, but they insisted. We sat around some more in front of the police station with a few coppers hovering about. I entertained the idea of escaping, but knew that it would be useless. I had no doubt that I could make it back to my hotel, but what then? The Nepali police, despite their support for me, would be left with no choice but to arrest me and return me to India. Then I'd really be in the shit. I still believed that this was a joke and surely someone of authority would step in, slap a few heads, and order my release and return to Nepal.

It was now 11.00 pm. It was beyond hot and very humid. I was exhausted and in desperate need of sleep. We were invited by the Sub-Inspector to dine at his house, but I needed a curry meal right now like a needed a solid kick in the balls. Despite this, with Ujwal and the other guy in tow, I wandered over to the Sub-Inspector's house and we sat on stools in a courtyard. Under instructions, a boy ran away and prepared food. We just sat there in silence. The Sub-Inspector had changed into a very long shirt (like a Pakistani shalwar kameez), but I sat there in the clothes I'd worn all day and sweated some more. The food arrived but, due to a power blackout, I couldn't see what it was, so I ate very little. The boy handed around glasses of water and, while I gratefully accepted it, there was no way I was going to drink it. Then the Sub-Inspector finally spoke.

'Don't worry, mister, you will be okay, I will not lock you in the cells tonight. Instead, I will supply you with a bed. Don't worry, you will be comfortable,' he said, trying his best to be reassuring.

'Thank you, Inspector, but with all due respect, you have been telling me not to worry since we first met. You told me in the car that it would be okay. The Nepali police have been telling me that it would be okay and my Nepalese friends have been saying the same, yet I'm still here and all because I mistakenly wandered a few metres across the border. So, I *am* worried, Sir, very worried.'

At midnight we were led back to the police station and to the Sub-Inspector's office. This was where we were going to sleep and a sheet was laid out on the floor as a bed. No pillows were supplied, but they did turn on the fan so that, when the power finally returned, we might have a breeze. It was still unbelievably hot and sticky. Ujwal and the other guy made themselves comfortable on the floor and seemed to fall asleep within minutes. I lay down but, despite being beyond shattered, I couldn't sleep. My mind was racing with concern tinged with a level of embarrassment for having allowed myself to fall into this situation. The process of reliving the day started, as did the continual self-inflicted kicks in the arse. The insects started to bite and that momentarily took my mind off my situation, but only momentarily. Damn, it was hot. I felt as if I was on patrol in the jungle. When you're wearing all your kit for a 14-day patrol and you first walk into the jungle, the humidity and heat under the canopy is horrendous — it's like walking into a wall of heat and humidity. Your sweat glands hardly get time to open as the sweat rushes out to fight off the assaulting furnace. The sweat comes so fast it actually hurts as the sweat pores are forced open and some people contract prickly heat — a rash on the skin caused by swollen sweat glands. In minutes you're soaked through with sweat and you spend the rest of the day fighting to replace the lost fluid.

4.
STANDBY PATROL

In the SAS, one of the squadrons maintains a standby patrol to respond at a moment's notice to any global or domestic threats involving Australians or Australian interests. A few years ago, I was fortunate enough to be the Squadron Standby Patrol Commander. We'd just returned from a two-week troop exercise to the Nullarbor Plain and were cleaning weapons behind the Q store when my Troop Commander approached me. 'Are you the Standby Patrol Commander?'

'Yes,' I replied, picturing myself doing a night parachute jump into some shit hole in the middle of nowhere as part of some bullshit exercise.

'The OC [Officer Commanding] wants to see you.'

The OC was a pretty good bloke, known as a bit of a micro-manager, but one of the smartest men I knew and I thought he was a bloody good boss. I'd known the OC for nine years; we'd done our selection the same year and had developed a pretty good working relationship.

Straight away the other blokes started suggesting an overseas trip and calling me a lucky bastard. Overseas trips were few and far between, so everyone was keen to get on whatever was going. I made my way back through the Q store, walked up the stairs and headed down the hallway to the OC's office. It was getting too close to the end of the year to be carried away with this warry stuff.

The blokes were right. The OC told me that my patrol was being deployed to an Asian country on an exercise with an Asian Special Forces unit. I'd heard some terrible stories about these exercises, but an overseas trip is an overseas trip, so I was prepared to make the most of it.

The squadron had deployed a patrol a few months before to Rwanda as part of the United Nations Assistance Mission, so everyone was pissed off that they had missed out on that and we'd heard that only patrol medics would be going on the next trip. While I was a trained patrol medic, my job was now patrol commanding, leaving the patrol medic work to the newer blokes. So, for now, this trip was as good as it was going to get for me.

It was Thursday and we were leaving on Tuesday morning. So I got together with my 2IC (second-in-command) Tony. Tony was a good soldier and mate; we had both come from the 1st Battalion and had completed the SAS selection course together. We put our heads together and finalised all the logistics associated with sending a patrol overseas for three weeks. I warned out the rest of the patrol who were more excited about flying business class than anything else.

My scout was John, who was also the patrol linguist. John had been a mechanic before completing the selection course and transferring to the Infantry Corps. In fact, John was one the few blokes to have successfully completed the selection course twice. The first time, he had indicated that he wanted to remain a mechanic and was marked accordingly. Then he decided he wanted to join one of the squadrons as a trooper, so he was forced to do the selection course again. Despite getting a fair bit of shit hung on him for being a loser, it was a real credit to him and the fact that he had successfully completed a bloody tough course *twice* showed just how determined he was. Most soldiers are unable to do it once. John was a bushy and had a real Paul Hogan Aussie accent. He wasn't a big bloke — maybe 5 feet 10 inches (177 centimetres) — but he was strong and spent a lot of time in the gym building muscle. Despite being under 30, he had more lines on his face than a topographical map of the Grand Canyon. Now he was learning the skills of being a scout.

Stuart was the signaller. He was the tallest bloke in the patrol, so I should have made him the scout so he could clear all the cobwebs for me. As the sig, Stuart had the most important job in the patrol — a sig who can't get comms is useless, and if the patrol can't communicate with Squadron Headquarters, then it's a wasted asset and of no use to anyone. So Stuart carried the radio and most of the spare batteries and had the heaviest load. Despite this, he could walk faster and for longer under load than anyone I knew. Stuart was new to the Regiment as was Cleave the patrol medic.

Cleve was part North American Indian and a real chick magnet. On the training we'd just completed in Kalgoorlie we managed to get a night off and had a few beers in the local pub. A group of young ladies walked in and, within five minutes, they were all gathered around Cleve making cow eyes at him. It was an amazing phenomenon to watch and damned painful for the single blokes in the troop. To try to keep Cleve's ego in check, the rest of the blokes gave him the nickname 'dances with pigs'. But the reality was that he was dancing with Vogue models. Cleve had not long before completed the patrol medic's course, so was still adapting all that knowledge to the requirements of the patrol.

Everything went smoothly, with most of the pre-deployment work completed by the Regimental Headquarters before we knew anything about the deployment. We packed a trunk which contained the patrol radio, two hand-held emergency radios, spare radio batteries, spare weapon-cleaning material, a primary and secondary weapon each and any spare equipment required to make our limited stay in their barracks a bit easier. We sent the trunk to Perth airport one day in advance so it could be sent as cargo.

We caught a direct flight from Perth to a dry (non-alcoholic) country. The flight was smooth (except for Cleve getting stuck with a big fat woman who chewed his ear off the whole way) and a Special Forces Warrant Officer met us on arrival. He was a great bloke and we ended up spending a lot of social time with him. We collected our kit and waited for our trunk to arrive, but for some reason they had put it on another plane and it wasn't going to arrive until the next day, so we boarded a small van and headed towards the barracks.

We decided we were bloody hungry after the flight, so I asked the Warrant Officer if we could stop for something to eat.
'Huh?' he answered, looking as if I was now speaking Swedish.
'Food — we're hungry.'
'Ahhhh … huh,' he replied, with a look of confusion.

Damn, how hard can this be? So I started using hand gestures and pretending to spoon food into my mouth. Again he shrugged his shoulders like I was trying to explain Pythagoras theory to a preschool kid. Alright, time to get John, our linguist, involved.

'Hey, John, come and ask the Warrant Officer if we can stop for a feed somewhere.'

'Okay.'

He turned to the Warrant Officer.

'Sir, can we stop for something to eat?' asked John in fucking English.

'Oh, food! Okay, no problem,' replied the Warrant Officer in bloody English. John leant back and looked at me as if the two of them had just had some deep conversation in the local language and said, 'He said he'll stop somewhere, no problem.'

'I fucking heard all that. What the hell was that? I thought you were going to speak in the local language.'

John just shrugged.

'Why? He speaks good English.'

Maybe my English was more like Swahili. The rest of the patrol laughed. After that, John was known as 'Mother Tongue'.

The Warrant Officer took us to the yacht club where we had a beautiful steak and about a six-pack of beer each. He surprised us with the beer — he'd bought it on the black market. The cold beers went down really well in this humidity. I think we flew to within two miles of the sun — damn, it was hot and sticky. I could have poured the beer over me.

The Warrant Officer drove us to our accommodation block and, by the time we arrived, it was about 10.00 pm. We were on the third floor and had one big room to accommodate all of us. There were five beds with mattresses and enough bedding to be comfortable. We had a cupboard each for our packs and webbing, and a large refrigerator stocked with milk stood in one corner. Next to the fridge was a table that had a hot water jug, plenty of brew gear and some biscuits to snack on. Along the balcony was the bathroom, but there was no hot water for the showers. The natives considered it a waste given that the temperature was always above 30 degrees. The toilets were just a hole in the floor in the shape of a toilet bowl. Next to the hole were two foot pads so you could line yourself up correctly. All in all, the accommodation was good and we had no complaints.

We spent the next day and a half preparing our kit for 16 days in the jungle with the rest of the Special Forces soldiers in the jungle training camp. We were issued 10 days' rations and, with each ration pack, we were given a bag of rice. We had flares, 300 bullets each, grenades, radios, medical kits, six litres of water, spare clothes, hammocks, hutchies, mosquito nets and mosquito repellent. I always had a particular pair of cams that I liked to wear when out bush — and this was no exception. I laid these cams on my bed and packed the essential lifesaving pieces of equipment into the pockets. Into the pocket on my left sleeve went my camouflage paint compact. Into my left shirt pocket I put my signal mirror and a US Army issue plastic spoon. I tied a can opener to the buttonhole of my pocket. Into my right shirt pocket I put my patrol diary and pen (wrapped in a waterproof wallet to prevent it from deteriorating from the effects of rainwater and sweat) and a pen torch with a red filter. Into my right trouser pocket I put my plastic-covered map, and into my left pocket I put my patrol SOPs (standard operating procedures), some emergency ration chocolate and a 20-round magazine. I placed my compass on top of my shirt. When I get dressed, this will be the first thing to go on. It has a piece of green cord attached to it so I can wear it around my neck. I also had the toe of an army sock threaded over the top of the compass to camouflage it when exposed. All items that could be tied to my pockets were. This prevented things falling out and compromising my patrol's position. My purpose in packing my clothes with all this shit was to be able to survive in a hostile area should I be separated from both my webbing and my pack. Ideally, this should never happen, but I liked to be prepared for anything.

We weren't really sure what we were in for once we got into the jungle, so we decided to pack for a 16-day tactical exercise. I loaded my ten 30-round magazines with 28 bullets, and then placed three magazines into the small pouch, and six into the larger pouch, with one magazine to go on my weapon. Into my right-hand pouch I put a red smoke grenade and a small hand-held patrol radio. I carried a large pouch on the back of my webbing which contained some basic weapon cleaning stuff, a strobe light, a torch with a red filter attached, mosquito repellent, personal medical kit and some emergency food. I threw my webbing on the floor and pushed it under my bed with my foot, noting the great pile of shit that I was supposed to squeeze into my pack.

I carried a US Alice Pack which I'd had modified into two compartments so that I could access my sleeping gear without digging through the top of my pack. I packed this bottom compartment first and put my winter-weight sleeping bag into my bivvy bag (a water-resistant bag that will keep the sleeping bag dry when there's heavy dew and light rain, but not a heavy downpour) and fed it into the sleeping bag compartment. Next to that went my mosquito net, then my hutchie and my hammock. A hammock is an essential piece of equipment in the jungle. It's not something that's used every night, but comes in very handy when the patrol has to sleep on a steep slope, in a swamp or in a non-tactical location for any length of time. I then had to break down the rations we'd been given into three meals a day. Breakfast consisted of a small sachet of meat and vegetables that was designed to be mixed with the small portion of rice I had packed, some biscuits, and some brew gear. Lunch was a quick meal and consisted of chocolate, muesli bars and/or biscuits, and dinner was the same as breakfast except that the sachet of food was bigger. Each meal was packed together in a plastic bag with a rubber band wrapped around it. This meant I only had to remove one package from my pack and then close it again so I was ready to bolt if I had to. Six days' worth of these small parcels of food were packed into the bottom of my pack. On top of the food went my raincoat, a spare set of cams and a pair of socks, both in plastic resealable bags, three water bottles and two spare batteries for the patrol radio. On the outside of my pack I had three pouches in which I put a further four days' worth of food in two pouches and a water bottle in the other pouch.

The rations didn't look too good, so we thought we would fill our bellies at the mess — but this wasn't meant to be. They tried to do their best for us and even gave us a spoon to eat with when everyone else used their right hand — the left was used for something else! For breakfast we feasted on two boiled eggs and a cup of sweet black tea. Lunch was better; we had chicken and some vegetables. We hooked into the chicken only to have chicken blood and juices run over our hands and drip from our elbows. To add to this we had to put up with a constant parade of cats across the table and around our legs. Part of going overseas involves immersion in another culture, and that's what we were doing. We just accepted what was happening and were grateful for everything. Our hosts took us to a fast food stand to have some 'roti with eggs'. This is a nice snack made from about five cups of pure cholesterol and dough that is spread thin and fried on a hot plate. The egg is then thrown on and the dough rolled up. These were 50 cents each and, while the locals had one each, we had four each. Aussie pigs yes, but we were bloody starving.

The Warrant Officer asked if we'd like to go on a hash house harriers run that night. 'Yeah, why not?' He picked us up that afternoon and off we went. We were late, so once we got to the start point we headed off straight away. We ran into the jungle deeper and deeper and it started to get dark. Tony and I became concerned, as did the Warrant Officer, so we headed back to the road. The Warrant Officer had obviously been over this ground before because he knew exactly where the road was. We arrived back at the start point as a few other blokes started to drift in. Once everyone was accounted for we wandered down to the beach to have a few beers. Apparently they had bought a heap of beer on the black market at $80 a carton. We had a few beers as we watched the sun go down over the South China Sea. It was a relaxing atmosphere until a squadron of mosquitoes practically chewed through to my bones. The Warrant Officer was pretty smashed, but nevertheless drove us back to the accommodation block.

On the morning of insertion we got dressed in our PT kit and wandered down to the mess to fight the cats for a feed. We had to be ready to go at 10.00 am so, at about 9.00, we started to prepare. We'd been delaying this because, once the gear goes on, the sweat starts to run; but it couldn't be delayed any longer so we got organised. I slung the compass around my neck then put on my pre-packed cams, then my black explorer socks and jungle boots. I checked around and all the blokes were pretty much ready to go. We had a jerry of water in the room and we all guzzled as much as we could stomach to replace what we were losing at a great rate. We threw all our kit into a rover and were driven to the helipad.

Waiting at the helipad to go into the jungle camp were another six people, eight crates of claymore mines, three crates of ammunition and a crate of explosives. I thought they were bringing in a Black Hawk helicopter to carry all this shit. But no, a Bell 212 (Huey) showed up and in we all squeezed. John pointed out that our hosts had life jackets and that we did not. We all accepted with indifference that we were going to drown.

The Huey finally got airborne after dragging its sorry arse along the ground for 100 metres and flew out over the South China Sea. I reminded the blokes of the helicopter underwater escape training we'd done recently and to dump all their kit before going out through the door. When a helo crashes into the ocean it quickly inverts due to the weight of the engine and rotor on top. Those inside have to wait until it inverts before opening the door or kicking out the window and scrambling out. It can be bloody frightening, especially if you happen to be flying over Bass Strait at night or the South China Sea in an overloaded helo during the day.

We arrived at a military camp some 15 minutes later. One of the officers told me that five people would have to get off the Huey so it could get over the ranges. I told my patrol to get off. Stuart was sitting in the gunner's seat when I told him to get off. As he was getting out, the loadmaster leaned out and, without seeing Stuart trying to get off, started to slam the door shut. Unfortunately, Stuart was only halfway out and had his head slammed in the door. The loady, without looking, obviously felt the door continue to jam, so he just kept slamming it harder into Stuart's head in an attempt to overcome the jam, not realising that Stuart's head was the jam. John and I watched the events unfold and could barely stand up we were laughing so much. It was something out of a three stooges show. Stuart finally got out and came over to us bitching and swearing with some bark missing from his head.

The Huey came back after 30 minutes and we were dropped on top of a little knoll in the middle of the jungle. Our first feeling was having flown even closer to the sun. Shit, it was hot under the jungle canopy. We had to go back and forth and hump all the equipment and ammo from the helipad down to the camp. We thought we were going to pass out — sweat was just pouring off us, but eventually we had all the gear stowed in the jungle camp.

The camp was just a section of jungle alongside a river — nothing spectacular. We were welcomed by an officer and then shown a place to set up our camp. We were next to the corporals' camp alongside a very cold, freshwater jungle stream. Life was very easy for the next 16 days because our hosts were more interested in training their own people than us. That was fine by me and we generally just took it easy, but when it came time to put in a solid effort, the blokes performed extremely well. Generally, the daily routine consisted of reveille about 15 minutes before first light and then standing-to until about 15 minutes after first light. Then we had about an hour to sort out our morning routine which consisted of giving the weapon a clean and oil, eating and drinking, morning ablutions and whatever else was required for the morning. Some units include shaving and boot polishing as a part of this routine — I don't. Shaving in the bush is a waste of water and there's a risk that the razor may cut the skin — cuts in the jungle quickly become infected. On the other hand, the growth of facial hair provides a natural camouflage. Polishing boots is a waste of time and pack space. It's far better to let the boots become the colour of the jungle floor rather than polish them black. After morning routine we joined our hosts for a PT session. This consisted of doing sit-ups, push-ups and a run to the helipad and back. Following a bath in the creek, we started the day's activities.

A day or so later, we were just sitting around when Cleve decided to build a bunk to sleep on and started cutting down trees to use in its construction. Cleve was up on the high ground above the corporals' campsite cutting down a tree. When it finally came down, it wiped out the campsite of our neighbours. Cleve ran around trying to fix up their camp as the rest of us were pissing ourselves laughing. Sure enough, about 10 seconds later, our neighbours returned to find their campsite demolished. Cleve could do nothing but apologise and call us a pack of pricks for not helping him.

Our hosts had some ranges set up in the jungle, one of which was a contact range. The patrol would contact the enemy and, after one bound of breaking contact, we'd put down a claymore mine on a seven-second fuse. Tony would pull the initiator and we'd patrol off. Seven seconds was a lot shorter than we'd used before, so I decided to rehearse with just a detonator. As we broke contact I told Tony to blow the detonator and we patrolled off. We got about three metres from the detonator and off it went. This gave us a good enough guide to the time we had to clear the mine, so we went for it. This time we blew the live claymore and, when I told Tony to pull the initiator, the patrol thought they were trying out for the fucking Olympic 100 metre sprint team. They bolted past me so fast I was lucky to catch them and — wouldn't you know it — we had a blind; the claymore failed to fire. We patrolled around to the rear of the mine to wait the required safety time (30 minutes) before approaching the mine. As we sat and waited, I heard the Captain, who was acting as the safety officer, calling for me. I stood up and called him over. When he approached, he held out the claymore and tried to figure out why it hadn't gone off. I glanced at the patrol who looked as though they'd seen a ghost. Good safety here.

One night we joined the rest of the blokes and practised our claymore ambushing. My patrol knew the drill from plenty of training, and the country was so close I knew I'd never lose sight of my men as they positioned the claymores, so all in all it was to be a very simple ambushing task. Just on dusk we patrolled to the site as a squadron. When we reached the site, patrols were being positioned along a track. We were last and were finally given our location. The Captain pointed to the track and told me where to position my patrol. The distance between the two was about four metres. The patrol gave me a look that said 'sort this shit out', so I told the Captain that we would be moving back a few more metres. Six claymores amount to 4.2 kilograms of plastic explosive, so I wanted to give us a few metres of stand-off behind the mines.

THE EASY DAY WAS YESTERDAY

We had the ambush set up in about nine minutes. The six claymores were joined using detonation cord and could be fired from a central location using one firing device. We only had to wait about one hour when the first ambush went off, then another and so on until we blew ours. Even sitting eight metres back from the claymores and behind our packs we still had a fair load of shit thrown at us. We dusted ourselves off and headed back to our camp.

Over the next few days the rest of the blokes went on with some booby trap training. They asked me if my patrol knew anything about making booby traps. I said they did, so they gave me a heap of explosives to do my own training. We played around a bit with booby-trapping, but still had a heap of explosives left over, so John went fishing in our little creek. When our neighbours came back to the camp at the end of the day, John had about 50 little fish for them. They were rapt and hurriedly cooked them. They tasted all right, but had heaps of bones. Our neighbours had caught a big frog that day and also cooked that up. They boiled it with three rocks from the creek and a piece of fungus selected from a tree. It turned out to be beautiful and the soup was good, very similar to chicken soup.

On our last day in the camp we packed up and prepared for a 45-kilometre walk to an ambush position that was near a small town. That was 45 kilometres as the crow flies, but in this place, with some of the biggest mountains and thickest jungle in the world, it could become 80 kilometres or more. We had seven days to reach the ambush position, so it would mean a fairly quick pace.

On the night before we left the camp, one of the corporals was being tested on his night attack so we took part as well. It was all live fire, which concerned me a little, but what could we do? We moved to a point about 200 metres from the enemy camp and were told to leave our kit there, and that we would move along another 100 metres and sleep there the night. This meant lying on the ground without a sleeping bag or a hutchie. I knew it would piss down with rain all night, so I told the patrol to grab their bivvy bags and a couple of hutchies between us and to give them to John who had a small pack to carry them in. This we did and, as night fell, I told John to pass out our gear and we got into our bivvy bags.

Chapter 4

About an hour after dark, it pissed down — I mean literally bucketed down. Now a bivvy bag is water resistant to an extent and will keep the dew out, but we were nicely located in a gully and, as I lay down, I found myself in a foot of water. A couple of hutchies went up, but you couldn't move under them because of the other blokes. Basically, it was a bloody miserable night, and in situations such as this you realise how long nights really are. The jungle is hotter than hell during the day, but at night, when you are soaked to the skin, it's bloody cold.

We completed the attack and didn't lose anyone to gunfire and commenced our walk out. We were given a local soldier to go with us to ensure we didn't get into trouble and that we took the correct route. I had already prepared and given orders for the patrol to the ambush site, and told my local man that he would be positioned between Stuart and Cleve. After breakfast, and a final briefing from the Captain, we patrolled off in a rough north-westerly direction with John scouting. I doubled as patrol commander and the second scout about five metres behind him, while Stuart, as signaller, patrolled behind me, then my local man, then Cleve as medic and Tony as the 2IC. Tony also had responsibility for acting as the rear scout. He had to ensure that no-one was tracking us, to protect us from enemy surprise from the rear and to ensure we didn't leave a huge trail behind us. We were patrolling well in primary jungle that followed a north-west ridgeline. The patrolling was easy and we made good time. While we knew there was no enemy, we still patrolled tactically — this was a great opportunity to refresh our jungle patrolling skills.

For a soldier, there is no greater challenge than patrolling, surviving and living effectively in the jungle. Everything wants to bite you, sting you, suck your blood, scratch or kill you. Everything is rotting and that includes you if you're not careful. Contact with the enemy is at a distance of 10 metres, which means if they see you first, it is hard to miss from that range. This also means you can't make a sound because noise travels and will give your position away. It is beyond hot, but worse still is the near 100% humidity. Your clothes are always wet and then they stick to you. Walking up a slight incline is difficult because your wet trousers stick to your leg making it difficult to lift. Night observation posts or ambushes mean lying on the jungle floor all night, usually in a torrential downpour.

After two hours we approached the end of the ridgeline which began to turn to the west, as I knew it would, so I was forced to search for a suitable spur that would take us in the general direction of the ambush site. I signalled John to stop and moved up behind him. John continued to look to his front and I whispered in his ear, 'Stop here for 10; I need to do a nav check.' John nodded in acknowledgment. The rest of the patrol could see we'd stopped and moved up behind. I indicated where I wanted them to be and then we sat. For five minutes we sat still and listened to the noise around us, adapting to our immediate environment. I pulled out my map and identified our position. We were making good time without rushing things, and were 1200 metres from our start point. According to my map, 100 metres up ahead was a spur extending from the ridgeline like a finger pointing towards the north. It seemed to extend for about 1000 metres and was quite high. The higher we stayed in the jungle, the better the patrolling. Down low in the re-entrants, the jungle was secondary and very thick. I got up and moved to Tony first to brief him on the plan. He had nothing to add, so I briefed the rest of the patrol and we moved off after a couple of good mouthfuls of water.

I clicked my tongue against the roof of my mouth and John looked around. I gave him a slight nod of my head and slowly John got to his feet. He inspected the floor of the jungle on which he'd been sitting, and moved some leaves to disguise the once-occupied area. He then moved off along the westerly spur. When he was about five metres away, I went through the same routine, as did the rest of the patrol, all spaced about the same. The whole patrol moved in a 'pepper pot' fashion. If John was moving, then I was stationary behind some cover giving John protection. If I was stationary, then Stuart was moving and so on. This style of patrolling was painfully slow, took a great deal of patience and discipline, but always ensured I had one foot on the ground if the shit hit the fan. No-one was getting the drop on us.

I'd counted out 180 paces, which for me was about 100 metres, but I checked with Stuart's count to ensure I was about right because there was a substantial spur branching off to the north. I clicked with my tongue to John who immediately stopped and I moved up behind him. As scout, John would never take his eyes off the axis of advance. If I needed to talk to him, I had to move up behind him and whisper in his ear. 'That's the spur, let's go.' I indicated to the rest of the patrol with a sweeping hand to the right that we were going to change direction. It was necessary to inform the patrol of any change in direction because, in close jungle, those at the rear of the patrol might see the fleeting movement of the scout and shoot, thinking he's the enemy.

As we reached the end of the spur we found ourselves back at ground level. The jungle was very thick. It was getting on for 1.00 pm and I could see the level of patrolling was slowly dropping off, so I caught Stuart's eye to indicate a lengthy stop, and pointed to an area that I considered suitable for the stop and defendable in the event of enemy surprise. Stuart passed this down the line, I informed John, and we moved in and occupied the position.

One by one we removed the small packages of food from our trouser pockets and ate. We'd had a long morning, so I told the blokes to brew up if they wanted to. Everyone took turns at preparing their brews and a feed so, at any given time, all five heads were not looking down rather than towards the perimeter. We sat in this spot for about 40 minutes when I decided to give each member a quick brief as to what we would be doing for the afternoon and to update the rendezvous points. We were going to continue in a north-westerly direction to a position about 300 metres away on a bit of high ground. I hoped to be in this night lay-up position by 4.00 pm.

One at a time we stood, checked our personal space and moved off. The jungle was thick and the patrolling was slow. It becomes very tiring when you have to bend over to get your pack under overhanging branches and through thick jungle, and when soldiers become tired they tend to make more noise. But this was just one of those occasions that separates regular soldiers from the SAS. This sort of patrolling requires extra discipline, strength, vigilance and concentration on the area surrounding each member. An SAS soldier would never forgive himself if he made the noise that gave the patrol's position away.

We continued on, but by now I knew we weren't going to reach the desired night lay-up position so, at 3.45, I started to look for a suitable location to hide the patrol for the night. To my half-right, I spotted a thick piece of ground on a slight rise. The area was covered in thick secondary growth and measured about 25 x 25 metres. I indicated the area to the patrol and we moved in. The growth was very thick and we had to struggle to get on top of the rise which was a little clearer and suitable for occupation. As the patrol members occupied their various positions, I inspected the surrounds and confirmed that no-one could sneak up on us through this growth. Normally I would send the blokes out some distance to check a piece of ground that we hadn't covered for dead ground and anything unusual, but in this area they would make more noise doing the check and that would defeat the purpose. We stood for five minutes and listened to the noises around us and had a good look at the surrounding area. I then sat down and the whole patrol followed. This action was standard operating procedure in the patrol. I figured it was better to make the noise of sitting down once, not five times. Again, we went through the eating process of one bloke preparing at a time, then each of the blokes cleared an area for sleeping. The sleeping area was wide enough to accommodate a sleeping mat which, when unfolded, was long enough to keep the hips and the shoulders off the ground, and a sleeping bag. The area was cleared only of twigs and anything that would make excess noise when compressed.

With the nightly routine almost complete, the patrol sat quietly and finished off the last of the brews while scanning the perimeter with their eyes. I moved around to each of them and asked how they were going, told them what I had in mind for the following day and what the rendezvous points were for the evening. When visibility diminished and the sun was all but gone, I told each bloke to lay out his bedding. Each patrol member had his pack rigged so that, while facing the perimeter, he could unbuckle, reach into a compartment and withdraw his bedding. So, at this stage, each man still had his webbing on, his weapon on his lap and only one compartment of his pack open. This meant that, in the event of a contact, he would, at worst, only lose his bedding, while everything else was still packed away. Some 20 minutes after dark we bedded down for the night.

Chapter 4

At 5.15 am the next morning I woke and sat up. The sun would not be up for another 45 minutes, but I always seemed to wake early in the bush. It's a good opportunity to have a bit of a listen and to adjust my eyes once again to the darkness. I'd done the same thing three times during the night and so had the other guys at different times. Slowly the remainder of the patrol began to stir and I could see them sitting up and slipping on their webbing. After a few minutes of sitting and listening, they slowly and methodically packed their bedding into their packs. Thirty minutes after first light I called the patrol closer in and said, 'We're never going to make it at this pace. So from here we step it out and move as quickly as we can to the ambush site.'

After breakfast we bolted for the ambush position. John set a blistering pace — well, as fast as you can go in secondary jungle — and, at the end of that that day, I was well and truly rooted. At the end of the next day both Tony and I had a bitching case of crutch rash. Having trousers that were continually wet meant some severe rubbing on the inner thighs until the skin was gone. It felt as though someone was running a blowtorch across my thighs. The worst was the local guy. He had his head down all day and just seemed content to follow and do nothing more. I had to stop the patrol more often for the local guy because I didn't want to lose him nor did I want to embarrass him should he go down with heat exhaustion.

At the end of the fourth day we were still 4000 metres from the ambush site. We found a secure spot inside some thick undergrowth to conduct our nightly routine and sleep. After a tactical breakfast in the morning we moved off on a general bearing of 5900 mils. This would take us pretty much to a position some 200 metres to the rear of the ambush position.

Patrolling in the jungle is very slow, and covering 4000 metres in one day is unheard of, but we had to cover this, so we patrolled at a speed that was faster than I would usually be comfortable with. We'd patrolled for about an hour and just got smashed by some bloody thick jungle that was almost impenetrable. We were making too much noise trying to find a way through this wall of foliage so I stopped the patrol and told John to push forward to see whether the jungle opened up. Moments later, I'd lost sight of John, but heard him swearing and cursing. I wanted to tell him to shut up, and I moved forward, taking the patrol with me, to see what was going on. John's cursing grew louder as I got closer to him but I still couldn't see him, so I called to him. He replied but, to our surprise, so did someone else. We froze, wondering who the hell it was. Slowly we moved forward and the jungle opened to reveal a small cleared area where I saw John. He had dropped his pack and webbing, his weapon was on the ground, his shirt was off and his trousers were around his ankles. At the same time another Asian patrol broke through on the other side of the clearing. We all looked at one another, then the semi-naked John and then back to one another. Their once narrow eyes were now as round as dinner plates as they tried to process the sight of this naked, cursing white man in the middle of nowhere. This was beyond confusing. What the fuck was John doing and who the hell were these guys?

I heard the guys behind me laughing. I looked closer at John and realized he was pulling green ants from his hair, chest and pubic hair. In fact he had ants all over him. Obviously he'd walked under the nest in a tree and it had collapsed on him. This other patrol saw we were laughing and did the same. John eventually got all the ants off himself and we sat and had a chat with these other guys. It turned out they were a patrol from Singapore doing their officer training and had been in the field for only a few days. We threw on a brew and shared a few stories with these guys before heading off again. Before we left, their patrol commander approached me on the quiet with his map in his hand and asked if I could show them where they were. No problem and we parted ways.

We continued on and, at about 3.00 pm that day, I located the track that we were to ambush. With the patrol dropping a little further back and John and I moving a little further forward, I located a suitable section of the track to ambush. I told John to lead the patrol to the rear of the ambush position so we could prepare to occupy the position at last light. It was to be a rifle ambush and, given that we weren't using any comms, there was very little preparation required. I located a reasonably secure lay-up position and, about 20 minutes before last light, we moved in and occupied the ambush site. I lay in the middle of the ambush, about six metres off the track and in a small hollow in the ground. I expected an enemy, possibly two or three, to move down the track at around 10.00 pm this evening.

Once the ambush was set, the only thing to do was to wait and be patient. At 7.30 pm I heard some people talking as they moved up the track from north to south. There were about ten people, maybe two families, laughing and chatting as they went, using torches to guide them. The children were all over the place and very unpredictable. They were walking off the track and into the jungle, and came within a few metres of us. In an ambush, the trick is to remain motionless. If they aren't looking for you, they won't see you. Children, being so inquisitive, are the best at compromising ambushes. I was sitting in an ambush near Daly River in the Northern Territory once, and we were trying to ambush the Americans at a creek road junction. The plan was to allow their humvees to cross the creek and ambush them with a few sticks of PE-4 (explosive) which would shower them with water to let them know they had been hit. While we were waiting, a car load of Aborigines pulled up next to the creek for some lunch. We waited, hoping they would leave, but they didn't. The men walked into the bush and started removing bark from a tree about two metres in front of me, and the kids spotted the explosive in the water and moved in to retrieve it. The men then walked to another tree behind me and were about to kick me when I let them know of our presence. They didn't say a word as the rest of the patrol recovered the explosives and we withdrew.

Back in our jungle ambush position, we watched as the family moved along and again we waited. About 15 minutes later, I heard more noise and saw more torches coming down the track. 'Fuck me,' I whispered. Then they came into view: four men wearing military uniforms and carrying M16s. As the middle man came to my front, I let rip with a 28-round burst from my weapon and the rest of the patrol followed suit. We didn't all fire 28 rounds, some only fired 20 and some 10 — we didn't want to risk everyone having a stoppage at the same time. The enemy went down and I gave the nod for my search teams to go into the killing ground to search the dead enemy. After two minutes my guys returned and we withdrew through the rear of the ambush.

We couldn't move far because it was as black as dogs' guts in the jungle, and our night vision had been destroyed by the gunfire and torches, so we propped and waited. One of the pretend enemy soldiers called out for us to make our way back to the track.

We followed the soldiers back along the track that would take us to a small township. When we arrived we moved into a military camp and were shown a piece of lawn to sleep on. More cats. They were everywhere. There were kittens all over the place and, while John was taking a piss, Tony shoved one into his sleeping bag and, less than a minute later, John crawled in after it. The kitten obviously decided to crawl up onto John's chest to get comfortable and warm. John screamed, and I thought he was going to kill it. Instead he just threw it about 10 metres away while we all sniggered like kids under our sleeping bags. Even exhausted we still had a sense of humour. John didn't seem to have one, though. Stop laughing and you grow old was our theory.

We slept in until about 5.30 the next morning when we were woken by the ritual call to pray at the Mosque. Over a loudspeaker a man would wail a prayer that seemed to go on for ages. None of us could sleep during this so we just lay there waiting for this guy to stop, but he just kept going. I knew the other blokes were awake when Tony said, 'For fuck's sake, stop mumbling, say what you've got to say.'

When the cleric stopped momentarily, John said in his best Elvis voice, 'Thank you very much, now here's a little number, I wrote on the way in tonight.'

Well, that was it, we all got up, and I went to find the Captain.

'Morning Sir, what's happening today?' I asked.

'Good morning. At around 1400 a long boat will pick you up from here and take you back to HQ.'

'No problem, we're going to secure our guns and kit inside the barracks and have a bit of a look around town, if that's alright with you.'

'Okay, that's fine, there are some good restaurants for breakfast and lunch.'

That was all I needed. To hell with the ration packs, let's get a decent feed.

Chapter 4

We had a bit of a clean-up as we hadn't shaved since leaving the jungle camp and were all looking a bit rough. We threw all our kit into a spare room and headed for town and some breakfast. We were in luck. There was a guy cooking some roti with egg, so we lined up and grabbed a couple each. That certainly filled a bit of the gap, so we went for a walk around town.

The place was like any other Asian town with the smells of food cooking in cafes and stalls on the footpaths, the open sewerage drains constantly moving with high rainfall, the markets selling vegetables, and fresh meat hanging in the windows or along the verges. We started to get a bit peckish again and found a small cafe. We sat down and ordered coffee and tea all around. We still had a few hours to kill, so there was no rush to eat. A young lady told us we could have nasi goreng (fried rice) or mee goreng (fried noodles). In conversation the name 'mee goreng' is often shortened to 'me', and when one waitress approached Cleve and asked 'You want me?' Cleve looked at the stairs going to the second floor and thought the woman was making him an offer of sex. 'No, no, no, no, I'm okay, thank you, just some food, thanks.' The poor woman had no idea what this crazy white person was saying, so she just smiled and walked away.

We made our way back to the jetty and sat around waiting for the boat which eventually arrived at around 3.00 pm. It was about 10 metres long, about 1.5 metres wide, and had a huge outboard motor hanging off the back. We gingerly loaded all our shit into this death trap and then slipped into a seat ourselves. Funnily enough, the boat was quite stable and, shortly after moving away from the jetty, the driver got under the bitch of a thing and we flew across the water heading for the Special Forces camp, which was an hour away.

The trip, though fast, was uneventful and when we arrived at the camp we unloaded our weapons and handed in all our ammunition. All leftover food was thrown to the shithouse and we sat and cleaned our weapons. Once that was done we put them back in the trunk and stored them in the armoury, then went to get cleaned up. We really needed a hot shower to get all the crap off our bodies and out of our skin, but there was no hot water, so we did the best we could with cold water.

The good Warrant Officer came up to our room that afternoon and asked if we'd like to go to the yacht club for dinner. Would we? Bloody oath we would! I could already taste the beer and steak. He picked us up at 7.00 pm and we all piled into his Pajero and headed for the club. On the way he pulled into his mate's place and said he would only be a minute. When he returned he had a bottle of scotch in his hand.

At the yacht club, we took a seat outside to enjoy the sea breeze. It was a wonderfully relaxing place to sit and spend some time. The wide landing we sat on protruded over the ocean. The steaks arrived and so did the coke, and that's when the Warrant Officer pulled out the scotch. Now, I'm not a big scotch drinker, in fact I hate the shit, I'd rather have a beer — the only thing scotch does is destroy a good glass of coke. But the Warrant Officer had gone out of his way to get the bottle and I wasn't about to offend the man, so I slowly sipped the poison.

Once again, I'm buggered if I know how we got home because the Warrant Officer was so pissed he had trouble finding his car, let alone driving the bastard. But get home we did and, after a bit of a sleep-in and breakfast with the cats, the commanders decided we needed a day out downtown. This was beyond boring. There was very little to do or see. We couldn't sit down and have a quiet beer, but we did decide to risk Kentucky Fried Chicken. We stood at the counter checking out the menu when a young local boy came in and stood next to us. No big deal, but suddenly this kid squealed like a cat having its tail stood on, then he meowed. Well, fuck me; I nearly shat myself. Initially we didn't know where the noise had come from, but when he meowed again we were hard pressed to control our laughter. John could barely get his order out he was in such a fit of laughter. Two of the blokes walked into the toilets so they could laugh. I hoped he wasn't making those noises from eating too much KFC. With that, we ate our order and walked around town for a while. Tony and I found a small cafe that was wall to wall with people, so we decided to sit and have another feed. The food was great so, with our bellies finally satisfied, we found the rest of the patrol and caught a taxi back to base.

Chapter 4

We said our farewells and, after a night of karaoke with Stuart thinking he was Barry Manilow, we headed home again, but this time with no beer for the trip.

Well, that was that. It was bloody hot in those jungles, but not as hot as the Sub-Inspector's office. Right now, I'd rather be in the jungle somewhere — anywhere but here.

5.
NIGHTMARE DAY ONE

Monday 26 May

At 3.00 am I decided sleep wasn't going to happen, so I got up and sat at the Inspector's desk. It was still very dark outside, but the power had come on and so had the lights. I sent a text to Sallie to let her know I was awake. She said that she'd spoken to a few people who'd advised her that this was a 'nothing' offence and I'd be released following court today. Well, that seemed to be good news and I certainly needed some right now. What a damned mess I'd gotten myself into. I should have been sleeping on the rock-hard mattress in the hotel instead of sitting here awake at 3.00 in the morning.

At 5.00 am the door was unlocked and we wandered outside into the fresh, cool morning air. The Sub-Inspector had set up a table in front of the police station to take advantage of the cool air and he now began the paperwork. He had a statement from Ujwal, the immigration guys and his own statement. The morning chai arrived in the traditional small glasses, pre-milked and sugared. It was very hot and sweet and I was grateful for it. My cell phone was almost out of battery, so I asked if the Sub-Inspector had a charger. He did, but there was no power. He then asked me to sign a statement that was written in Hindi.

'No, I'm sorry, but I don't read Hindi, so I have no idea what I'm signing,' I told him regretfully. He seemed annoyed and considered this for a while. Then he said, 'Perhaps you can write that you were asked to sign this, but you did not know what it meant or said.'

I gave that some thought and asked Ujwal to read the statement and confirm that it read exactly as it should. Ujwal told me that it did, so I wrote the agreed words and signed the statement.

I still believed this would end and I would make my flight to the next course at 1.00 pm. In hindsight I realise that I was the only one who believed this. I'm pretty sure those around me knew what was coming but decided not to tell me. I'm glad they didn't. After an hour or so, Ujwal and the others walked away to chat and it was just the Sub-Inspector and me at the table. I leaned over and asked for the Sub-Inspector's support and told him I just wanted to finish the job I came here to do and then go home to my kids and Sallie. I reminded him that I'd done everything that had been asked of me and that he had told me many times yesterday that all would be okay. The Sub-Inspector looked me in the eye and said sincerely, 'Mister, I will support you with all my heart. This is all wrong, and I will do all I can to help you.' I hoped that would be enough, but I couldn't ask for more from him.

The Sub-Inspector asked if I'd like to take a shower.

'Yes,' I said, thinking that I had better spruce up a bit for court.

'Okay, wait and we will prepare it,' he said.

I wasn't really sure what all that meant, so I just sat there until told to do otherwise. Ten minutes later, Ujwal gave me a plastic bag that contained a towel, a pair of massive boxer-style underpants, a toothbrush, toothpaste, a comb and this bizarre piece of thin metal that looked like half of a paper binder — the type of binder where one flat half slides over the two metal ends that have been pushed through the holes in the paper. I soon discovered that the strange device was a tongue scraper! Why they thought I needed a tongue scraper was beyond me. I asked Ujwal what the story was and he told me it was a common Indian bathroom item.

Ujwal directed me to the shower which turned out to be an old-fashioned water pump out in the open for all to see, and when the big white man had a wash everyone came to look. Ujwal told me how the shower routine was to work. I wrapped a sarong around me, pulled down my jeans, took off my shirt and, in my underwear and sarong, I poured water over my head and washed 24 hours of sweat off. When

I was done, I dried myself as best I could with a wet sarong and underpants on. I then removed my jocks and pulled on the massive new jocks and got dressed. Bloody hell, what a drama — a shower would be easier and, by the time I was dressed, I would be covered in sweat and need another wash. This is shit, I thought. I wanted to strangle that old prick at the border for fucking me around like this. I should have had a nice sleep-in this morning followed by a lazy walk around town before going to the airport to fly west for another training course. Bastard!

Again I called the High Commission guy to keep him updated. He asked if I'd like them to find me a lawyer. I agreed, but they rang back and said I was too remote and they couldn't find one nearby. They also needed me to confirm who they could pass information to. I gave them Sallie's details. I also spoke to Sallie to tell her the latest and sent her my son Sam's contact number in case I was going to gaol. Sallie told me to stop being so dramatic. I hoped I was being dramatic, but I had an uneasy feeling. I also sent her my brother Trevor's cell number just in case. Again, Sallie gave me the standard reassurance that I'd normally give people in sticky situations like this. So I wasn't sure if she actually believed what she said, although I thought she probably did.

By now my cell phone was almost flat, so I asked the Inspector if he had a charger for my hardened Nokia. The good news was that he did and lent it to me. The bad news was that there was still no power, so the charger was useless. So I decided to turn my phone off until after court to preserve the battery.

The same police jeep that was used to take me back to the hotel last night pulled up, driven by the same old police sergeant. The Inspector motioned for me to get into the jeep. I grabbed my plastic bag of worldly possessions, including my new tongue scraper, and slipped into the back seat. The jeep was pure vintage and looked to be straight out of an old World War II movie. It had no doors, a canvas roof and bugger all room in the back seat. The Inspector jumped in the front seat and turned, handing me a lunch box full of sandwiches. Ujwal sat next to me looking very glum as I started munching on a sandwich.

Chapter 5

The small compass on my G Shock (watch) told me we were heading south and, while we crossed the railway line several times, we generally followed it the whole way to the courthouse in Araria. I wanted to know where I was going in case I needed to make my way back to the border. I just had a feeling that this wasn't going to work out too well, so I needed that back-up plan. Always have an escape plan … I could still hear myself telling my students that yesterday. The railway line ran conveniently north–south. If the opportunity presented, all I had to do was to parallel the line north and I'd get to the Nepali border.

We only drove about 40 kilometres, but the roads were absolute shit. The potholes were so big that it sometimes took a few minutes to drive out of them. I was absolutely knackered, but even if I could have slept, the seats were uncomfortable and the continuous bouncing would have had me pissing blood by the end of the day.

We arrived at Araria courthouse at 10.30. The place looked terrible. It was very poor, crowded, run down and filthy. Everyone stared and pointed at the white man in the police vehicle. The Inspector led me into an overcrowded administration room and pushed me into the corner telling me not to move. One policeman stood outside the crowded room to ensure I wouldn't escape. The clerks all looked at me with disdain from behind their desks which they clearly assumed gave them some sort of power. I suppose in this case it did. I noticed folders and papers being placed in front of them and also noticed the only folders and papers receiving any attention had money discreetly attached to them.

The Inspector brought an old bloke to me and introduced him as my court-appointed lawyer. God help me. This guy had to be 50 years old. His teeth were badly stained with red betel nut juice. His white collar was severely sweat stained and his breath made me feel faint. But apparently he was the best, so I was grateful to the Inspector. My new lawyer, Mr Debu-San, told me I'd meet the Magistrate then have a bail hearing tomorrow. At that time it didn't occur to me that I'd spend the night in gaol.

'What?' I said, 'No, no, no, this can't be right. I've got a plane to catch in a few hours and work to do tomorrow.'

'This is not possible,' said Debu-San. 'This is the system.'

Ujwal just looked at me with blank eyes and I sensed he already knew this but had kept it from me — probably not a bad idea.

My lawyer disappeared just as the Inspector took me to front the Magistrate. I expected to walk into a courtroom and see the magistrate at the bench, but instead I was taken to the Magistrate's office. The Magistrate's office was unbelievably small — about 1.5 x 1.5 metres and made even smaller by a bookshelf on one wall supporting old, tattered law manuals that appeared to be holding more mould than law. It was dark and miserable and I could see by the scowl on the Magistrate's face that the office had a pretty ordinary effect on him too. Well, I hoped it was the office that gave him the shits and not my presence. The Inspector spoke to the Magistrate in Hindi for a minute or so and, when he finished, Ujwal came into the already overcrowded room only to be told to get out by the Magistrate. The Magistrate was Mr Triparthy and he was the senior man in the Araria court. Triparthy stared at me for a while and then said, 'Well, what's your story?' with a tone that said, I've heard them all, now what bullshit will you come up with?

Fuck you, you dried up old has-been, I thought, and then launched into my rehearsed speech.

'Well, Sir, I took a rickshaw ride with my Nepali friend to look at the border between India and Nepal when my rickshaw driver accidently rode across the border. As you may know, Sir, the border is very open and crowded with people and shops, so I didn't even see something marking the border. I had no intention of crossing the border, but the rickshaw driver didn't know that the border is only open for Indians and Nepali and not foreigners. This was an honest mistake. I barely crossed the border and didn't even get as far as the immigration office. I have the support of the Nepali senior police who have agreed to accept me back into Nepal if you would be kind enough to release me.'

Triparthy continued to read the police report for a few more minutes without saying anything, while I stood in front of him like a school kid shitting himself in front of the Headmaster's desk. Then he said, 'Well your story is unbelievable and I have no choice but to wait for the police report from the Superintendant of Police. You will have to be remanded until this is completed.'

Chapter 5

Oh shit, that didn't sound too good.

'No, Sir,' I said in disbelief, 'I can't do that. I have work to complete and need to be on a plane in a few hours. I can't stay here, surely this can be dealt with now — it was a simple mistake.' Now I was pleading. I didn't want to be remanded anywhere.

'My hands are tied and now that you are here I must follow the law. The best thing for you to do is to get your High Commission to talk to the Home Office Secretary who can order your release.'

He then motioned for the Inspector to remove me.

As the Inspector and I walked back through the staring throng of people, Ujwal rushed to me to ask what had happened.

'The Magistrate thinks I'm a liar, so I have to go to prison,' I replied in a tired and 'I'm over this shit' kind of tone.

'Oh,' said Ujwal and, although I waited for him say more, he didn't.

The Inspector told me I could keep my cell phone until we got to the gaol and then I would have to give it to Ujwal. He told me that, in all other cases, the phone would have been removed when I arrived at the police station, so I was grateful. I asked if I could charge it somewhere as it was nearly flat and I needed to call the High Commission and Sallie. We got back into the car and drove to the police station. All the young police jumped to their feet and one raced off to find a charger in response to the Inspector's demand. When it arrived, I plugged it into the nearest power point and had to move it around the get a flow of power through the line. This was getting a little tough. Finally it worked and I quickly made a call to Sallie.

'Hi there, how did it go?' she said in a very upbeat way, clearly expecting to say, 'I told you so.'

'They don't believe me and I have to go to gaol,' I said.

'That's fucking ridiculous, did you tell them it was a mistake?'

'They don't believe me so I have to go to gaol,' I repeated. 'I'll call the High Commission and tell them, but the Magistrate said that the High Commissioner should contact the Home Office Secretary to ask that I be released.'

'Okay, I'll push for that from here as well. Keep your chin up and we'll fix this.'

I hated the idea that others had to fix my mess.

'I will. Don't tell the kids, okay?'

'Don't worry, I won't.'

'Bye.'

'Bye.'

I called the High Commission and told them what I needed them to do. The representative said they were sending someone to assist in securing my release. He also told me — once again — that the Australian government could only ensure that I was treated fairly and no different to others in custody. They could not interfere or try to persuade a foreign government and had to let justice take its course. Damn, I thought, but fair enough. I handed the phone over to Ujwal and told him to keep it on and pass on any messages when he could. The phone was my link to the world of help and losing it meant I no longer had any control over my destiny. I was now in the hands of others and that made me uncomfortable and miserable.

We all got back into the police car for the drive to the gaol, but it was only next door. Bugger. Having a police station full of cops right next to the prison was going to make any escape attempt a little interesting. The prison was a shock to all my senses. I'd visited plenty of gaols before, including some pretty rough gaols in Iraq; but visiting was interesting, being sent to live in one was a nightmare in the making.

We pulled up outside the prison and a guard opened the gates to let the old police jeep in. The prison wasn't what you'd imagine; it wasn't surrounded by double chain link walls topped with razor wire. The guards weren't standing in towers with assault rifles. The guard was standing in a roughly made corrugated iron shelter and carried an old .303 blot action rifle. Through the gates of the prison there were people everywhere crowding a small concrete building with a wire mesh around the front. There were people at the barred windows yelling at people inside and the people inside doing the same back. I don't know how they could've heard anything as they all competed to be heard over the people around them. The Inspector and the other police with us pushed and shoved people out of the way so we could access an old gate to enter a single-storey building that looked more like a hut.

Chapter 5

Once through the crowds of visitors, the inside of the administration building was dark, filthy, smelly and crowded. The Inspector cleared a path through the people who momentarily stopped their loud chattering and stared at me as I was ushered through a series of very small rooms into the Warden's office. The administration building was shaped like a long, narrow rectangle and consisted of four rooms next to one another, each measuring about three metres square. The first room was the entry room into the prison, the next was the clerk's room; next to that was the Warden's assistant's office and then the Warden's office. The walls were once white, but were now filthy with tobacco spit stains and dust. The place was dark and depressing. I followed the Inspector into the Warden's office and, assuming an introduction would take place, I thrust out my hand to shake hands with the Warden. He looked at my hand and clearly wasn't in the habit of shaking hands with prisoners. Reluctantly, he took my hand and gently shook it, while directing me to a chair next to the Inspector.

The Warden's office consisted of two desks: one large and one small. The Warden sat behind the large desk on a plastic chair; behind him was a bookshelf stacked with some old dusty folders. I would have expected to see a computer, even an old one, but there wasn't one in sight. The Warden was Mr Sing. He was probably in his late fifties, balding, wore glasses and smiled constantly despite this intrusion. As I sat in front of him, he chatted to the Inspector, occasionally looking over at me. While this was going on, other people dressed very plainly kept walking in and asking the Warden to sign a document or review some figures. It was difficult to tell the prisoners from the prison employees. Mr Sing seemed sympathetic to my situation, but I was confused and thought this building was the remand prison and all these people were locked in this building. I asked the Warden if I could sleep in his office just like I did last night in the Inspector's office.

'I'm sorry, that is very impossible, but don't worry, you will be well treated,' said the Warden.

The Inspector then spoke in English and said to the Warden, 'This man is not a criminal and should not be here. You cannot put him in with the murderers and rapists. Is there a place for him to be protected from the other prisoners?'

The Warden cradled his chin in his hand and considered this for a few minutes then called in a man wearing only a sarong and white singlet. They spoke briefly in Hindi and Mr Sing appeared to be giving orders and asking a question or two. The man in the singlet left the room on a mission. The Inspector then gave Mr Sing 1000 rupees in case I needed anything and Mr Sing gave it to another man to record under my name.

The Inspector told me he had to go back to Jogbani and that I'd be well looked after. I didn't want this bloke to leave me in this damned toilet. I knew he had done me some favours and was only doing what he was told, but I felt as if I was being abandoned to the wolves to be forgotten. Another person directed me to wait in the clerk's area to be processed and two prison clerks began my administration after telling me to sit on a stool.

'Name?' one of them barked. I looked at him and sensed he was trying to act commanding. Both these guys were in their very early twenties, just boys really; they both chewed some sort of packet tobacco and tried talking with a continuously full mouthful of spit. Eventually one leaned behind me and spat into a bucket while the other spat juice through the window, causing visiting prisoners to scramble.

'Paul Jordan.'

'Father's name?'

'Why do you want to know that?'

'Just give it.'

I wanted to say, 'Mister, go fuck yourself,' but thought better of it. 'William Jordan,' I said.

They then grabbed my arms and started looking at my freckles and moles. 'What are you looking for?'

They pointed to a freckle and asked, 'This is a needle mark, is it?'

'No, it fucking isn't, mate.'

'We need to see a scar or mark on your body to identify you.'

'Right. Do you have any other white people in here?' I said in a smart arse tone.

'No, just you,' he said with a red-toothed smile, putting me right back in my place. I showed them some scars on my arms. They searched the plastic bag that contained my worldly possessions and declared that I could keep them all.

'Okay, you just sit and wait.'

I tried to get up and move out of their way, but they insisted that I stay where I was.

Prisoners began to parade through the small room and just stop and look at me until someone told them to leave, but they were only replaced by others. The staring was unbelievable. The room was only about three metres square and these people would just stop about a metre away and stare. Initially, I locked eyes with them and stared back, hoping they'd be embarrassed and look away; but they didn't, it didn't seem to worry them and they just kept on staring. So eventually I just looked away and decided to ignore it as best I could and remain on my plastic chair in the corner. These guys would be really good in a staring competition.

I sat in that chair for about an hour and began to get very tired — in fact I really hit the wall. After last night's effort and the stress of this morning I was now really bloody knackered and started to micro nap, but I really needed to piss and wondered how disgusting this experience was going to be.

'Excuse me mate, I need to use the bathroom.'

'What did you say?'

'I need to go to the toilet.'

'What is this?'

Bloody hell, am I talking Swedish? 'I need to piss,' I said and motioned with my index finger the action of pissing. He got the idea and asked me to follow him. We walked through a large wooden door on the back wall of the entry room to a yard behind the administration building.

'Holy shit,' I whispered as I went into sensory overload and now realised where the prison really was. I couldn't believe what I was seeing: a sea of people, 580 people jam-packed into a space built for 120 people, people strewn all over the place. The best way to describe it was an overcrowded third-world toilet that smelt a lot worse. I was directed through the crowd of prisoners who all stared at the new guy. The ground was dirt and covered in chewing tobacco residue and green phlegm spat everywhere. I told myself I'd have to sterilise my shoes when I got out of here tomorrow, or throw them out, and I made a mental note not to touch the soles any time in the near future. The clerk pointed to a drain. The drain was about 15 centimetres wide and seemed to run along the entire length of the wall and had a constant trickle of water running through it. How the hell am I supposed to use this? I thought.

I saw another prisoner crouching about three metres away and I tried to follow his example. However, trying to crouch down and balance was difficult and I didn't want to touch the wall or ground or anything, and peeing in jeans was bloody difficult and I nearly sprayed my face with urine. Eventually I just thought 'bugger it' and stood up to pee properly. So what if I didn't do it the same as others, what are they going to do, arrest me? As I pissed, I looked at the wall in front of me and to my left and right. It was about five metres high and clearly a rendered brick as I could see that bits of the concrete had fallen off in sections. One thing was clear, free climbing the walls wasn't going to be easy. I turned to wash my hands and a prisoner who was already there pumped the water for me. I thanked him and moved on.

On the way back to the administration office, a prison guard motioned that I should come to him. He sat on a big round pipe turned on its side and used as a planter box. He had his flip-flops off, his feet were up on a chair and he held a length of cane in his hand that I imagined had probably been across a few backs before and would hopefully not be used on mine! He looked quite relaxed as if he owned the place. All he needed was someone to stand next to him dropping grapes into his mouth, because he already had a man on the other side fanning him.

'ARE YOU OKAY?' he yelled at me. I actually reeled back a little as this guy spoke with the volume on high.

'Yes, I'm okay, thank you, Sir,' I said quietly as a huge crowd gathered around us.

'MY NAME IS PANDI BUTTON AND I AM THE SENIOR GUARD. YOU MUSTN'T WORRY. YOU WILL BE IN THIS CELL,' he said and pointed to a large building close to the entrance to the administration building. This guy was a classic. He was about 6 feet 2 inches (188 centimetres) tall, spoke good English, had a head of thick black hair, a well-trimmed moustache and a huge set of teeth that I struggled not to look at. But the yelling was hysterical.

'IF YOU NEED ANYTHING, YOU MUST ASK ME, OKAY?'

I shook his hand and said, 'It was nice to meet you, Mr Button.'

The clerk took me back to the administration building and I waited and waited while watching as the guards processed new prisoners. I looked at these new prisoners and wondered if I looked like they did. They seemed lost, frightened and resigned to misery. Then a truck arrived and the clerk told me that the truck had come from the courthouse. I got up to watch through the window as the guards and police secured the area before unlocking the back of the truck. About 30 prisoners fell out of the truck and all filed into the now very crowded administration building to be processed before going back to the prison.

After what seemed like another hour of sitting in the chair, I was led back into the prison. I expected to be taken to the cell indicated by the loud-talking guard, but instead was directed to a smaller block in the south-eastern corner of the yard. Thankfully, I seemed to be on my own. My cell was 13 of my feet long and eight of my feet wide. It consisted of a front area and a back section. The front section was like a courtyard and had no roof, but 15-feet-high concrete walls, and my cell was at the rear. Someone had been kind enough to make what seemed to be my bed which consisted of a hessian bag spread on the wet concrete — excellent. The guard remained at the front of my cell to control the hundreds of prisoners who had gathered to stare at me. There were others in my cell. One man was hooking up a power lead with a light bulb and was assisted by another. The clerk brought a small steel fan into the cell and the same two men hooked that up to the power as well. Then they hammered a series of nails into the concrete wall and I wondered what they were for until the man who seemed to be taking the lead picked up my plastic bag and hung it on one nail. I took my wet towel from the plastic bag and hung it on another. I suppose I had to be grateful for being on my own and the fact that the Sub-Inspector had organised for this fan was a blessing.

Everyone left the cell, I thanked them and the loud talker walked in. 'I WILL LEAVE MY GUARD AT THE DOOR TO MAKE SURE YOU ARE NOT HARMED, OKAY?'

'That's very kind of you, thank you.'

Then I was on my own except for the entire prison population trying to get a glimpse of me in my cell. The ugly guard positioned at the door didn't let them into my cell, but he allowed them to gather and look. I truly felt like a caged animal in a really small enclosure at the zoo with all the people looking at me. I paced the cell and wondered how the hell this had happened to me. I got people out of situations like this; I didn't get into them myself. Yesterday at this time I had just finished the course and was having lunch with a fun bunch of students and now I was in gaol. The prisoners continued to jockey for a good vantage point to look at me. Two prisoners then walked to the ugly guard, slipped him some dirty notes and he allowed them to pass and walk right up to my cage for a closer look. These two skinny little pricks just stood there gawking at me at a distance of about a metre. One of them held the palm of his right hand out and started to shake it as though asking what I was doing. I replied by saying, 'What the fuck does this mean?' as I imitated the move. The loud-talking guard returned and went off. He started swinging that cane of his at everyone in sight and seemed to go into shock when he saw the two prisoners right up at my cage. The prisoners nearly collapsed with fear because they knew what was coming and the only way out was past the readied cane. If Loud Talker was yelling before, he really opened up the volume as he abused the two prisoners while simultaneously flogging the shit out of them. Whatever got in the way was hit as they ran out of the cell. Within seconds there wasn't a prisoner in sight and it was just Ugly, Loud Talker and me. Loud Talker turned on Ugly and gave him a mouthful of abuse then open palm slapped him across the face and walked away. Fuck me; where the hell am I? This was the last thing I needed because now the prisoners would want revenge and old Ugly was giving me a filthy look.

Chapter 5

I decided to lie on the hessian bag and try to think — and sleep if possible. I just wanted to disappear, or wake up and have this nightmare over. I expected someone to call me at any minute to say the problem had been worked out and the Magistrate now accepted that this was an accident and I could go. An hour later, as I drifted close to the edge of sleep, I was summoned to the clerk's office. The Nepali Superintendent of Police had arrived and expressed his deep disappointment. He gave me a blanket, sheet, towel, sarong and some water. He told me he would continue to apply pressure to have this resolved as quickly as possible and then, as quickly as he had arrived, he rushed off. This time I made my own way back to my cell and noted that I now walked very slowly. I accepted that there was no rush, I didn't need to be anywhere at a particular time and there was nothing to do when I got there.

No sooner had I settled into my cell when I was again summoned to the office and Ujjwal was there with more bottles of water, biscuits and a set of massive underpants. I stared at the underpants with a questioning look on my face and he told me I'd work it out. Some former students had come too and Ujwal said to me, 'Don't worry Paul, we will talk to the Magistrate and lawyer before we go back today and push to have this sorted out. Do you need anything?'

'Freedom!'

'I know, don't worry, everyone is working on this. All the journalists in the district on both sides of the border are going to blockade the border tomorrow and protest your arrest. Don't worry, we'll get you out of this.'

'Thanks, Ujwal.'

'We must go now. Is it bad back there?'

'I can handle it, but I don't want to spend too long here.'

'You won't. Bye.'

I was only back in my cell for 20 minutes when again I was told to go to the administration building. Each time this happened I fantasised that I'd be told to grab my kit as I was out of here, but it didn't happen. When I arrived, a guard pointed out a strange-looking guy as if I knew him. The Indian guy stepped forward and told me he was from the Indian International Federation of Journalism (IFJ) and handed me a loaf of bread. He told me that the IFJ in India was aware of my problem and was working hard to resolve it quickly. I thanked him very much, he left and I returned to my cage.

Sitting in my cage up against the wall looking at all the visitors to the zoo and then gazing down at the loaf of bread and all my water, I couldn't help remembering my mother's warning when I was boy. She repeatedly told my brothers and me that if we were bad we'd have to go to gaol and all they'd feed us would be bread and water. Well, Mum, here I am and you're right, but I have some biscuits as well — must be the luxury gaol.

Despite the some 200 to 300 prisoners staring at me, I felt totally alone with no control over my fate. I suppose this must be prison life. I had no freedom to do as I pleased. I was forced to rely on everyone else for food, water and assistance to get out of here. The only freedom I had was the freedom of thought, so I lay down on the hessian sack, pulled the sheet over my eyes, and thought and thought and thought until I started to hit that spot close to sleep. I was quickly pulled back from the point of sleep by someone yelling. It was Loud Talker and, if he had swung that cane any faster and harder, he would have started to lift off the ground. The prisoners never seemed to learn or they must have found me incredibly interesting. When all the prisoners were gone, he again approached Ugly and delivered another nice smack across his left ear. It was a pretty solid hit. Loud Talker must have put his hips into the delivery because Ugly fell up against the wall and I thought I saw a tear in his eye. Damn, this could end badly for me.

I lay down again and then opened my eyes to thick smoke pouring in through a barred window on the back face of my cell about three metres off the ground. This is great, I thought, and just pulled the sheet over my eyes again. One of the clerks came into my cell. He seemed to have some authority as a prisoner as he walked straight past the guard and into my cell with a plastic bag in his hand.

'Mr Paul, I have some stuffs for you.'

'Thanks, what is it?'

'A plate, cup, spoon, bucket for washing, bucket for toilet and soap, okay.' God help me, I thought. 'Great, thanks,' I said instead. 'What is your name?'

'My name is Manish.'

I shook his hand and said, 'Nice to meet you, Manish. Why are you here?'

'I'm accused of kidnapping.'

Manish got up and walked to the front of my cage to spit a great gob of red tobacco juice on the dirt. Oh, God.

'Kidnapping,' I said, 'why?'

'The other clerk and me is accused, but we innocent.'

I'd seen enough movies to know that everyone is innocent in gaol.

'That's terrible, Manish. How long do you have to stay here?'

'We don't ask this question. It is not polite.'

'Oh, sorry mate.'

'It is okay, I must do 20 years.'

'Shit! How long have you done?'

'Nine months.'

'Shit! Sorry to hear that, mate.'

'We are still waiting for the appeal, we are innocent.'

'Well, good luck, mate,' I said, but I thought it was time to change the subject.

'Tomorrow I'm going back to court and will hopefully leave here, so maybe I won't need all this stuff.'

'No, you do not go to court tomorrow. You go to court in 14 days' time.'

'What! No, you're wrong. My lawyer told me I'd go back to court tomorrow for a bail hearing.'

'No, this is not possible. You are already listed to return to court on the 7th of June, I think.'

I was convinced Manish had no idea what he was talking about so I let it go. 'Okay,' I said, 'no problems.'

Manish left and I wondered what the hell was going on. There's no way I could still be here in 14 days, just no way.

At 5.00 pm I lounged in my cage with absolutely nothing to do but think. I hadn't even been here one day and I was sick of thinking this through. I've 'what if'ed' this thing to death already. What if I had just stayed in my room resting? What if I hadn't gone for the rickshaw ride? What if I had paid more attention to where we were? What if Ujwal and I had just bolted through the police? What if I had tried to pay them off earlier? Why me? Why fucking me? What else does one man have to go through in one life? Surely I've already done my share?

Ugly Guard entered my cell and stood at the grill staring at me for a while. I looked back and he said nothing, just kept looking. Again, I felt like the animal in the zoo. Eventually I said, 'You all right, mate?' Ugly just grunted a few times and made some noises like a caveman. Excellent, he'd be back with a knife later, I thought. I soon worked out that he was trying to tell me to shower. Okay, I thought, it's been a hot, sweaty day and I've still got a good sweat going, so I could use a wash; but I won't be dropping the soap. I've seen enough movies about prison life to know what that means.

The bathing process was simple. In the massive underpants with my new sarong wrapped around me, I used the very old fashioned pump and filled a bucket with cold water. I placed my boots and sarong to one side and used the small blue bucket to pour the cold water over me until I was completely wet. I soaped up, then poured more water over me to wash the soap off. As I was doing this, 580 prisoners stopped what they were doing and came closer to watch me and stare. I suppose they'd never seen a white man shower before. A few prisoners stepped in to hand me my towel and boots and I became concerned that this meant I owed them something now. When I was totally finished I bowed to the audience and returned to my cage only to be followed by what seemed like the entire population. Loud Talker soon sorted that out with his cane and booming voice. And he had another go at Ugly.

Back in the cage I realised that I had just killed 15 minutes. I changed into the dry pair of jocks and wrapped the sarong around again, deciding to stay like this as it was much cooler. I hung the Calvin Klein jeans on one of the nails and decided not to wear them again until I was released or went back to court. I wondered if Calvin Klein had ever had a pair of his jeans in an Indian prison before. Probably plenty of fake pairs, but these were definitely the real deal and were my favorites. I wished I hadn't been wearing them yesterday as I didn't want there to be bad memories in the future when I wore them again.

Chapter 5

It started to get dark and I noticed fewer people hanging around my door. In fact, it seemed as though people were only walking past with a few stragglers hanging around to gander for a while. I ventured outside and saw the guards pushing people into their cells. There appeared to be three other dormitory-style cells with prisoners shoved in wherever they could fit. Poor bastards. An identical cell attached to the left of my cage seemed to be for the sick guys as there were some badly damaged souls in that joint. I realised how lucky I was to have the Sub-Inspector and Nepali SP's help when I arrived. I had my own cage and there were eight guys in the cell next door that was the same size as mine.

As there was no toilet in the cage I decided I had better visit that repulsive drain again before I got locked in for the night. It was easier this time in the sarong and jocks, but still required some balancing so as not to touch the wall or anything else that might have the Ebola virus waiting in ambush. As I walked slowly back to the cage the yard was almost deserted and Ugly Guard waited for me to return. He motioned for me to get inside and, at 7.00 pm, the gate was locked for the night.

About 15 minutes after I was locked in, the Hari Krishnas started with their tambourines, drums and songs. Where the hell did the Hari Krishnas come from? I wondered; but, to be honest, it was something different and wasn't too bad. Oh God, I hope I'm not here for so long that I end up shaving my head, leaving a small pony tail and start wearing a yellow frock. Maybe I'll get my own tambourine?

As I sat and listened to the Hari Krishnas belt their tambourines, the Warden and his prisoner assistant walked to my gate. I got to my feet and welcomed the chance for a quick chat in English.

'Hello, Sir,' I said with as much respect as I could muster.

He always seemed to have a smile on his face.

'Good evening, are you okay?'

'I'd be happier if I wasn't in here, but aside from that, I can't complain, Sir.'

'That is good. Just be patient and pray to God. I'm sure everything will be fine.'

'I hope so, Sir, and thank you for your kindness.' A bit of sucking up never hurt either.

'It is no problem. Okay, good night.'

'Good night, Sir.'

My G Shock told me it was 8.30 pm when Manish walked to my cell with some food.

'Oh, thanks mate,' I said as he handed me some roti rolled in newspaper and some thin yellow liquid in a steel tin.

'Why are you outside your cell, Manish?' I asked, looking for some conversation.

'I have privilege until 9.00 pm because I work as a clerk.'

'That's good.'

'Yes, I go now.'

'Okay, bye.'

When Manish disappeared into the darkness I threw the food into the plastic bag I had designated as my rubbish bag. I didn't expect to be here for long, so didn't want to suffer any stomach problems; besides, I still wasn't sure how the toilet issue worked at night.

It occurred to me that I hadn't eaten since those sandwiches the Inspector had given me on the way to court this morning, so I cracked open a packet of biscuits and guzzled some water and decided there was nothing else to do except sleep. I used some of my clothes to fashion a pillow and, as the squadrons of mosquitoes were already trying to carry me away, I knew I had to cover myself for the evening otherwise I'd end up with dengue fever or malaria. The best I could do was to cover myself with the sheet and hope the fan would blow the mozzies away from me. The last thing I did was to remove the light bulb and store it for safekeeping in the pocket of the Calvins. About five minutes later, a few guards arrived in a mad panic and wanted to know what had happened to the light. I guessed everyone else slept with the lights on, but I wanted to push this point, so I screwed the light back in and out again and said I can't rest with the lights on. They seemed to accept this and left. Every hour thereafter the guards shone their torches in my face to make sure I hadn't escaped. One of the guards grunted at me every time he did it. Excellent.

Sleep was a challenge as, every time I came close to sleep, I'd be quickly brought back to reality by the dread of what my future held.

Chapter 5

How could I be so fucking stupid? I'm so much better than this. In my line of work, I just couldn't afford to drop my situational awareness even for a moment, otherwise this sort of shit happened. I decided sleep was a waste of effort and sat up to watch the guard patrol pass the gate. As I sat in the dark I discovered I wasn't alone in my cell. Two rats scurried in and out of the cell and ran right past me without fear — their fear not mine. I suppose it was because these rats looked massive, like cats with short legs. I was worried about the diseases they might bring. It'd be just my luck to survive this and then get some terminal illness from the place. I really needed to focus now and change my mindset so I could get through this night and get out of here tomorrow. As far as my life went till this point, I'd certainly done much harder things than this —much harder.

6.

SAS SELECTION COURSE

In 1987, I'd been in the army for about 18 months and was doing quite well. I was already the acting 2IC of my section, but I had become disillusioned with the army. Most of the guys just got by; they weren't really into the army way of life and didn't really accept soldiering as a profession. I felt out of place, but had no option but to plough on as best I could.

One day two blokes from the platoon approached me and said that they wanted to do the SAS selection course. No worries, I approached the Platoon Commander and explained the situation. Given that the course was to start in March 1988, he said the men could spend the time after Christmas break training for the course. To me this sounded great because, at the time, a few of us were competing in every triathlon held in the Townsville area, and full-time training would be perfect for our triathlon program. So, off the cuff, I told the Platoon Commander that I was also interested in doing the course. 'Great,' he said, 'you write up the training program and take care of it.'

So the three of us applied to the SAS and were accepted to do the pre-selection test in August 1987. This consisted of doing 20 chin-ups and 80 sit-ups in two minutes, and a five kilometre run in under 20 minutes. Then, two days later, we had to do a 3.2 kilometre run in under 16 minutes wearing greens and boots, carrying a rifle and wearing webbing that weighed 10 kilograms. The 3.2 kilometre run is one of the hardest runs that I've ever had to do, but I managed to pass with a minute to spare. We then had to do a monster psyche exam before being interrogated by a shrink. With these results in hand, we all had to front the Board for an interview. The Board consisted of the Commanding Officer (CO) of the SASR, the Regimental Sergeant Major (RSM), the Officer Commanding Training Squadron and the shrink. I managed to pass this part of the pre-selection although, at this time, I still had no idea what the SAS was all about. All I wanted was time off to train for triathlons. Everyone I asked had a conflicting story and I don't think anyone really knew what the SAS was about apart from the members of the SAS themselves.

Now let me take this opportunity to dispel a myth commonly circulated by loud-mouth wannabees. The process to get onto the selection course and, if successful, into the SAS, is the same for everyone. People who brag, 'the Army asked me to go to the SAS, but I said no,' are spouting bullshit. No-one ever gets asked to go to the SAS. You ask them and, if you are very lucky and a good soldier, they might give you a go at the selection course.

For me, 1987 was a great year. Two months after we returned from the Fiji coup, we went to Malaysia on a three-month deployment. For a single bloke, the three-month deployment was just great. I spent the first month of the deployment at the Butterworth RAAF Base. I was fortunate enough to be nominated to do my first promotion course for corporal while in Malaysia. This took four weeks to complete and I managed to come third in my class. The second month was spent on exercise in the jungles of Johore Bahru in southern peninsular Malaysia. The month spent in the jungle provided excellent training. While we never saw the enemy, it was the perfect opportunity to sort out our ability to survive and operate in the jungle for long periods of time. When we were extracted from the jungle, we went straight to Singapore for a week of R&R. This was a pretty good week, although Singapore is an expensive place. We then spent a week in Bangkok and Phuket in Thailand. We had a great time. I was 21 years old, the women in Thailand were beautiful and the more money I gave them the more they loved me. It was excellent — damn, it was like throwing a kid into a lolly shop with a $100 note in his pocket.

I never got used to walking into a Penang nightclub. They were so dark inside you'd always assume they hadn't paid their power bill, but in fact this was just the way these places were. Before my eyes could adapt to the darkness, I'd feel my way to the bar and then to a seat, and on the way I would trip and fall over couches and/or people.

Butterworth was a great place to train for the selection course. It was always hot and damned humid, so it was a great venue for some long, hard runs and pack work. But that was Malaysia and, in early December, we headed back to Townsville. In fact I arrived with just enough time to fly to Brisbane to help my old mate Dave celebrate his 21st. When I arrived back at the battalion I was promoted lance corporal and then sent on Christmas leave. But my holidays were over; it was time for the training to start. I decided I had better get serious about training for the selection course because I didn't want to look like a dick, nor did I want to suffer too much.

I drove from Townsville to Brisbane for my annual leave. I had my pack, webbing, boots and greens with me to train while on leave. I also took my bike so I could vary my fitness training. During the six weeks I spent in Brisbane, my training schedule consisted of cycling 20 kilometres first thing in the morning, then having breakfast and relaxing for a while. Before lunch I went to the gym and spent two hours working out. I only worked out four times a week, the other three days I went to the pool to swim two kilometres. In the afternoon I would run eight kilometres in shorts and T-shirt, but I'd wear my boots with soft weight belts wrapped around my ankles. Again, I did the run four times a week, did a 15 kilometre pack walk twice a week, and then had one afternoon off. This may seem like a lot of training, but most of my mates in Brisbane were working, so I had to keep myself occupied during the day. I also knew that, if I didn't do the training, I wouldn't have a hope of surviving the selection course, let alone passing the thing. I'm not one of those naturally fit people who can run a marathon with little training. I need to train hard to maintain my fitness level. There's a great old saying in the army: 'train hard, fight easy', and this became my mantra. For me, that translated to: 'train bloody hard before, so the actual event is a little easier and I could perform better'.

Early in March 1988 I boarded a Hercules C130 at the Townsville RAAF base and, with a heap of other blokes, flew direct to RAAF Base Pearce in Western Australia. It was a strange situation on the plane with everyone checking one another out. The big goose across from me asked the bloke next to me what corps he was from.

'Engineers,' answered Cookie.

'Hah! There's no way in hell an Engineer will pass the selection course,' replied this big mouth twit. This guy withdrew himself from the course on day five and Cookie went on to attain the rank of warrant officer in the SAS and I'll bet he never forgot that wanker.

The Herc landed at Pearce and an SAS Corporal got on board. I was ready for a rain of abuse but, as calmly as you please, he said, 'Okay fellas, grab your kit and jump on the bus.' Gingerly and quietly we all located our packs and webbing, threw them into the storage compartment and then climbed on board. No-one said anything. They probably all felt the same as me — wondering what was going to happen next. I just wanted to play the grey man. I didn't want to be noticed. I just wanted to be the bloke who was always there but never seen.

We arrived at Swanbourne Barracks at about 3.00 pm on Sunday afternoon, and the first thing I noticed was that the guy on the front gate doing guard duty had this great mop of hair hanging out from under his sandy beret, and most of the blokes seemed to be wearing camouflage uniforms when the rest of the Army still wore greens. This is great, I thought, these guys weren't worried about how short your hair was and were wearing fatigues for war — either that or the guy was on guard duty because he hadn't got a haircut. That was it for me; I really wanted to be part of this and intended to work hard to get that sandy beret.

We moved into the old mess on the hill and handed all our paper work to the clerks. The same corporal who had collected us from RAAF Base Pearce then told us that the course was going to start on Tuesday morning at 8.00 am and that was when we would next be required. Then out he walked. Bloody hell, we were all shocked. We had expected to be busting our arses by now, not being given two days off. A few of the blokes were originally from Perth and showed us around the joint for the next couple of days. I didn't do any physical training though. I figured that two days wasn't going to make any difference, but I ate as much food as I could get into my gut. The selection course is famous for turning blokes into something that looked like it had just escaped from a Japanese POW camp, so a bit of extra weight wasn't going to hurt. At this point in my life I was in the best shape I'd ever been — I just hoped it would be enough.

By Tuesday morning, about 120 men had assembled from all over Australia to start the SASR selection course. Every one of us had a dream. Some wanted the glory of being in the SAS — but that wasn't me, because six months ago I didn't even know what the SAS was. Some wanted to get some time off in Perth when they pulled the pin from the course — again, not me as I didn't know anyone in Perth. Some wanted to be part of something special, to be the best soldier they could be and be surrounded by like-minded men — that was me. I had decided a long time ago that I wanted to be the best soldier that I could be and, from what I'd heard in these past few months, these guys were the best and I wanted to be part of it; that's why I was here. I was hugely disappointed with the calibre of soldiers in the battalion. Most just viewed their military life as an opportunity to fill a gap and did just enough to get by. When a platoon is only as strong as its weakest link and 70% of the platoon couldn't give a rat's arse about being the best they could be, you ended up with a very ordinary product. You ended up with a handful of blokes busting their arse to be the best while dragging along too many fat, last fucks. As I looked around the bus I tried to work out who was going to be still around when the course was over. History confirmed that most wouldn't be. I was realistic in my outlook. I expected to be around at the end of the course, but then I also expected the SAS to send me back to my unit. My estimation of the SAS standard had become so high that I just didn't think they would select me.

We arrived at the Northam Army Camp at about 4.00 pm. Northam is an old camp originally built to house Italian immigrants after World War II. The buildings were small dormitory-style wooden buildings with gaps in the floorboards that allowed plenty of dirt and dust through. As I got off the bus I saw about 20 SAS soldiers, who were obviously going to be our Directing Staff (DS), and instruments of torture — trailers and massive logs etc. — lying around the place looking quite harmless for now. We were divided into different groups; some had to go to the medical centre for a check-up, others had to go to the Q store to collect various bits of equipment required for the course, including self-loading rifles (SLR). When I received my kit and SLR I walked outside and started trying to organise myself. A DS approached me and asked, 'What do you do when you receive a weapon?'

'Clear it,' I said.

'Did you clear your weapon?'

No point lying. 'No, I did not, Sir.' We had to call every DS 'Sir' regardless of rank, and we were called 'rangers', regardless of our rank. 'Give me 50 push-ups.'

Far out, I've only just got off the bus and I'm in the shit. A mate from the battalion, Col, was with me on the course and started pissing himself laughing at my misfortune. There are 120 people and I'm the first one to get 50 push-ups.

We were allocated to a patrol, and two patrols were allocated one hut to live in. I wandered off with my patrol and found my hut. I was fortunate to be in the same hut as two other blokes from the 1st Battalion. Col was one and the other was John. Both John and Col were from Recon Platoon. The hut consisted of a number of beds in an open dormitory-style wooden building. There were no lockers and, because there were so many of us, the beds were about ten centimetres apart. There was no time to sit around chatting, my bed had to be made, I had to sort out my webbing and pack, my weapon had to be cleaned and the DS was coming to the hut to give us a brief.

When the DS arrived he began to search all of our kit. Any item that wasn't on the list of things to bring was confiscated, and wasn't returned until our time on the course had finished. The DS was a sergeant and when he went through my kit he asked very quietly what unit I was from.

'1 RAR, Sergeant,' I said.

'Five minutes ago, you were given a set of instructions as to how you are to address the DS. Do you recall those instructions or do you have trouble retaining information?' he whispered.

You're shitting me, I'm in trouble again, and Col is grinning. 'Yes, Sir, I recall the instructions, and …' Shit, what else did he say?

He looked at me expecting more, but I said nothing. 'And do you have trouble retaining information?'

Oh, that's right. 'No, Sir.'

'Then why did you call me "Sergeant" and not "Sir"? Were you being a smart arse?'

'No, Sir, it slipped my mind.'

'So you do have trouble retaining information. Give me 50 push-ups.'

Bloody hell, I've officially been on this course for half an hour and I've done 100 push-ups. So, as I'm pumping out the push-ups, the DS begins his brief.

'You blokes came to us, we didn't come to you. The DS on this course will not give you any encouragement; it's up to you to motivate yourself. If you've had enough and wish to withdraw from the course, then all you have to do is tell me and I'll make sure you're on the next bus out. However, you cannot pull the pin before the fifth day; after then, do what you like. To pass this course you will need to continuously put in 110%. I do not need to impress you; you need to impress me if you want in. At the end of each day a program will be posted on the door. It will inform you of the timings for the following day. You will never know what you are doing more than one day in advance, so don't ask. You have all been issued with a weapon. That weapon is never to be any further than arm's length from you at all times. Any questions? Good, continue preparing your kit, I'll be back later.'

I continued preparing my kit when the DS returned and called for me, 'Ranger Jordan.'

'Yes, Sir.' I got it right this time, as I wasn't too sure if I could manage another 50 push-ups right now.

'Outside now, the RSM wants to see you.'

Oh shit, maybe 100 push-ups was the cut-off and I'm being removed after 45 minutes on the course — that must be a record. I walked

Chapter 6

outside and saw the meanest looking bastard on earth. He had eyes that appeared to look right through to my heart and I actually felt my heart jump.

'Yes, Sir,' I said.

'Are you Ranger Jordan?' Again, another quiet talker.

'Yes, Sir.'

'Was your father in the army?'

Where is he going with this? 'Yes, Sir, he was.'

'Is his name Bill Jordan?'

'Yes, Sir.'

'I know him. He helped me on my RSM's course.' He then leaned in and said, 'I'll be watching you, Jordan; get back inside.'

'Yes, Sir,' I mumbled and ran back up the three steps and into the hut. You've got to be fucking kidding me; so much for trying to play the grey man. I've been on this course for 45minutes, I've done 100 push-ups and the RSM is going to be watching my every move — I haven't got a hope. Thanks, Dad.

Apart from everything else, we had to write our names on the front and back of two white T-shirts that we were required to bring with us to the course. We would wear these at certain physical training (PT) sessions. We had a quick dinner at 6.00 pm and then continued preparing our kit until 11.00 pm when I decided that I would need some sleep because I had a feeling that tomorrow was going to be big. That turned out to be an understatement.

Wasn't I right; at 5.00 am shots were fired around our huts and one of the DS yelled for us to be on the roadway in ten minutes, dressed in boots, trousers and white T-shirt — it went without saying that we had to take our rifles with us. PT was like nothing I'd done before. It was never meant to be interesting, was very monotonous, incredibly painful, and the session always went for over an hour. To top it all off, it seemed as though I had my own personal DS permanently attached to my ear and he didn't stop abusing me. 'What's that? You're piss weak. You call that 110% effort? You might as well fuck off right now.' These phrases, and others just as encouraging, were continually fired at me for the entire session. I wondered where the whispering guys had gone as

I had liked them better. At the end of the session I had to clean out all the spit the DS had donated to my right ear.

After PT we were told to shower, shave and have breakfast. The food that was served on the selection course was always great, there was always heaps of it and we were encouraged to take as much food as possible. This was due to the high level of physical activity we had to endure. However, it was difficult to eat a big meal after having come very close, on several occasions, to throwing up; but I knew that I had to eat so I forced the food down. After breakfast, and dressed in greens, we were seated in the classroom and were addressed by the CO of the SAS.

I thought we were going to be welcomed to the course, but the CO spoke to us as though our mere presence had offended him in some way. His attitude was the same as the DS: 'you came to us, it is up to you to prove you are worthy of entry into the SAS'. There was no encouragement in his words, but he did say that if we were still here at the end then we had a 90% chance of moving onto the next phase of selection. I admired the CO and the DS for their attitude. They were clearly all professional soldiers who only wanted genuine professional soldiers to join them. What a great set-up this was. Soldiers of the Regiment got to decide who got in and who didn't. They were saying that there is no place in the SAS for dreamers, only performers — and they were right.

The CO left and we began navigation theory lessons. The DS started from lesson one and went through every navigation lesson. Morning tea was served and again the amount and quality of the food was unbelievable. At this time people were starting to get sore from the PT that morning. I found this amazing; it was only the first session and we had another one planned for the afternoon. These blokes had sore muscles and couldn't lift their arms above their shoulders. Obviously they had not put in the hours of training. One poor prick was given 50 push-ups, but he couldn't swing his arms when marching so the 50 push-ups promised some entertainment.

Week one went by with PT twice a day. The only day we didn't do PT again in the afternoon was the day we did the 20 kilometre forced march. This entailed carrying a pack weighing 20 kilograms, our webbing weighing 10 kilograms and our weapons, and we had three hours and 15 minutes to complete the distance. We were despatched by patrols at five-minute intervals; my patrol was the fourth patrol to leave. It was still dark when we left and we were told that water would be positioned every five kilometres. I calculated that, if I could complete each five-kilometre distance in less than 45 minutes, I'd be on target with time to spare. Initially, most of the blokes decided to make up the weight of their packs with water and then drink it on the way, which would lighten the load. But this idea was quickly squashed. The DS said that our pack had to weigh 20 kilograms when we started and when we finished. So, in went the sandbag of dirt to make up the shortfall. We also carried a 77 set radio with us at all times, so with that and the water, I didn't have to add a great deal of dirt.

Off I went, and was feeling pretty good. I quickly got into a run-walk cycle and reached my first five kilometre mark in 40 minutes. I didn't stop for water, but continued on. I had six water bottles on me and drank every time I walked, whether I was thirsty or not. A few kilometres later, the sun came up and it started to get hot. My back started to ache in the lumbar region and on my shoulders as the pack bounced up and down, so I had to hoist the pack off my shoulders, bend over as much as I could, and continue running. Some blokes passed me, but generally I passed more. At the 15 kilometre mark I was 15 minutes up, so decided to have a quick water break and fill my bottles to ensure I had the right weight at the finish. I had no idea what was going to happen after this was over, so I thought it was good to be ready. I set off from the 15 kilometre mark with one hour and 15 minutes to complete the last five kilometres. My pace didn't slow and I ran-walked the remaining distance. However, 45 minutes later, I was still running and could not see the finish line. One hour after making the water break I was still running and still couldn't see the finish. By now I was starting to panic. I hadn't walked for the last 25 minutes and certainly wasn't about to walk now. As I rounded a sweeping corner a DS appeared and yelled, 'What group are you with?' 'The fourth,' I managed to force back.

'Well, you'd better pull your fucking finger out then, hadn't you?'

Then I saw the finish line and, as I passed, the time-keeper yelled 'three hours and 25 minutes'. Fuck it, I was gutted. I'd failed. How could this be?

'No,' I said, 'that can't be right.' I couldn't believe that I was talking to the DS like that, but I was sure I'd passed. The DS looked at me with a bored face and replied tiredly, 'What group are you with, Ranger?'

'The fourth group.'

'Well then, stupid, you have to take 20 minutes off that time, don't you?' Oh yeah, that's right. I walked off and gave my time to the timekeeper while bracing myself to get my arse handed to me for talking to a DS in such a way. But nothing happened and, after a few minutes, I was happy to lift my head again and stand up straight.

Once again the cooks had outdone themselves. There was a buffet of cakes and snack foods that we were encouraged to eat. So I dumped my pack and webbing and, with my rifle in hand, I pigged out. John and Col had beaten me over the line and were already hooking into the food. John had some cramps in his back so the dopey medic told John to take off his shirt and he began to rub in the Deep Heat. As soon as the Deep Heat hit his back, John started to swear and curse, because the pores of his skin were open and the Deep Heat got right into his skin and began to burn his back. The medic ran water over his back and we used his shirt to wipe the Deep Heat off. John was still in some pain, but it wasn't as bad, so Col and I hung some shit on him for good measure, just for being a sook.

At the four-hour mark, blokes were still coming over the line. This was unbelievable. Sure it was hard, damn hard, but certainly attainable with the training hours put in. The DS were disgusted with the general performance and told us that this time, as a group, we were going to do it again, and do it right. So, with packs and webbing back on, we formed up on the road. John put his shirt on (the shirt that I'd used to rub off the Deep Heat) and again got burnt, but he didn't want to complain at this stage. The DS set a blistering pace and I had to run to keep up. I couldn't believe that we were going back. I looked around and everyone looked as depressed as I did. But I just thought, bugger it, I might as well just suffer through it. We had done about five kilometres when we rounded a corner and saw the trucks. You beauty, I thought, as did everyone else, and the pace picked up marginally. But we got to the trucks and kept going past them and the pace backed off again. A couple of hundred metres later, we stopped and the DS told us to get on the trucks.

The 20 kilometre march was just one of the tests we had to pass during the first week. We also had to do the 3.2 kilometre run. Now the difference between the one we had to do on the selection course and the pre-selection run was that, on the selection course, we did the run on day four and were pretty run down by then. We were suffering from lack of sleep and the effects of doing two gut-wrenching PT sessions every day. To make matters worse, the first 200 metres of the run was uphill, so it was bloody hard to pass. I made it by 15 seconds and I was well and truly shattered when I had finished. That run is the hardest of all runs in the army.

Another run we did was known as the airfield run. In patrols, we marched up to the airfield dressed in PT gear (shorts, T-shirt and runners). As patrols, and in single file, we approached the airfield and, to my alarm, I noticed that there were tents set up on the side of the airstrip. In those tents the medics had set up intravenous drips on stands next to a stretcher — there were five of these set up. This is going to hurt, I thought. The patrol of 10 started to run around the airstrip with the last man continually sprinting to the front. We just kept going and going, and it was bloody hot. After about half an hour of this, the stretchers were full and some blokes were on the ground getting filled up. My patrol started to get smaller and smaller until there was only Col, John, one other and me. Then a DS decided to join us and we picked up the pace. Another two laps later and, having run for an hour, we stopped. Thank Christ, I thought, I didn't have much left in me. Again, I was well and truly rooted.

Day five of the course presented an unbelievable sight. I hadn't given any thought to pulling the pin and I assumed everyone else was the same; but on day five there was a mass exodus — half the course withdrew. Call me selfish or whatever you like, but I drew an enormous amount of strength from their failures. One of the original blokes from

4 Platoon also withdrew on that day. From this day, we were continually asked, 'Who wants to pull the pin? Pull the pin now, and tonight you'll be having a few beers down in Fremantle.' Sounded nice, but no way. I'd come to realise the SAS was indeed special. You couldn't get into the SAS because you were rich and could buy your way in. You couldn't get into the SAS because you came from a privileged family and went to the right schools. The SAS was available to anyone in the Defence Force and the selection course treated everyone as equals. If you wanted it badly enough and were willing to go beyond anywhere you'd been previously, then maybe you'd get through. But pulling the pin wasn't happening.

Most nights we were finished by about 10.00 pm unless we were in the field. But, instead of getting a good night's sleep, a DS would calmly enter the hut at around midnight, turn on the lights, and tell us to be standing outside the classroom in 10 minutes dressed in greens and runners with a notebook and pen. Then we'd be given a maths exam, or English exam, or we'd watch a video and have to answer questions like what was the written on the number plate of the jeep in the first scene, or what rank was the officer giving the brief? The movies usually went for about an hour; foolishly, some of the blokes would get some sleep then obviously fail the exam. Quite often a few of the students would arrive incorrectly attired. The DS would say, 'There will be times when you have had little sleep, and you will be given a set of quick orders. You must listen to these orders and absorb everything that is said, because the orders will not be repeated. Perhaps we need to wake everyone up a little, so that they will hear what is being said in future.' With that, we would set off on a five kilometre run at 1.00 in the morning. By the time we were back in our beds we were so pumped it was hard to get to sleep, and then we were up again at 5.00 am to the sound of gunshots for a gut-wrenching PT session.

Every day more and more people left the course and others were withdrawn for their own safety. We went out on several navigational exercises known as Pacer 1 and 2. These were only short in duration, but all built up to the Stirling Ranges week. We boarded a bus and drove south for eight hours which was a great opportunity to sleep. When we were about 50 kilometres from the Stirlings, I could see the peaks that I would have to scale over the coming week. The idea behind the Stirlings was for the students to complete a navigational exercise by themselves over a five-day period. The aim was to see which students could motivate themselves and complete the task. Some soldiers needed others to push them along, and the selection course was no exception; but, in the Stirlings, we were all on our own and had to complete the task under our own steam. I was relieved to finally get to the Stirlings. It was the first time I had been alone in 14 days; there'd be no DS abusing me and I would get to sleep through the night. The task was to navigate to five different peaks over the five days. The rules were simple: no walking on the roads or tracks unless walking up the side of the feature; no walking after dark when climbing a feature; and all walking to stop at 10.00 pm. Navigation was reasonably easy because, when I arrived at each peak, I was told my next peak and, most of the time, I could see it from where I was. My daily routine never really changed; I'd get up and get ready before first light; as soon as I could see where I was going, I'd start walking and eat on the move. About half an hour before last light I'd stop and eat a decent meal. The only down side to the Stirlings was that it's a national park and therefore no fires were allowed, so a hot brew was out of the question.

When I completed my fifth peak, the DS told me to make my way back to the base camp. It took me about two hours to get back and I arrived at 9.00 am on the last morning. There was already a group of blokes there and others continued to pour in. It was then that I learnt that the other bloke from 4 Platoon had pulled the pin, as had plenty of others. Bloody hell, I then remembered that originally I'd only decided to come to the course because two blokes in the platoon wanted to do the course and were getting time off to train and that had sounded good to me. Now they were gone and I was still here. But my initial intentions had now changed. I still didn't think the SAS would accept me, but I was determined to go back to the battalion having completed the course — I wasn't going back a failure. However, the reality is that you either get in or you don't and, if you don't get something you've been fighting for, then you've failed. It's no consolation to say, 'well at least you finished, mate', because you still end up at the same place as those who pulled the pin.

We ate some fresh food then boarded the bus for the trip back to Northam. The next phase was called the 'low intensity' phase. I liked the sound of that because, even though I got to sleep every night in the Stirlings, the hard walking during the day, and the preceding 14 days, were taking their toll on my body. I felt absolutely rooted; I was tired, my body ached from carrying my pack; my hands were scratched to the shithouse from fighting my way through the dense scrub in the Stirlings, but I was pleased that, at this point in time, I had passed everything.

The low intensity phase was a four-day period that included gaining a qualification in airborne rappelling. Now I must confess that I have a fear of heights and I was not looking forward to that activity. We boarded some trucks and went to some huge grain silos at a railway yard not far from Northam. I couldn't believe the size of these things and wasn't at all keen to jump off them. We were shown how to fit the harnesses and then we all lined up on the ladders ascending the bin. This part of the training had nothing to do with the airborne rappelling qualification; it was merely to see who had the balls to go over the edge head first. I certainly questioned the size of my balls and lined up last. Then it was my turn. I'd been listening intently to what the others had been told and had a fair idea of what the DS wanted to see. The DS handled the activity really well and talked me over without any dramas. In fact I even enjoyed myself once I was over edge. It gave me a lot of confidence for the next day when we were to jump from a Huey (Bell 212 helicopter). Again though, there were some blokes who said 'fuck that', and pins were popping all over the place.

Rappelling from the Huey was great, and I managed to get through the day reasonably unscathed. At lunchtime that day, a few blokes were talking and the subject of the parachute course came up. Yeah fuck that, I thought, but it didn't bother me because I was only concerned with completing this course. I was having trouble understanding why this was called the low intensity phase, because that afternoon we did one of the hardest PT sessions of the course. As patrols, we wrapped our SLR slings around a giant log and raced each other up and down this damned hill.

Chapter 6

We ran down and back once and were all pretty rooted, but then we did it again. On the last day of the phase we went for a run in PT gear. We basically just followed the Senior Instructor (SI) of the course. Now, at the start of the course, I was always finishing with the top 40 or 50 blokes, but now there were only 40 or 50 blokes left and I was down the back dragging my sorry arse, and John wasn't far away from me either. When we finished, the SI approached John and I and said, 'Don't worry, Rangers Ellery and Jordan, when we get you into the Regiment, we'll have you running five kilometres in 18 minutes.' Bloody hell, this was the first sign that I'd been given that I might actually pull this off. Immediately I started to feel pretty good about myself, but that was quickly squashed with Exercise Lucky Dip — the final phase.

Exercise Lucky Dip is a 'can you hack it' exercise. It involves various tasks that require solutions to problems. The solution always involved a bloody heavy load to be carried, pushed or pulled. I found myself continually trying to deliver something to some ungrateful resistance fighters. At one time, everyone in the patrol carried two full jerry cans of fuel to the resistance. The restriction was that we also had to carry our full kit and then patrol tactically at the same time. So we tied both jerries together with our ropes and slung them over our packs — damn it was heavy. Then we arrived at a lake and had to get all our kit across the lake. The resistance supplied two large tarpaulins and, with our ropes, the patrol got across by wrapping our packs and the jerries in the tarp and then floating it all across. I was left behind to untie the safety line and the rest of the patrol were going to drag me across. All I had was my webbing, rifle and life jacket. I tied the rope around my waist and the blokes pulled me over. As I left the bank, the DS told me not to get my rifle wet and not to inflate the life vest unless I really had to. Well fuck me if the blokes didn't really start pulling on the rope and the water forced me straight to the bottom. They said the last thing to go under was my rifle. I decided that now was a good time to inflate the life vest, and I shot to the surface spitting out muddy water. The jerry can problem was a carry exercise — the next was a push exercise.

This pattern continued for five days. We'd do two tasks during the day and one at night. During each task someone different would be the nominated patrol commander. I drew the short straw during a night ambush. I positioned the patrol in three groups in a linear ambush. Given that we were all totally shattered, I gave orders that one man in each group was to be awake at all times while the other two slept. We were expecting a three-man patrol to move along the road and my task was to kill, search and deliver the intelligence to the resistance. As I settled into the ambush with the two other members of my group, one bloke volunteered to do the first picket. Sometime later in the night I woke and lifted my head. I turned and looked at my group and everyone was asleep. I then heard a noise coming from the killing ground and fuck me if the patrol wasn't moving through the ambush. I fired immediately and, by the time I had fired almost 20 rounds, the rest of the patrol was awake and had started to fire. It was the worst ambush ever, but thank God something stirred my sleep and I sprung the ambush in time. After the search we withdrew back to the firm base and the DS said we could eat the food that we had recovered from the ambush. I looked at my searchers and they shrugged their shoulders. They had seen the food but hadn't taken it. 'Too bad,' the DS said. This was devastating because we hadn't eaten for two days, and didn't look like getting any food in the near future.

On the fourth day, and at the end of the first task for the day, we were given food by the resistance. There were several hot boxes waiting for us, but instead of TV dinners we were served sheep's heads boiled in water. But hey, we were starving and hooked right into the feast. By now the end of the course was in sight, and I believed that, even though I felt absolutely shattered, I was going to make it — I only had two more tasks to complete.

When we arrived at the second task for the day we were shown a land rover, and we told that it had to be taken to the resistance, but could not be driven. We were given long, thick ropes to attach to the front of the rover so we could pull it. We got it moving and everything was going sweetly; the road was flat and, in parts, slightly downhill. But this quickly changed when we hit the hill. It would have been a bit easier to push and pull the rover up the hill had the back not been full of rocks. We found ourselves tying truckies' knots and moving the rover six inches at a time. I was on the rope with my back to the hill pulling the rover. Two blokes were in front of me, and one was behind me. We were dressed in full kit and were leaning right into the hill when suddenly the rope broke. We all crashed to the road and I landed on the rifle of the bloke behind me. The magazine rammed into my ribs, immediately followed by indescribable pain. I couldn't fucking believe it. This couldn't be happening to me — not this close to the end. I was so close to finishing this thing, but now it was all over. I stayed on the road, struggling to gain a full breath and fighting the tearing pain every time I breathed, until the ambulance came and took me to the base camp. The medics gave me some morphine for the pain and I was sent back to Northam. I became very depressed. I would now have to go back to the battalion as a failure. The Q store approached me and told me to hand in all my issued equipment including my rifle. It took me a long time to get used to not carrying my rifle with me and, for days, I kept looking for it before going anywhere. The next day the course was over and the rest of the blokes were on their way back to Northam. The SI of the course came to the hut and told me that yesterday's incident would not affect my result on the course, and then left. What the bloody hell did that mean? Would yesterday's incident not affect my passing — or ensure my failure?

The blokes arrived back a day later and told me what I'd missed. They got cleaned up and also handed in their issued stores. For the rest of the day we sat around and did nothing but eat. We were all so underweight and found ourselves continuously hungry. I'd eat at the mess until I could barely walk, and would then regret eating so much. But come the next meal time, I'd do the same thing. At lunchtime the following day, a DS called out about ten names and told those people to report to the SI. Bugger, I thought, they must have passed. Then the rest of us were told to be in the mess at 1.30 pm, dressed in greens. We all sat down, and even though we had showered, had a good feed, and had a good sleep, everyone looked as rooted as I still felt. The SI of the course marched in and we all braced up.

'Sit easy,' he said. 'Look around you, men. These are the other men who will continue the selection process with you. Well done.' He looked at us for a response, but no-one said anything. 'You can say something if you want to.' No-one said anything until one of the blokes said, 'Shit hot!' That was it, most of the blokes smiled, but if the others were like me, I had mixed feelings of excitement and exhaustion. At this point in time I wasn't looking forward to starting another 'can you hack it' course. The SI then said, 'Grab all your kit and get onto the buses. You will be taken back to Swanbourne and will not be required again for the rest of the week.' You beauty, five days off. So, out of 120, there were 27 left who were to go on to the patrol course. This was unexpected and fantastic. The selection course was brutally hard, but not impossible. There were times when I had absolutely nothing left in the tank, but had to keep going and make tactical decisions. You have to dig deep and look for some heart. Damn, I got through.

So, if I can get through 28 days of hell, I can survive one night in this toilet.

7.
NIGHTMARE DAY TWO

At about midnight I needed to go to the loo, so I put the light bulb back in and called to one of the guards. No-one heard me, but I heard a prisoner in the cell next door say something to a guard and he came in. I motioned with my hand that I needed to pee. I hadn't seen this guard before, but he was a true caveman with the guttural grunts and 'arrghs' to go with it. He motioned for me to go to the toilet where I was, before walking away. I realised that he was the grunting guard who had been shining the torch in my eyes all night. I got one of my water bottles, drank the remaining water and then peed into the empty bottle. I'd hate to have a stomach problem at night in this place. I decided to remove the light bulb and try to sleep. As I did I noticed how many cockroaches were running across the floor and the hessian bag — oh God, what else can you throw at me, old mate? I pulled the light bulb back out and lay down to try to sleep. Trying to sleep on a hessian sack on damp concrete was almost impossible. I normally sleep on my side, but the concrete was just too painful on my hips and shoulders. So I lay on my back wondering what the next day would hold and hoping that I'd be released to get on with my work.

Tuesday 27 May

After very little sleep, I woke at 5.00 am as the caveman guard unlocked my cage and gave me another 'aarrrgh' to make sure I really was awake. I didn't know the morning procedure, so I got straight up and rolled up my bedding and then had bugger all to do. I decided to have a look outside and empty my pee bottle. Within minutes my crowd was at the gate staring again to see what the animal was doing this morning. I decided to go and visit the drain and wash my hands and face under the pump. Those prisoners not watching me were laying out their bedding from these great stacks of hessian in the yard so they had something to lounge around on all day. Others were cleaning their teeth with what looked like ash and a piece of chewed stick. They dipped the frayed end of the stick into the ash and rubbed it over their teeth. They seemed to take a long time to do their teeth, but I guess if you're using a stick it won't be as good or as quick as my Oral B. The final thing they did was to jam the stick down their throats until they nearly coughed up a lung. They'd dry retch and hawk things from the back of their throats and nasal passages for a good five minutes. Now I'm not saying only one or two did this — they all did. All 580 of them spent the first 30 minutes of every day cleaning their nasal passages, and I was certain there were several cases of bronchitis and several cases of pneumonia in this prison. To describe this as disgusting is a gross understatement; it was way beyond repulsive. I quickly retreated into my cell so I wasn't in the line of fire of any green and yellow missiles. I was getting a bit older now and I really didn't think I could have handled getting slapped in the leg by an oyster.

Back in the cell I could visually block out the spitting, but not the noise, and that was enough to have me close to dry retching. Fucking animals. The other prisoners just took it as normal; in fact, they didn't even seem to notice. I supposed it was because, in a few minutes, they would start doing the same. Maybe this was normal outside prison as well. When the group nasal-passage purging was almost complete, I decided to have a morning bucket wash and damn, the water was cold! As I poured the water over my head in front of my massive audience, I prayed that this would be the last time I had to do this. It was an interesting experience, but one I didn't want to repeat. The massive undies were really pissing me off and I wondered what would happen if I just got nude and had a proper wash like a normal bloke. Then I quickly reminded myself that I was in prison and it was probably not the best place to show one's fresh, white butt. After the bucket bath I washed my Calvin Kleins and hung them over the rope outside my cage so they would be clean and dry before my appearance in court and (hopefully) release from prison. I hoped the hearing would be early enough for me to get back to Nepal and get the flight to the next training course. Damn; I had really stuffed those poor students around through my stupidity.

My cage floor was covered with dust, dirt, dead ants and flies, rat shit and broken bits of concrete, so I asked Ugly Guard if I could have a broom to sweep it out. He looked at me as if I was suffering from the effects of LSD, rolled his fat eyes and walked away without giving any indication as to whether he was going to help or not. I wandered back into the cage and started pacing back and forth. A few minutes later, Ugly Guard reappeared with an old man following him carrying a broom. The brooms they use in India are just a few hundred lengths of straw bound together. It's rudimentary, but effective. As the old man approached I put out my hand for the broom, but the old man waved me off and started sweeping himself. I insisted, but he just kept sweeping. Okay, I thought, if you really want to do it, mate, then fill your boots. The old man did a great job and I couldn't believe how much rubbish he managed to sweep out of the cage. When he was finished I thanked him profusely and he was gone. Ugly Guard looked at me and shook his head. Why are you shaking that ugly mug at me? I said to myself.

At about 10.00 am I heard Manish calling names, so I stood at the entrance to my cage waiting for my name to be called. My Calvins were almost dry, as was my shirt, so at least they no longer smelt bad. I quickly ducked back into the cage and ran the toothbrush with some toothpaste over my teeth to try to make myself look a little more presentable. About 25 names were called, but not mine. Manish saw me watching and just shrugged and went back to the clerk's office. I felt as if someone had hit me in the heart with a sledgehammer. Perhaps Manish was right, I thought as I slumped against the wall of the cage. Maybe I *was* going to court on the 7th of June; maybe I would be stuck here until then. It seemed impossible. It couldn't be right; people knew I was here. I just couldn't accept that this could be happening. How could I still be here for something so ridiculous? Yes, I cocked up, but I didn't try to smuggle a kilo of heroine across the border. Fuck me!

Manish came to my cage at about 12.00 to tell me I had visitor. Thank God. Maybe I wouldn't have to go to court. Maybe those wankers at the border had come forward to confess their mistake and I would now be released. I didn't care who it was as long as they told me to grab my bits and pieces and got me out of hell. It was Ujwal. Ujwal had biscuits and more bottles of water with him. The sledgehammer hit again. You don't bring water to someone leaving gaol. Ujwal told me that I wouldn't be going to court today because if I got bail then I could be re-arrested for not having a valid visa and away we would go again. Ujwal told me that the Magistrate was now sympathetic and believed it was all a mistake, but needed the completed police reports before he could release me.

There was a moment of quiet and then Ujwal said, 'Is it bad in there, Paul?'

'It's beyond terrible, but I have it better than the other prisoners.'

'Sallie rang and said to tell you she loves you,' said Ujwal with a hint of embarrassment.

'Tell her I love her too.'

'We will go and talk to your lawyer and give him some money.'

'Okay, mate.'

I wandered back to the cage trying to stop myself sliding into the depths of depression, but I was losing the battle. I had so many other issues on my mind. My dear old dad was terminally ill with bowel cancer and didn't have long to live. I now realised I might be in here when my dad died. That would be unforgiveable. I hoped I would be away from this mess in time to see him again. As the eldest it also fell to me to help my stepmother, Carole, and my brother, Trevor, with the funeral arrangements. I took that responsibility very seriously and didn't want Trevor to have to do it alone. I couldn't accept that I might actually not get to say goodbye to Dad because of some vindictive, racist arsehole at the border.

Let me tell you about Trevor. He's a person for whom I have loads of admiration. You'd describe him as a really good bloke. Unlike my half-brother, Colin, and me, Trevor remained a homebody and never strayed too far from where we grew up in the northern suburbs of Brisbane. Trevor trained as a cabinet-maker, married young and had two girls.

That marriage was destined to fail and he met the most amazing woman, Carissa — she is a saint. Carissa is a lot younger than Trevor, but is a mature influence in his life. With Carissa at his side, Trevor rebuilt his life. They now have two kids, Jack and Lily, and a great house and life in Joyner, northern Brisbane. Trevor is the linchpin of the family. He holds us all together and is a great brother.

Colin is my half-brother. What a life he has led. Colin has never let anyone stand in his way in the pursuit of his one love — BMX. At the tender age of 18, Colin gave up his life in Australia and left for the USA to ride BMX. In Australia the sport was in its infancy and no-one was really into it, so he went looking for like-minded professionals. Once he got to the USA he never came back. He was the first Australian to make it big in the USA — he led the way where many have now followed. He's made a bundle from the sport and continues to enjoy celebrity status to this day. He's a champion bloke with a great wife and I wish I could see more of them. I'm blessed with two unbelievable brothers.

The other thing playing on my mind was that my ex-wife had a new boyfriend and my youngest son, Zac, and my daughter, Sayge, seemed to get on well with him. I knew my eldest son, Sam, was loyal to the core. Not that I blamed Zac and Sayge — they were two beautiful people and seemed to like everyone. Sam was more measured and, while a little difficult as a child, had grown into an intelligent, deep-thinking young man. I was really concerned that my ex-wife would seize the opportunity while I was away and have the boyfriend move into my house and take over as a dad for my kids. It seems silly now and I'm sure it wouldn't have happened, but in prison when you have 24 hours a day to think, you can convince yourself of some bizarre things — your worst enemy is your mind. Your mind can be evil and play tricks on you. Your mind has you contemplating things you would never otherwise consider. Your mind knows when your security barriers are depleted through stress and that's when it attacks.

8.
GROWING UP

I didn't really know my dad as a kid, and I didn't know it at the time, but he really left a huge hole in our lives when he left the family for another woman. But when he finished his time in the army, he re-entered our lives, and we enjoyed a cordial relationship, although we would never have that bond that a bloke should have with his dad. Bonds are built on the foundation of history and experiences, and we really didn't have any. Dad went on to remarry — a lovely lady called Carole. In reality, Dad left Mum for Carole, but that's life and we all liked her. In fact, she was great at always filling the gaps on the many occasions when I had nothing to say to Dad.

Despite a few setbacks in my childhood, it was actually good and I have nothing to complain about. Dad left the family when I was about eight or nine years old, but that's all right. Dad's a good guy, he just wanted something different out of life and that didn't include us kids or mum. He did call in every couple of years to say 'hello', which was a bonus, and it kept his image alive in my mind. I don't really remember much about Dad when he was living with us, even though my memory goes back a long way. Dad was in the army and always went away for lengthy periods, but I also suspect some of those trips were to see his girlfriend at the time — Carole. My older brother Steven and I would see him loading gear into his car and ask, 'Where ya goin' Dad?'

'Going to see a man about a dog,' he'd reply.

'Can we come with you, Dad?' we'd ask, all excited and bouncing around the driver's door.

'Not this time, boys,' he'd say and then drive off.

'Do you think he's fair dinkum this time and he's gunna bring us back a dog?' I would ask Steven. Steven was older than me by 18 months and, as the eldest child, was deemed to be the leader with all the answers. 'Nah,' he would say, 'he says that all the time, but never brings back that dog. Besides, we've got Tina and she'll do.'

Tina was our little Pomeranian and possibly the smartest dog on earth. When Trevor was small and got lost or went for a walk, Mum would ask Tina where Trevor was and Tina would somehow find him — he'd usually be a few doors down, sitting on someone's front lawn. Tina would lead Mum, Steven and me down the road straight to Trevor. When we saw him, Steven and I would yell to Mum, 'He's over here, Mum, she's found him again.'

Trevor was four years younger than I was but, by some strange twist of fate, he was born on my birthday. I know it's hard to believe and I hated the idea of sharing my birthday with someone else. We weren't even twins! I remember the day he was born — in fact I think that day is my earliest memory.

We were living in Casula Street, Arana Hills, in an army married quarter in the northern suburbs of Brisbane. The day is memorable not only because Trevor was born at the Royal Brisbane Hospital, but also because it was Easter and my birthday. I recall my paternal grandmother, Hazel, looking after Steven and me while mum was in hospital. On that day Nana presented both of us with an old jam tin with some grass clippings from the lawn in the bottom with three small chocolate eggs on top. We were excited, but were more excited about having a baby brother.

Anyway, back to the dog that Dad was always going to see that bloke about. Sure enough, a few days or weeks later, Dad would come home from his trip away without the dog. Steven would say, 'Told ya, didn't I? He's never bringing that dog home.'

A year or so later, Mum and Dad bought a block of land in Cestrum Street in the same suburb and built a house on it. The house and land package cost them $9000. I recall periodically visiting the house while it was under construction, and my dad pinching some tongue and groove timber which he later used to build a sandpit for us. Our enjoyment of that sandpit was short-lived when the cats decided it made a damned good toilet. Quite late one night, my dad lifted me from the couch and placed me in the car where the rest of the family was waiting and we drove the short distance to the new house. Steven and I shared a room and Trevor, who was just a baby, had his own room. I spent the next 15 years of my life in that house.

We were very lucky as kids because my dad's parents, my nana and pop, lived at Mooloolaba on the Sunshine Coast. My pop fished for a living and they lived in a great apartment directly opposite the Mooloolaba River. Pop had a fantastic shed out the back where he kept all his bait and the catch. There was also a shower outside so that, when we came back from the beach, we could wash all the sand off before going inside. Pop was a big man and I thought he was the strongest man in the world. Some afternoons we'd all walk along the shore of the river at low tide and collect soldier crabs to be used as bait for fishing. There'd be thousands of crabs scrambling along the sand, all in the same direction. If we wanted to look under a rock for crabs, Steven and I would push and shove, but never budge the rock. Pop would stroll over and, with spectacular ease, roll the rock over while we chased the scrambling crabs. Pop was strong.

Staying at Nana and Pop's house was an adventure and we all looked forward to it. We'd sleep in massive beds with huge, white mosquito nets draped over them that also kept the sandflies away. Nana cooked good food that always consisted of seafood of some description. Mum would help her in the kitchen while Dad was at the bowls club with Pop having a few. Dad's sister, Aunty Carmel, lived in the house as well. She was a really nice lady who always had a kind word for us kids. There was a corner shop only a few doors up and Aunty Carmel would ask Steven and me to go to the shops and buy her a packet of Benson & Hedges cigarettes — in those days kids could do that. She would always give us one or two cents each as a reward so we'd buy lollies that were two or three for one cent. Aunty Carmel wasn't in the best of health. All we knew was that she'd been pushed down the stairs by her former husband and now had trouble walking and talking. Nana worked in

Chapter 8

,a fish shop up on the esplanade where Pop sold some of his catch. When they weren't working they always seemed to be at the bowls club drinking. We seemed to spend a lot of time there. My grandparents, my dad and his sisters were all heavy drinkers. For Mum it was a case of 'get on board or you won't survive in the family'. But Mum had never been a big drinker and was content to let them go for it.

In 1974 I was eight years old and in grade 3 at Grovely State School. One day, after walking the two kilometres home, I saw my mum watering the garden and, as I got closer, I realised she'd been crying. 'What's wrong?' I asked. She was really upset and I started to panic. Mum never cried in front of us — this was the first time I'd actually seen her cry. 'Your pop died today,' she whispered.

I was stunned.

'Why?' I asked.

'Because he had a weak heart and it was his time.'

I couldn't work this out and wondered what it all meant. Pop was such a strong man, how could it be possible that he was dead and what did that mean? Where was he and when was he coming back? Mum sent us to Sunday school every week and they taught us that, when you died, you went to heaven. Heaven was supposed to be a paradise where all the nice people went. It seemed pretty simple, but even at that age I struggled with this concept. Sunday school for Steven and me was simply an opportunity to make a little money. Mum gave us ten cents each for the plate that was handed around. We didn't put our money on the plate, but kept it for later in the day when we'd go down to the creek and search for penny turtles. On the way we bought matches for a small campfire and some lollies.

Anyway, five days later, we went to the Albany Creek Crematorium for Pop's funeral. When we arrived, Dad came over to the car and told Mum that we boys had to wait in the car. Mum said, 'No,' and that we were all attending the funeral. That's the only recollection I have of that day.

A year or so later, I saw Dad loading some of his stuff into his car and we thought he was going to see that man about that dog again, but this time he seemed to be taking more stuff than usual. Steven and

I were playing in the front yard and asked him where he was going. He said he was going to visit Nana for a while. We got all excited because we loved visiting Nana at the beach and pleaded to go with him. He said, 'No,' then left. We rarely saw Dad after that. Mum was a scorned woman and, understandably, wasn't going to make life easy for Dad. He had met another lady and left us for her. Years later, we met her — Carole — and we all liked her. She was very nice to us and never tried to play the role of a second mother. We remained fiercely loyal to Mum.

I really didn't think much about Dad leaving because he was always going away with the army and this seemed just like a long trip away. But he didn't come back from this one. It wasn't a case of them sitting us all down and telling us that their marriage was over. We were too young for all that, I suppose. I don't remember Mum crying about her marriage falling apart and Dad running off with another woman. I'm sure she did, but she did a great job of keeping it from us. To us kids, life just continued as normal.

There were times when we missed having a dad around. Steven and I had to learn how to fix our bikes ourselves, and when my friend's dad built him a bird aviary I had to make my own and the end result was a pile of crap. I'd saved my pocket money for a few weeks and had enough to buy six Zebra Finches. They were white with red eyes and made a tiny squeak. I carried them home in a shoe box balanced in my lap as I peddled my bike. I watched with joy when I released the finches into their new home and then horror as they all followed each other out through a gap in the chicken wire. I just sat there and watched them all head for the hills. Bugger; I couldn't believe it and wondered how I had missed that gap in the wire. It was massive. A pelican could have flown through it. But I fixed the hole and went over the cage very carefully looking for more holes, but there was only the one. As kids without a dad around we had no choice but to adapt and get on with it. There was no point complaining about it because who'd listen and who'd care? We learnt how to make do and managed as best we could.

I remember not having a great deal of money. Mum always made sure we had enough food, were always dressed nicely when we had to be and, every second year, we'd visit my relatives in Sydney. But it was clear we were doing it tough. I was aware that we didn't have those small things that all my friends had. We didn't have a phone in the house and were the last house in the street to get a colour television set. In the school holidays my friends would go to school camps while we stayed at home on our own. We were doing this before Trevor started school so we were quite young. You can't get away with that sort of stuff now, but in those days it was not considered anyone else's business and we really had no choice as Mum certainly couldn't afford holiday care. While we knew we didn't have much money, it didn't seem to bother any of us and we just made the most of what we had. We learnt to fend for ourselves very early in life. We had to make our own fun and look after Trevor as the need arose.

I remember one year when we were lucky enough to go to a school camp — run by the local church group so I think it was free. The camp started at around 9.00 am, but Mum started work at 7.00 am, so we had to wait in her car in the car park at her work. I wouldn't consider doing that now with my kids, but in those days it was okay and we just sat there waiting for Mum to come out on her morning tea break. It was worth the two-hour wait; we had a great time at that camp. An Aboriginal guy showed us how to make a fishing spear and then he showed us how to spear fish. This guy was an expert and there was no way we could match him, but we had a great time trying and I really admired this guy's ability to make a spear out of almost nothing and then fend for himself in the bush.

Mum had a boyfriend who was also in the army. Jack was his name. Jack was okay and Mum seemed happy with him. They used to go to functions at the Sergeants' Mess and Mum would get dressed up in a beautiful, red, full-length dress and have a great night. One night we were asleep when they got back from a night out. Steven and I slept in bunks in one room and were woken by Mum screaming from her room to be left alone. Steven came down to my bunk on the bottom and we talked about what we should do. I was really scared because Jack was yelling at Mum to be let into the room. We heard a loud crash and we both jumped as Jack rammed the bedroom door with his shoulder, smashing the lock in the process. Jack must have fallen and Mum ran to the bathroom crying and screaming. We could tell she was scared and I became terrified as well. Only a few months before this, Mum had told us about her mother and how she was burnt alive by a boyfriend who was drunk and angry with her. I think Mum was also worried that Jack would do something similar to her by the way she was screaming and pleading to be left alone. Steven was very brave and, despite my pleas, he went to the bathroom to confront Jack. I think the act of being confronted by a 10-year-old boy who wanted to defend his mother brought Jack to his senses and that was the end of the fight. But the relationship survived a while longer — at least until the next time Jack got drunk and decided to use Mum as his punching bag again. That was the end of it for her. I always wondered why she didn't dump the shithead the first time it happened, but I think she just didn't want to be alone.

Steven and I launched ourselves into rugby league at West Arana Hills Football Club and, while we were only mediocre players, we made some good friends. We hung out with these guys nearly every day and, as Steven was only 18 months older than I was, we generally had the same friends who all lived within a kilometre of one another. Shane and Graham Brown lived a few streets away and we'd known them since we were five or six years old. Allan and Brett Ford lived a similar distance but in another direction. Shane, Graham, Brett and I played in the same football team and Steven and Allan played a grade higher. Mum became friends with the parents of our friends. Football was good, and every weekend we were both off playing somewhere different. Of course Mum couldn't go with both of us, so she picked one and the other had to get a lift with Shane and Graham's parents or Allan and Brett's parents.

I liked football, but was generally an on-the-field spectator until part way through the game when I'd be discovered doing bugger all by the coach. He would alert me to his discovery by screaming that I needed to pull my finger out and do something. The first time I heard this I thought I must have been discovered picking my nose or something similar, but I couldn't remember putting my finger anywhere that it wasn't supposed to be in public. I'd then get angry at the coach for disrupting my viewing of the match and take my anger out on the opposition. So I suppose he had the desired effect.

But I remember attending most games on my own and I missed the encouragement and support the other players got from their parents. Mum couldn't help it of course; she had Steven to consider and Trevor who was only young. When I was 11, my team went through the year undefeated and won the grand final. I knew the game was important and really tried hard and was eventually awarded the trophy for the best forward on the field. When the whistle blew at the end of the game, I remember being absolutely exhausted, with nothing left in the tank, but I was really happy. We'd just won the grand final; I had a grin so big. All the parents ran onto the field and straight past me to their children and hugged them tight and smothered them with kisses. I looked for someone to hug me, but Mum had to be with Steven that day. So I just walked off and got my football bag sorted out. After the celebrations off the field, we all went to someone's house for more celebrating and I got a lift with the coach, Greg.

Even though Pop had died and Mum and Dad were divorced, we continued to spend weekends with Nana on the Sunshine Coast. Apparently when Pop died, they didn't have a great deal of money and Nana had to leave the apartment at Mooloolaba as it was only rented. So Nana was living in a rented house at Maroochydore. We'd drive up the coast on a Friday night and meet Nana at the Mooloolaba Bowls Club where she, her friends and Mum would sit through the endless chicken raffles and drink plenty of beer. Every hour or so Mum would buy us a coke, but we generally spent most of our time outside running around with the other kids. Late in the evening we'd all head back to Nana's house and go to bed without any dinner — I think they just forgot. Mum knew this would happen so she always bought us a packet of chips before we left the club.

Nana met a new fellow — Arthur. Nana and Arthur were married and Nana moved into his house a bit further up the road. Arthur seemed really old to us, but he had a great shed in his backyard with a wood-turning lathe. He made nice wooden bowls and anything else he could turn out on that lathe. Arthur smoked a pipe and once said to me that he was on a five-year plan to quit smoking because he'd gone from cigarettes to cigars and was now on pipes. Nana introduced Mum to a new fellow as well — a guy called Lex.

Mum liked Lex and we started spending every weekend up the coast, but we stayed in a caravan park so Lex and Mum could spend time together. We all liked Lex, he was a good guy and made Mum happy. Lex's mum owned a sugar cane farm and that was where she lived. We sometimes visited the farm and Steven and I had a great time. Lex had an old mini-bike with a lawnmower engine and Steven, Trevor and I would ride this thing non-stop all day long. We started to feel like the kids who had money.

In about year 6 at school there was a beautiful girl in another year 6 class called Susan. Well, I thought she was fantastic and she became my girlfriend. Each lunchtime I'd forgo my lunch (I thought it was un-cool to eat a sandwich in front of a girl anyway) and Susan and I would meet behind the log and kiss for 45 minutes. Steven had a girlfriend in year 7 and another friend, Wayne, had Susan's sister as a girlfriend and they joined us for a group kissing session at the log. This continued each lunchtime for about a week until one day, as we all made our way across the oval towards our classrooms, a teacher stopped us all and told us to go and see the Headmaster. Visiting the Headmaster was nothing new to me as I'd paid him a few visits before. Mr Barton was a straightforward sort of person. You only really got in trouble if you did something wrong. I thought he was okay even though he'd given me the cane a few times in the past. So on this day, as the six of us stood in front of him in his office, he accused us three boys of kissing the girls behind the log. Well, with complete indignation we all declared we were doing no such thing — we were simply telling stories and talking. I added (and in the process totally blew our cover story) that we were also telling jokes. My brother Steven and Wayne both gave me death stares as Mr Barton said, 'Well, please tell me one of your jokes.' I couldn't for the life of me recall even the lamest joke, so I just looked at Mr Barton with an 'all right you got me' look on my face. Meanwhile, Steven and Wayne retained

Chapter 8

pleading expressions that begged for my plan to go beyond that one death sentence statement. I avoided their pleading looks because I had nothing and had walked all of us into an ambush.

Mr Barton then explained in his very proper voice that we were to be punished with three canes each, but (and this was a bloody big but) as he couldn't cane the girls, then we boys would receive their canings. Apparently, if we wanted to act like men, then we'd take responsibility for our actions and those of our girls. As an 11-year-old, I wanted to yell, 'ARE YOU SHITTING ME?' Susan seemed pretty happy with the outcome and the three girls were told to return to class and never allow us boys to do this to them again. Now, by my calculation, I was about to get whacked across the hand with the cane six times — three times on each hand. I was no stranger to the cane. Mr Barton was quite an expert in its use, but his predecessor, Mr Topping — now he knew how to swing the cane. Mr Topping almost had his cane screaming a vicious tune of terror as it flew towards my hand. Mr Topping also had a voice — man could that guy yell — and when he let fly at some student a few hundred metres away, we all froze in panic hoping we weren't next. Mr Barton had a number of canes which he kept in a basket in the corner of his office. He selected three canes and, like a baseball player selecting a bat, he had a couple of practice swings with each, finally settling on a long, thin cane that swooshed as it flew through the air.

I went first and held out my right hand. Mr Barton lined up his trajectory and, without warning, let fly. The cane swooshed loudly through the air and cracked as it connected with my palm, where my fingers joined my hand. The normal reaction is to pull your hand away, but then there's a danger of the cane connecting with the fingertips and this pain has been described as beyond belief. There was also the threat of getting an extra cane if you moved. I chose not to inspect my hand as, from previous experience, I knew it would bruise immediately. I left my hand where it was and Mr Barton went on to give me two more on that hand. Without a word, I rolled up my beaten palm as best I could and presented my left hand. In quick succession, Mr Barton completed my sentence: six of the best. That was enough for me. The sting in both my hands was enough to drag out some tears. I watched Steven and Wayne receive their floggings and was glad I had gone first. Like me, they were now also in tears. Mr Barton was never one to drag things out after he'd dished out his punishment and, after delivering 18 canes, he probably needed a rest, so we were told to return to our classrooms.

On the way back we examined the damage to our hands and tried to reassure one another that it didn't look as if we'd been crying, as we certainly weren't keen to return to class looking like wimps. After school, the girls found us and were really nice about the whole thing. I became the chivalrous one yet again and declared, 'It was nothing.'

I would have liked to have had my dad around in those early days, but really I didn't know what I was missing. Sometimes a kid just needs to know his dad is there for him, I suppose. We just didn't have that sense. But we did have a great mum who more than filled that gap.

9.
NIGHTMARE DAY THREE

The cage was a lonely place, but it had become my sanctuary. I sat up against the side wall so the visitors to the zoo would have trouble seeing me. I wished I had a book to read just to kill some time. The boredom was torturous. I wondered how prisoners who didn't have a prison job survived years and years in this place. This prison had nothing to do with rehabilitation. It was a place to lock people up and that's it, nothing more. I was surprised more people didn't go insane.

Then a crazy man came into my cell. He had a crazed look in his eyes, like a drug addict. He walked straight past Ugly and even my glaring at Ugly to get this guy out failed and I realised Ugly was afraid of Crazy. Another prisoner followed Crazy into my cage. I stood up so I could better defend myself when the action started. Crazy started trying to talk to me in Hindi and continuously spat when he spoke. His offsider played interpreter, but he couldn't speak a great deal of English either. Crazy then showed me a cell phone and asked if I wanted to use it. 'No problem,' he said. Crazy had disgusting, infected, self-inflicted wounds on his left forearm. He'd used a cigarette to burn his initials into his arm; each letter was about 10 centimetres high and three millimetres deep. I began to realise that Crazy was a stand-over guy and was trying to offer his protection services to me, but to do that effectively he had to move into my cell. He said he would ensure no-one came into my cell and caused me harm. As he said this, the old man walked in. Crazy turned and threw a pile of abuse at the old man who quickly turned and retreated. I called the old man back and then told Crazy that I didn't understand what he was saying. He tried to explain himself and again I said I didn't understand. Eventually he got the idea and left. As he walked out, Ugly reappeared from nowhere. 'Thanks for nothing, you ugly prick,' I said to Ugly, who smiled as if I had just told him I thought he reminded me of Brad Pitt.

About an hour after Ujwal left, I was again summoned to the office. The Nepali police SP was waiting for me. He again reassured me that all would be okay. He also brought me a small pillow for which I was very grateful. I asked him if he was able to influence the Indian SP to write his report quickly so I could leave this terrible place. He said he was trying to do just that and that the SP owed him some favours. I thanked him for his efforts, realising that he didn't have to do what he was doing and had done.

I went back to the cage and noticed fresh flies and ants had moved in and a crowd of admirers was waiting at the front. Excellent, just what I needed. The other issue of real concern was that I needed to go to the toilet for 'number twos'. I'd been dreading this and knew it was going to be a drama. There was no hanging on any longer and I had to make a move, so I grabbed my small red bucket and made my way to what I thought were loosely referred to as toilets. I waited in line out the front of the five shitters that reminded me of very old style outhouses. A prisoner walked out of one and another prisoner waved me to the now empty outhouse. As I passed the prisoner he called me back and handed me a filthy bucket full of water. So now I had my little red bucket and another larger bucket of water. I entered the outhouse and nearly threw up. Oh fuck, this can't be happening to me. The toilet pan was level with the floor — a squatter. It had a very small drain hole and two foot pads on either side. I'd used a squatter before and was not generally bothered by them. I'd even used a few long-drops in my time, but I'd never used something as disgusting and repulsive as this. The walls were covered in shit stains and there appeared to be about three years of skid marks in the bowl. It was absolutely horrendous. I lifted my sarong and lowered my jocks making sure neither touched the floor. Then I placed my feet on the footpads and slowly lowered myself making sure I didn't lose my balance or touch anything. I tried to line myself up with the previous years of leftovers while trying not to look down. When I was done I had to work out how to use the red bucket water as toilet paper. Let me say, the result was a bloody disaster and I ended up with more on me than in the bowl, and had to use half the water from the filthy bucket to finish the job. Why me? When I thought I was done I slowly rose and lifted my jocks to a very wet bum then used the rest of the filthy bucket water to flush. I had no choice but to touch the spit-covered door to get out, but was grateful another prisoner pumped water for me to thoroughly wash my hands and arms. There must have been an easier way to do this, but I certainly wasn't asking for tips — I'd work it out myself. I made doubly sure I separated the red bucket from my blue washing bucket.

Sitting in the cage was beyond boring and I was looking for something to do. I wished I had a book to read — just something to take my mind off this crappy situation. Then the loud-talking guard walked into my cage. 'ARE YOU OKAY TODAY?' he yelled.

'Yes, thank you, Sir, I'm okay.'

'ARE YOU A JOURNALIST?'

'No, but I train journalists in safety,' I replied, wondering where he got his information.

He handed me a newspaper. 'YOUR JOURNALIST FRIENDS ARE PROTESTING AT THE BORDER TODAY, AND THERE IS A STORY ABOUT YOU HERE,' he yelled and pointed to an article written in Hindi. He read the article aloud; it said something about an Australian journalist being arrested at the border for not having a visa. I asked if I could keep the article and he gave me the paper.

Indian police arrest IFJ officer
POST REPORT
BIRATNAGAR, May 26 — Indian Police arrested Paul Jordan, training officer of International Journalists Federation (IFJ), along with Post correspondent Ujjwal Acharya from the bordering Jogbani area, Sunday.
Upon completion of a three-day training program for journalists of eastern Nepal, Australian citizen Jordan and Acharya had reached Jogbani when they were suddenly arrested by the

Indian police. Following the arrest, Jordan and Acharya were taken to the police station in Jogbani.

Since no charges were pressed against Acharya, he was released the same day while Jordan is still in police detention. Jordan was shifted to Arriya Jail in Bihar on Monday.

Acharya said, "The police arrested us from near the no man's land area while we were being questioned by the local Indian Immigration Office."

Meanwhile, Morang Chapter of Federation of Nepalese Journalists (FNJ) has appealed the Indian authorities to release Jordan as there is no legitimate grounds for the arrest. However, the Indian side has claimed that Jordan has breached international law.

"The Indian Police has decided to press charges against Jordan at the district court on Tuesday," said Shambhu Bhandari, FNJ Morang chair.

Jordan had come to Nepal at the invitation of FNJ to facilitate training for Nepalese journalists. He was to facilitate another training session in Mahendranagar from Tuesday, which has been cancelled following his arrest.

As I flicked through the pages looking at the ads and reading the odd English words, I came across a Sudoku puzzle. I'd never done one of these puzzles before but I was bored like never before and the Sudoku was just what I wanted, although I realised I would need a pen. I walked into the administration office and asked Manish if I could borrow a pen from him. He didn't look too happy, so I asked if the money left by the Inspector could be used to buy a pen. He reluctantly agreed to lend me a pen. Back in the cell I got to work on the puzzle. Apparently this one was listed as hard and, after about five numbers, I had totally cocked it up. So I found a blank place in the newspaper and drew a new puzzle, entered the original numbers and started again. This time I took it slowly and considered each entry and it occupied my mind for some time.

Manish came to my cage and told me to go to the Warden's office immediately. I thought this had to be good news and that I'd be released from this hell. I walked into his office and he pointed to the phone. I had no idea who could be calling me and, as I picked up the phone, I hoped for a miracle.

'Hello.'

I didn't get the miracle, but the next best thing — Sallie.

'Hi there, are you okay?'

'I'm okay, how are you?'

'Good, but listen, the Australian High Commission guys are coming tomorrow to see you. Don't worry, you'll be out of there soon. I went to SBS last night and when Amrita finished reading the news she spoke to the SP. He said you have nothing to worry about and will be out of there as soon as the reports are written.'

'That's great, thanks so much.'

'Trevor is aware of the situation and I brief him a few times a day on any changes. He has also spoken to Dave. Between both of them they will keep an eye on your house.'

'Okay, that's good, but ask Trevor not to tell Mum or Dad. They don't need the worry. Hey, I need to go. The Warden has been very kind to me and asked that I keep this very short.'

'Okay, I love you so much.'

'I love you too, bye.'

'Thank you, Mr Sing.'

'It is okay, but it is against regulations to accept a call. She cannot call again.'

'Okay, I understand, thank you.'

I wandered back to the cage walking ridiculously slowly and contemplating being in this dump for another night — unbelievable! I decided to have a bucket bath and wash some of the sweat off and then spend some quality time pacing my cage; there were areas of my new house that I hadn't explored. At 7.00 pm Ugly Guard motioned for me to get inside the cage and locked the sliding bar. I stood holding the bars wondering if I should get my steel cup and drag it along the bars like they do in the movies. As I thought of this, I contemplated the bars and, more importantly, how I could get through them.

The only time I could escape this rat-infested dump was at night and through the bars. The bars were painted a filthy red, rusty colour. I thought that if I had a small hacksaw (perhaps baked inside a cake)

I could cut 90% of the way through two bars and then fill those cut marks with some putty made from ground rust, paint and water. On the night of my escape I could simply cut the rest of the way through and be outside my cage. Another option was to only make one cut through the sliding bar, although with all the movement of the sliding bar the putty could fall out of the cut and might be noticed by a guard. And anyway, that would only get me outside my cell. I would then have to get past the guards and over the five-metre flat concrete wall. Sure, I could free climb the sections where the concrete render had fallen from the brickwork, but the reality was that I was crap at climbing in the Regiment, and had spent most of the time as the second climber hanging from the protection rather than the rock face. There was one section of the wall that offered a better chance of scaling. Next to the big door to access the administration building there was an outdoor kitchen where some prisoners churned out hundreds of chapattis every day. If I was able to get on top of the kitchen roof then I would only have a three-metre wall to climb, which would be easier given that I'm 6 feet 2 inches (188 centimetres) tall and so would have more than half the wall covered. But I would still have to get across the yard and over the wall without being seen by the patrolling guards. Without outside help, this would be a challenge. However, I believed I'd only be here for a day or so and therefore I didn't need to spend too much time planning my escape. But it was always good to have a plan just in case.

About 15 minutes after lock-up, the Hari Krishnas opened up with their tambourines and happy songs, so I leaned against the bars and enjoyed the nightly chant. The Warden arrived at about 7.30 for his nightly rounds and a quick chat and, shortly after, Manish came with three chapattis and a bowl of vomit — well, that's what it looked like, anyway. We had a quick chat, then Manish was gone into the darkness. I threw the food into the plastic bag hanging from a nail which was my daily bin and dragged my hessian sack and pillow up against the back wall to lean against while I worked on the Sudoku puzzle. At around midnight I decided to try to get some sleep, so I removed the light bulb and stored it in the pocket of the Calvins, then pulled the thin cotton sheet over me to try to fend off the mosquito squadron during the night.

10.
NIGHTMARE DAY FOUR

Wednesday 28 May

At 3.00 in the morning a prisoner in the hospital cell next door started singing. I use the term 'hospital' loosely as that's what it was called. There were eight prisoners crammed into a cell the same size as mine with no special care or treatment. They were sleeping on the ground just like me, only they were jammed in where I at least had space. In fact, compared to the rest of the prisoners, I was in the penthouse while they were in the shithouse. The singing was bloody awful and enough to prevent any further sleep, so I got up, dug out my light bulb from my Calvins, connected it and did some more Sudoku. In the last six hours of Sudoku, I'd managed to add one number. I'm crap at Sudoku, but it certainly occupied my mind. Obviously some prisoners in the hospital cell thought as much of the singing as I did, because about 30 minutes into it, an argument started. There was yelling and screaming and then it stopped, and I could hear someone copping a solid beating. The beating was ruthless and the sounds of the hits were joined by the victim's screams of pain and cries for help. Those damned guards shone their torches in my eyes every hour, but didn't appear when someone needed help. How had this become my life?

At 5.00 am the cage was opened with a morning 'arrggh' from the caveman. I didn't bounce out of 'bed' as fast as I did on the first day, but slowly sat up and got myself together. I could feel my body suffering from the effects of only a few hours' sleep over the past few days and the dramatically reduced food intake. I threw on the sarong and my boots and joined my fellow prisoners at the drain. On the way I noticed that I was now getting nods and the odd 'morning Sir' from my fellow prisoners. 'Morning,' I would always reply, although I remained intent on keeping my distance as much as possible. I'd seen the film *Midnight Express*, so I knew what could happen in prison when a group of men is thrown together for years on end. I knew if any of that was pushed in my direction, it would be violent, people would be hurt and I could lose my single cage. So I stayed clear of the others as much as possible.

When I wandered back into my cage the same old man was in there sweeping out. This time he had a bucket of water and was using his straw broom to mop the place. So I waited out the front until he was finished and watched the prison come to life. Some prisoners undid their bundle of blankets stored in the yard and spread them out for the day using the blankets to stake their claim over a small area of the yard. Some went for a morning walk around the yard, while others started the nasal-passage-cleansing process. At this point I retreated to my cage. The old man had finished and I thanked him and then wondered what the hell I was going to do. The old man reappeared and motioned for me to have a wash. I picked up my towel, small blue bucket and soap and walked to the pump outside my cage. It seemed the best location for a wash as the pump was positioned next to a raised slab of concrete which provided a relatively clean surface on which to stand or squat while bathing. The old man had the big communal bucket full of water waiting for me. So I dropped the sarong on a dry section of concrete and, in my massive jocks, began the process of bathing in front of an audience of 580. Even though I had a layer of sweat on my body and looked forward to a wash, the water was very cold and always a shock to the system — like when you first dive into a mountain stream. After emptying the first bucket to wet my body, I soaped up while the old man filled another bucket to rinse off. I lathered up to clean all the sweat off and placed the soap on the concrete. The old man grabbed it and went to wash my back. 'Whoa there, mate, don't even think about it.'

He insisted and so did I and I'm sure he wasn't going to try that again. I poured a couple of blue buckets of water over me to rinse the soap, then the old man picked up the entire big communal bucket and poured it over me. Bloody hell, I thought I was going to drown. I dried myself and forced my wet feet into my boots being careful not to touch the soles where I was certain some as yet undiscovered hideous disease was waiting to pounce. Perhaps I should donate my shoes to science when I got out of here. Back in the cage I hid from the prying eyes behind the narrow wall of concrete that supported the gate and changed into dry jocks. Then the old man came in, took my wet jocks, washed them and hung them on a piece of string in front of my cage. I protested, but he insisted. Okay mate, whatever rocks your boat. I started to think I had my own slave.

Back in the cage, I wondered what the hell I was going to do to kill some time. The Sudoku was good, but it was getting boring. A fellow prisoner wandered straight past Ugly Guard and into my cage and told me we should walk in the mornings. I had rejected all other offers and approaches by other prisoners, but this guy seemed genuine and certainly had the measure of the guards. 'Okay then.' I walked past Ugly Guard and nodded to him. He knew where I was going, but there was no indication he gave a shit. We did a very slow circuit of the yard and the other prisoner told me that most prisoners walked in the morning and evening as it was good for the health.

'My name is Satya,' he said, speaking reasonably good English.

'My name is Paul,' I said, shaking his hand.

'You are very interesting for the other prisoners.'

'Yes, I can see that. I hope they get bored with me soon.'

'Maybe. Why are you here?'

'I mistakenly crossed the border by a few metres and they arrested me.'

'Oh.'

'Yeh, oh. What did you do?'

'I was a politician.'

'Oh, okay. But that's not a crime.'

'I fought against corruption.'

'That's admirable, but a challenge in this country. So, fighting corruption is a crime?'

'No. But the magistrate in my district was very corrupt, a dishonest man, so I crushed him.'

'What do you mean you crushed him?' How?'

'With a piece of wood. I hit him over the head. He bled a lot.'

I had to stifle a laugh. This was brilliant.

'How long are you here for?'

'Three months. I only have four weeks to go.'

'Do you think what you did was right?'

'Next time I will take a different action, maybe diplomacy.'

'Yeh, probably a good idea.'

We completed three slow laps of the yard before he deposited me back at my cage. I decided to rest for a while. The old man entered the cage and, motioning with his hands to his mouth, said the word 'kanake'.

'I'm okay,' I said, 'I'm not hungry.'

The old man proceeded to give me his first lecture which went on for about 10 minutes. He knew I couldn't speak Hindi, but that didn't stop him from serving it up to me. To appease him, I picked up a packet of biscuits and ate one. He shook his head and walked out.

My cage had dried from the morning mopping, so I lay down and tried another Sudoku number. As I settled in, the cage began to fill with smoke; it literally poured through the barred hole in the back wall. This hole was about three metres up and near the top and was about 30 centimetres square. I threw on my boots and walked around the back of the cell block to see who was making smoke signals. Three blokes were gathered around a small oven made from clay trying to get a fire going, but the thing was just spewing white smoke, most of which went straight into my cage. I didn't actually mind because the smoke cleared out all the mosquitoes. The three blokes shared the oven and spent most of the day preparing food and chai. The oven itself was a simple construction and there were about five of them scattered around the yard, all owned by someone. The oven was about 30 centimetres square with a hole in the front for the wood and air intake and a hole on the top where the frying pan and pot sat. One man prepared the food, another sorted the coals, while the third cooked and sat in front of the oven fanning the fire. When they saw me watching them they smiled and offered me some chai. I said no, but thanked them and went back to my cage to continue with Sudoku.

Chapter 10

About an hour later, Manish came and told me to go to the Warden. I slipped on my boots and one and only shirt and wandered to the office. There were three people in the Warden's office: the Warden and two others. A young Indian bloke introduced himself as the Sub-District Magistrate and the older bloke with him was his assistant. Both were clearly well educated and spoke very good English. I felt embarrassed that I was talking to these important men wearing my sarong. They told me not to worry about what I was wearing. Apparently the Sub-District Magistrate had seen the article in the newspaper and, as the prison came under his jurisdiction, he had decided to visit me. We spoke for over 30 minutes and he explained that his position was similar to the district Mayor, except that it was a government-appointed position. He told me not to worry. He had read the charge, Magistrate Triparthy was a friend of his, and both believed I'd only be here for a few more days. He told the Warden to send someone to buy lemonade and we all had a glass. It tasted good. As he left he asked if I needed anything. I couldn't think of anything, so said I was fine.

'What about a mosquito net, do you have one?'

'No I don't,' I said.

'I will have one sent to you this afternoon. You must treat me as a friend and ask for whatever you need; don't hesitate. The Warden has my number and you can tell him you want to talk to me any time, okay?'

'That's very kind of you, thank you.'

I walked back to the cage wondering what all that had been about and whether the Sub-District Magistrate was just another guy who wanted money or something else from me. Frankly, at that moment, I'd have paid anything for this drama to be over. After a nap and a battle with the swarms of flies, I was again summoned to the office. On the way I asked Manish if one of the visitors was a white man.

'I do not see, but I think.'

The Australian High Commission guys had arrived. Apparently they had a hell of a time getting to the gaol as Araria is so remote. They had flown two hours from New Delhi then driven for five hours. At the end of the day they would drive four hours back to a hotel. I felt for the poor bastards and cursed myself for a wanker for asking them to make this effort for me, but I really needed their help. One of the guys, Craig, was a consular officer and the other was a locally employed staff member. They didn't have much for me at this early stage and really had little to offer. Their powers to intervene or influence were nil. I asked them to speak to Ujwal, the Sub-District Magistrate, my lawyer and the SP. I also had to sign some papers to say that I would pay back any money lent to me by the Australian government and to confirm the names of people to whom DFAT could release information. I confirmed Sallie's name. Craig handed me an envelope containing paraphernalia offering assistance to those in gaol overseas. Many of the brochures I'd read during my time inside foreign embassies around the world and there I was scanning the brochure for any clue for a way out of this mess. Craig also gave me a bag with some bottled water, a bar of chocolate and a novel. He asked how I was being treated, but added that he couldn't doing anything to ensure I received better treatment than the other prisoners.

'Mr Sing is being very kind to me and I'm grateful for everything he is doing,' I said, using the opportunity to suck up to Mr Sing in front of Australian government officials.

'Thank you Sir, for your treatment of Mr Jordan,' added Craig helpfully. Mr Sing just wobbled his head and said, 'It's our duty to look after him properly.'

'Well, thank you again. Would it be okay if Mr Jordan used my cell phone to make a two-minute call to his family, Mr Sing?'

'That would be fine,' said Mr Sing, wobbling his head.

Craig entered Sallie's number into his cell phone and pressed call. I tried to leave the office for privacy, but Mr Sing asked that I stay in his office. Fair enough, I thought.

Sallie answered and I felt myself plummet into depression. The visit from the High Commission staff had made me feel like Schapelle Corby or the Bali nine, and then hearing Sallie's voice had made me lose focus on what I needed to say to her. But Sallie took control and described Amrita's conversations with the SP and his reassurance that everything would be fine. The IFJ had gone into full swing in Australia, Nepal and India. The Federation of Nepali Journalists was visiting the

Indian High Commissioner to Nepal and the Nepali Prime Minister demanding action. Sukimar, the IFJ representative in India, was talking to the Home Secretary daily demanding action, and my journalist friends in Australia were calling government ministers there demanding intervention in this matter. In fact, Sallie said there weren't too many federal ministers who didn't know who Paul Jordan was. Bloody hell, more embarrassment. She told me she loved me, I told her the same and she was gone. Craig told me they had to go and visit a number of people, but would be back tomorrow, hopefully with some good news. I shook their hands and returned to the cage.

About an hour later I was again summoned to the office. I thought Manish would be getting pissed off with all my visitors by now. It was Ujwal and I had to talk to him through the gate of the entry room. Ujwal had brought two other Nepali journalists with him for support. He had just come from Magistrate Triparthy's office with good news. Triparthy had said I could be released today, but most likely tomorrow, if the paperwork from the police arrived in time.

'That's great news, mate. Let me tell you, Ujwal, I won't be letting you take me for any more tourist rides,' I said with a laugh.

'Yes, we made a huge mistake and I don't want to come to India again.'

'Me neither. What will you do now?'

'We will go to the SP's office and ask him to write the report quickly.'

'Thanks, mate. Hey, do you have my wallet?'

'No, but I took some money from it to pay for the lawyer and some other things.'

'No problem. Can you give me some money, but in small notes. I need to give some to someone in here.'

'Are you being threatened?'

'No, no, no. There's an old guy helping me and I want to give him some money.'

Ujwal handed me some notes and got smaller denominations from the other two journos.

'Is there anything else you need?'

'Yeh, could you please go to my bag at the hotel and get my book and my thongs?'

'Okay. I will bring them tomorrow,' Ujwal said as he wobbled his head and handed me a plastic bag with three bottles of water and two packets of biscuits.

'Okay. Thanks, mate. Bye fellas.'

Three heads wobbled and they were gone.

Back in the cage I immediately started reading the novel Craig gave me. I wondered whether this wasn't some perverted humour on Craig's part. The novel was called *Primal Fear* and was the story of a nutcase in gaol for murder. But it was a good, thick novel and was a great relief from the Sudoku puzzles. The fan wasn't working due to a power outage, so it was hot and the flies were torturous. It occurred to me that the fan never died at night. They obviously had a generator to keep the lights on all night, but it didn't matter during the day. When the fan was on it was enough to blow the flies off me and give me some respite from their torment.

The old man walked in and was followed by Sanjay Pandi. For some reason that I couldn't determine, Sanjay was also in the sick cell next door. Sanjay was about 6 feet 2 inches (188 centimetres) and built like a toothpick. He spoke a little English and insisted on calling me 'Sir' despite my pleas for him to call me 'Paul'. Sanjay was a nice guy, but beyond annoying. You know the type of bloke? He would give you the shirt off his back, but had no social skills or comprehension of personal boundaries, and it could be painful to be around him, but I could never say he did anything wrong. I'm sure Sanjay wished he had been selected on the first day to sweep the floor of the cage and then he might have been my helper, but thankfully he wasn't.

Sanjay spent a lot of time telling me about his crime. He'd been found guilty of murdering his wife, but insisted she had committed suicide. Having only known Sanjay for a short period of time, I thought he didn't seem to have it in him to murder someone, but I could see why his dear wife might have considered taking her life. After five minutes with him I considered the idea myself. Sanjay was a former policeman who was arrested by his colleagues for the murder. Apparently the local police commander told him he would drop the charges if Sanjay paid him US$1000. Of course Sanjay didn't have that sort of money so he went to prison and then his five sons lived on the streets begging for money. We were in the poorest state in India so I don't know who they begged from. Sanjay annoyed the shit out of me by walking into my cage at times when I just wanted to be alone. Both Sanjay and the old man sat against the wall and just hung out. I decided to pull out the bar of chocolate and broke it onto three and we all munched on Cadbury's chocolate. They were both ecstatic. I was certain they hadn't had chocolate for a very long time. In fact, the look of surprise mixed with delight on the old man's face made me think he'd probably never tasted it before. When we were done the old man got up to leave and told Sanjay to leave as well. I was starting to like the old man. I couldn't understand a word he said, but he seemed to have taken over caring for me.

Sanjay walked back to his cell and I called the old man back. I dug out 200 rupees and pressed them into his old, wrinkled hand. The old man's face lit up and he thanked me over and over. I felt guilty because 200 rupees was about $3, but we were in gaol and the old man was beyond poor. I settled into the hessian-covered concrete and read some more.

About an hour later, a guard walked into the cage and threw something at me. I started, wondering if I was about to get the beating I'd been expecting all along. The object landed at the entrance to the cage and the guard walked away. I hadn't seen that guard before, but he didn't look too happy. I retrieved the bundle and realised it was the mosquito net promised by Sub-District Magistrate Bala. A few minutes later, the same prisoner who put the nails in the concrete walls so I could hang my clothes walked in with four nails and a hammer. He belted the nails into each corner of the cage so I could tie the mosquito net up every night. I thanked him and he was gone.

At around 5.00 pm I was again summoned to the Warden's office. When I walked in, Mr Sing pointed to the phone and told me, 'Your wife is on the phone. She is not allowed to call on the phone. It is not allowed.'

'Okay, Mr Sing, thank you.'

Mr Sing acknowledged my thanks with a wobble of his head.

It was nice to hear from Sallie and I wondered how I'd go tomorrow not hearing from her, although I was convinced I'd be out of here tomorrow anyway. Sallie told me everything at home was fine. Trevor had told my son, Sam, who was handling things well. Sallie was upset that she couldn't call me any more and said she would keep pushing it with the gaol. I asked her not to as I didn't want to piss the Warden off. She told me the company had agreed to send her over if I wasn't released in the next few days but, like me, she believed I'd be out of here very soon.

The old man was waiting when I walked back to my cage and put pressure on me to have my freezing bucket bath. Then Satya, the politician, came by and we went for walk around the yard.

I now looked forward to the nightly lock-in as it was the only time I had any peace and quiet. As I now had the book, I decided to read for as long as possible into the night. I thought I'd start staying awake at night and sleeping as much as possible during the day. My rationale was that the nights seemed to go faster while the days just dragged on forever. I spent the first 30 minutes setting up the mosquito net ensuring the correct tension on the strings so the net touched the floor and the sides were tight enough not to pull out the nails. The fan blew the net all over the place so I put full bottles of water at each corner to hold the net down. Finally I was set for a night without the threat of being carried away by the usual mosquito squadron.

11.
NIGHTMARE DAY FIVE

Thursday 29 May

At 3.00 am the singing started followed by a beating about 20 minutes later. I didn't mind the early wake-up as I wanted to sleep during the day and had only been asleep for three hours. The singing was awful and, to be frank, I felt like digging a hole through the wall and giving the singer a decent beating as well. The screaming and crying stopped at around 4.00 am and, by then, I already had the light out of the Calvin Kleins and into the socket and had read about 10 pages of the book. The caveman walked past and, despite the light being on, decided to shine his torch in my face and deliver his usual greeting, 'arrrggghh'.

'Hi there, mate, how are you doing today? You're looking good as always, you grumpy old shit,' I said to him with a smile on my face. He stopped and came back to the bars and for a moment I thought he had understood what I said. Then he shook his head, grunted some more and spat something chunky on the ground.

'All righty then, see you after, me old mate.' Damn I was bored, but in a jovial mood, as I was leaving this toilet today.

Primal Fear kept me entertained for another hour until the caveman returned to unlock the cage with another 'arrgghh'. I got up and emptied my water bottle, then walked to the drain dodging the spitters on the way; it was like a bloody obstacle course or running the gauntlet. I didn't want to get hit with one of those flying combinations of phlegm and rotten lung, or even receive some splash. Back in the cage I lowered and folded the mosquito net then slowly started to pace in front of the cage under the watchful eye of Ugly. Satya arrived and said, 'Come, we walk.'

'Yeh, okay.'

Satya was an interesting guy who would ask me questions that bounced from one diverse subject to another.

'Paul, do you know William Wordsworth?'

'Well, not personally, but I've heard of him,' I said, thinking that he was a classical novelist, but not sure.

'I do like William Wordsworth. I like his words. What is your favorite William Wordsworth novel? This is what I'd want to know,' said Satya, chewing on a twig.

'Well, to be honest, mate ...'

'Yes, yes.'

'I haven't actually read any William Wordsworth novels.'

'Yes, yes,' Satya said, and I wondered if he even knew what I was saying.

'Also, I want to know about babies and how they are born in Australia.'

Bloody hell; does he want me to explain the birds and the bees to him?

'Well, a lady goes to the hospital and the baby comes from her vagina.'

'Yes, yes. In India many babies and mothers die during childbirth. Does this happen in Australia? This I want to know.'

'Child mortality rate is low in the cities, but still too high in the remote Aboriginal communities.'

'Yes, yes.'

'But it is now mostly controlled, because expectant mothers have monthly check-ups with their doctor to ensure both are healthy, and most mothers have their babies in hospitals, so if something goes wrong there is a surgery and specialists close by. So that helps,' I explained.

'Yes, yes.'

By this time we had done three laps of the yard and Satya deposited me back at the cage where the old man was waiting.

Following the ice cold bucket bath, which I was certain was my last, I returned to the cage and tried to get into *Primal Fear*, but could only think about getting out of this disgusting place. I lay down on the hessian to get comfortable and, with the fan keeping the flies at bay, I dozed off for a while. At 11.30 Manish came in and woke me and told me to go to the office. This time I put my Calvins on and my boots with no socks and wandered to the office. I was more than excited at the prospect of leaving and had even considered the information I'd receive about the whole mess being sorted and the call I would make to Sallie. She'd be excited and I could get on that plane tomorrow and go home and Sallie and I could take that holiday to Fiji. As I entered the Warden's office I could see Craig and the other High Commission guy waiting for me. I greeted them, the Warden and Ujwal, who was also there. When I sat at the table next to them I turned and saw something I hadn't considered and my heart sank — a plastic bag with bottles of water. They wouldn't have brought water for someone about to leave prison. I tried to stay positive as the guys told me the Magistrate had the report, but that it had no conclusion and the conclusion needed to say that I had made a mistake. At this stage it didn't, so the Magistrate couldn't do anything but leave me here. Ujwal said the police would not write this as their conclusion because then they'd look stupid for arresting me in the first place. But it got worse. Craig had spoken to SP Siddiqui. Siddiqui told Craig I'd be lucky if I got six months.

'How can this be happening? How can I get six months in gaol for mistakenly crossing an open border? I barely got to the immigration office!'
'I know,' said Craig.

'No you fucking don't. You go back there and sleep in that shithouse for one day and then you can say you know how it feels. What is the government doing to sort out this scam?'

'As you know, the Australian Government will not do anything to interfere with this country's laws — laws which you're accused of breaking,' said Craig a little timidly.

'I think I've done a fair bit for my country and I'm not asking for much in return, but you're telling me you can't do anything,' I replied, totally exasperated. 'You must know that this is all ridiculous and a waste of everyone's time and effort.'

But the look on Craig's face made me realise that maybe they didn't believe my story and I suddenly felt like Schapelle Corby pleading her innocence on TV. Guilt seemed to have nothing to do with it; it was what people believed.

'All right,' I said, looking for another angle, 'am I supposed to bribe someone? Is someone waiting for a payment?'

'We have heard mention of this.'

'Right, how do I do it and to whom?'

'We can't advise you on this, and if that's the way you want to go, then we'll have to step away from it all.'

'Fuck me, I'm just asking for some cultural guidance here.'

I turned and looked at the local bloke assisting Craig and said, 'You're local, what do you think I need to do?'

'I also cannot advise you on this as I too work for the Australian High Commission.'

To change the subject, Craig asked if I was happy with my lawyer.

'I don't know, I've only meet him once for about two minutes,' I replied, more than a little annoyed.

'Okay, well this is a list of lawyers who seem to have good reputations from this area,' replied Craig as he handed me a list with names, addresses and telephone numbers of local lawyers.

I scanned the list and asked, 'Which one do I pick?'

'We can't advise you on that, it's up to you.'

For fuck's sake, this was becoming too much. 'Are any of them in Araria?' I asked, seeking some direction.

'No, but this one is the closest and he is about four hours away. We've tried to call him, but haven't received a reply yet.'

'This is hopeless, I might as well just stick with the court-appointed advocate.'

'Yes, that's probably a good idea.'

Are these guys for real? I thought. Why did we just have that conversation?

Craig handed me a letter from Sallie that she'd e-mailed to him and he had rewritten as there was no printer in his crap hotel. I put the letter in my pocket to read later. Craig and the local guy decided it was time to leave and I sensed a coldness in their manner, as if they wanted to distance themselves from the condemned man. As they prepared to leave, I extended my hand to Craig and it seemed to take him by surprise, as though he just wanted to get out of the place as quickly as possible.

Ujwal remained behind and he and I discussed the issue of bribing the SP. Ujwal said he would look into it, but thought the SP wouldn't accept the bribe at this point, but that he would try. Ujwal also mentioned the hearing tomorrow and was optimistic about the result. He said the journalists from Biratnagar were preparing a welcome-back party for me. Ujwal left me with a sense of hope, but this feeling was clouded by the sense of hopelessness left by Craig. I guess he was doing what he had to do, but when your life is placed in everyone else's hands you tend to cling to hope and, at the moment, I was left with none. People who have committed genuine crimes — like those arrested at an airport with heroin strapped to their bodies — prepare themselves to spend time in prison. But even these people look for some light at the end of the tunnel, some glimmer of hope that they will get 10 years rather than the death penalty. Would you say to these guys during their first days in custody, 'You'll be lucky not to get the death penalty?' Everyone needs hope and Ujwal knew how to provide this.

Back in the cage I fell into the depths of depression. This was just dragging on and there seemed to be no light at the end of the tunnel. I should have been in a nice hotel in Katmandu having a cold beer while preparing for my flight back to Australia the next day, but no, not me. I was stuck in a cage on the cold floor with the mosquitoes, ants and rats waiting for the Hari Krishnas to start their nightly chant.

I reflected on the morning's events and felt grateful to the Australian government for sending Craig and his assistant all this way to help me get out of a hole that I'd foolishly dug. I knew their hands were tied and that they were doing all they could. Just their presence and interest in this matter had to help.

Ugly locked the cage at 7.00 pm after I closed the gate myself. I was on my own and appreciated the solitude, but certainly didn't want to start thinking again, although it was a battle not to. That night Manish brought a sumptuous meal of three cold rotis and a small bowl of watery dhal that resembled and smelt like the results of a night of cheap wine and pizza. Manish also thought I looked depressed. He said he would do me a big favour if I promised to eat the food. 'Okay, I will,' I said. Manish then handed me his cell phone. I couldn't believe he had a phone in this joint, but I suppose that sort of stuff goes on in gaols. Manish told me to call my family and give them this number to call back immediately.

Manish stood outside the cage as I tried to think of a number to call. I didn't have any numbers committed to memory except my father's and stepmother's, but I really wanted to chat to my brother Trevor. I decided to call my father's number and get Trevor's number from him. My stepmother answered the phone, as expected, as my father was too ill to talk on the phone and would be sleeping deeply with the aid of a sleeping pill. In Australia it was almost midnight so my stepmother was obviously sleeping and the phone rang five times before she answered.

'Hello,' said a sleepy voice.

'Carole, it's me,' I whispered.

'Hello love, what's wrong?'

'Nothing much, but I need Trevor's phone number quickly, do you have it?'

Yes, love, hang on. Now where is that number?'

'Please Carole, you have to be quick.'

'Okay love, here it is, are you ready?'

'Yes, send.'

Carole read out Trevor's number and I wrote it on my Sudoku paper.

'Is everything okay, love?' Carole asked with an edge of concern. I decided to tell her.

'No, I'm fucked. I'm in gaol in India, but I'm working hard on getting out.'

'Oh, God.'

'I have to go because I'm using someone else's phone and calling illegally.'

'Okay, love.'

'Don't be concerned, I'll sort it out,' I said, regretting telling her of my situation.

I rang Trevor and got the answering machine. I left a garbled message including Manish's cell phone number. Manish was getting anxious so I hoped Trevor would get my message and call me back — and soon.

He did, and just in the nick of time, as Manish was approaching and I'm sure he was going to tell me to try again tomorrow.

'Hello mate,' I whispered.

'Hey, how's it goin?' Trevor said in his heavy, jovial, Australia accent.

'Bloody excellent, mate. Listen, I only have a few more seconds. Sorry for waking you both so late.'

Chapter 11

'No worries, mate. Are you okay?'

'I'm surviving, mate, and thanks for helping Sallie and keeping an eye on things.'

Then I heard Trevor's wife, Carissa, on the other phone telling Trevor that my ex-wife was on the other phone. That's when I learnt that my ex-wife was staying with my stepmother and father for the night and had woken to hear my conversation with Carole. Carole had no choice but to tell her that I was in gaol and she was calling Trevor to learn more. Carissa did the right thing and didn't say much. My ex-wife meant well, but had a habit of turning everything into a major drama and making it about poor old her rather than anyone else. I knew that once she realised my predicament everyone would know and I was trying to avoid that.

'Do what you have to, mate and don't worry about what's happening back here. It's all under control. Sam has been good and won't let anyone near your house,' Trevor said reassuringly.

'Thanks mate, gotta go, my love to Carissa,' and I hung up.

Manish came back to the cage and took the phone. I thanked him very much as he disappeared into the night. I was on my own again. It was great speaking to Trevor, but I wondered what sort of shit storm I'd created back in the world.

I set up the mosquito net for the night, placing bottles of water on the corners as weights to ensure the blowing fan didn't allow the edges to lift and let in the squadrons of mosquitoes just waiting to clean me out and leave some nice dengue fever or malaria behind. The idea that I might be here for some time started to creep into my mind and I decided it was best to get used to it. In fact, that's what I teach people to do when they're a hostage or in prison. I teach people to expect to be a hostage for months rather than days, but teaching it and putting it into practice were two different things.

Mentally, I was struggling. I couldn't get my kids out of my head. Every time I thought of them I came close to tears. I thought my kids would quickly forget me and accept my ex-wife's boyfriend into my house and that would be their new family while their loser dad was in gaol in India. And the idea that I could be here when my dad died was pulling me apart as well. I was really struggling. Then I remembered the letter in my pocket.

How could I have forgotten Sallie's letter? I got up and retrieved the light bulb from the Calvins. I dug the letter from the other pocket and got comfortable back under the mosquito net. The letter was written in another's handwriting, but the words were clearly Sallie's and beautiful. She told me not to worry about the house as Sam had said that no-one was getting anywhere near it. That allayed my concerns a little. There were also instructions from Colin Rigby (our psychologist friend) about positive thinking, exercise and meditation. Positive thinking and exercise I could handle, but I don't meditate; I find it boring and get distracted too easily.

Exercising was a good idea though, and something I would have started day one if I had thought I'd be here this long. I removed the light, put it back in the Calvins and got under the mozzie net. I wanted to exercise without the caveman seeing me and reporting my efforts. I started doing push-ups. I placed my hands a little wider than shoulder width and went down very slowly until my chest touched the hessian and then slowly pushed back up. After 20 of these very slow push-ups my chest was screaming and I couldn't get another one out, so I rolled on my back and started doing sit-ups. I raised my feet about 20 centimetres off the ground and, as I brought my knees to my chest, I raised my upper body at the same time to meet my knees, keeping my hands on my abdomen. I managed 50 and then rested for five minutes before repeating the cycle. Then I was rooted and just lay there for a while before putting the light back in and reading some more *Primal Fear*. It wasn't much, but it was enough to keep me going for now.

12.

NIGHTMARE DAY SIX

Friday 30 May

Thankfully, there was no singing this morning. I suppose someone had finally got the idea after being bashed twice. Reminds me of that joke: what do you tell someone with two black eyes? Nothing, you've already told him twice.

I was awake at about 3.00 am anyway trying to mentally prepare myself to be here a bit longer; but it was impossible, it just couldn't be done. I thought more about Colin Rigby's advice. He suggested just getting through each day, that I shouldn't get excited about leaving, but that I should establish a routine, exercise and eat. This was all good advice and all strategies I knew as that's what I teach. But it's bloody hard to put into practice — almost impossible when all I could think about was sleeping in a real bed that night, not having to bathe with a bucket of cold water, and not sleeping with rats and the constant smell of piss and shit. I also missed freedom, but felt like a whinger for thinking like that after only a few days in the big house.

The caveman grunted at me at 5.00 am and opened the cage. I sat up and grabbed my boots so I could challenge the morning obstacle course when I felt some pain in my toe and noticed some blood surrounding a small wound. My immediate thought was that one of the many rats that entered my cage at night had decided to make a meal of my big toe. The taste of disgust and repulsion rose in my throat and I nearly vomited; dirty, filthy, fucking thing. There was nothing else to do but forget it had even happened. Maybe I had stubbed my toe at night and didn't notice. I didn't have any antiseptic.

I emptied my bottle and wandered over to the drain for my morning leak. Then I waited and waited and waited. The old man nagged me to have a bucket bath and reluctantly I did. Kneeling on the concrete slab, I was deep in thought soaping up my body when I suddenly realised that the old man was washing my back with his old, weather-beaten, calloused hands. Oh God, I hope this is the last time I wash in this shit hole, I thought, as I carefully monitored how far his old hands went down my back. Then it was back to the cage where I kept waiting; every minute became an hour, every hour an eternity.

Finally I was called to the office where I was surprised to see Debu-San, my lawyer, and the High Commission guys sitting in the Warden's office. As I entered the office I looked for the death sentence — plastic bag full of bottled water. It was there and I was crushed. I wanted to go off. I wanted to kick and punch out. I wanted to scream 'what fucking now?' I wanted to yell, 'what's wrong with you fucking imbeciles?' But I didn't. I just sat there and prepared to listen to what old rotten teeth had to say to me.

Apparently the police paperwork wasn't as complete as we had all thought it would be, and a petitioner had presented a petition against my release. They didn't know where this man had came from, but he was old, had a grey beard and suffered from severe vitiligo. Bloody hell, it was the angry man from the border, the criminal and police informer. But I couldn't understand why he would go to so much effort to ensure that I was not released. I could only assume that the SP had pushed him to do this. The High Commission guys told me that Ujwal had gone to deal with him so he wouldn't visit today. Old rotten teeth Debu-San told me there would be a hearing tomorrow, but only to deal with the petition and not my release. Debu-San told me not to be concerned with the petition as it was illegal and would be thrown out, but that I would be here for a few more days. I told him I'd heard the 'don't worry,' line before and that, in here, there wasn't much else to do but worry. Craig let me use his phone and I made a two-minute call to Sallie. I felt absolutely destroyed and this came

Chapter 12

through in my voice when I spoke to Sallie. She told me to be strong and that she was on her way to help. Craig handed me a letter from Sallie with comments about Trevor and the kids and more advice from Colin Rigby. The letter lifted my morale slightly and I was relieved to hear that the kids were well. Trevor seemed to be doing a great job handling the family. Craig and his mate decided to leave and pointed to a mattress in front of the prison that they said they had brought for me. The mattress would make the nights easier on my bones, but confirmed that I would be there for longer than anyone had expected. Maybe I was the only person who had thought I'd be out of here in a day or so. Maybe everyone else realised that this was bad and that I was in here for the long haul but no-one wanted to tell me. I thanked them for the mattress. Craig told me he was returning to Delhi, but that a local replacement was on his way to help. I thanked Craig for his efforts and was genuinely grateful to him, as I knew he could only do what the Australian government allowed.

Back in the cage, I cried like a baby. I couldn't stop and had to ensure that no-one saw me in this state. Once I started, I just kept on going. This was getting crazy and ridiculous, but I couldn't stop. The old man walked in and saw me in this condition and started rubbing my back. That was enough for me to stop and think about something else very quickly. I stopped as quickly as I had started and lay down for a while. The old man had a fan and started to fan me. I couldn't handle the fanning and didn't want to treat the old man like a slave, so I asked him to stop. A few minutes later, I dug out some old notes from my Calvins and gave the money to the old man. Then he started to bawl uncontrollably and I picked up his fan and started fanning him, and had to control my laughing — this was getting ridiculous. The old man eventually regained control of himself and left and I started laughing again. Could this get any crazier?

Crying was an interesting experience for me, because I hadn't really cried since 1977.

13.
STEVEN

Remembrance Day, 11 November 1977, and Shane, Graham and I were walking down the road heading to Shane and Graham's house. Trevor was at home and we had just said goodbye to Steven as he rode off to a friend's house on his bicycle. I was 11 that year, Trevor was seven and Steven had turned 13 two months before. 'Tell Mum I'll be home later,' he had said. Steven hadn't wanted to come with us as he had somewhere else to go. Mum had taken to stopping at Shane and Graham's house for an afternoon coffee with their mum, Trish. We'd known Trish and her husband Kel for a long time and they were both actively involved with football — Kel was the manager of the team. Steven and I spent a lot of time with Shane and Graham. Most weekends, when we weren't playing football, we were at the Keperra Golf Course looking for golf balls to sell to the Pro Shop or to golfers. We managed to save quite a stash. As we ambled along Patrick's Road, an ambulance screamed up the road past us and we heard it turn the corner and stop quite close by. We debated whether to go and see what had happened but decided we couldn't be arsed.

Mum and Trish greeted us as we walked through the door. Mum was sitting at the table with Trish while Kel was standing in the kitchen. 'Here comes trouble,' Trish said, 'where have you been?'
'Just at Paul's house,' Graham replied.
'Where's Trevor?' Mum asked.
'He's at home doing nothing,' I said.
'What about Steven?' asked Mum.

'He went out, but said he'd be home for tea,' I answered.

Satisfied with this, Mum and Trish slipped back into their conversation. Then the phone rang. Trish answered and I noted the change in the pitch of her voice — it told me that something was wrong. All she said was, 'Yes, yes, yes, where? Yes, yes, okay, we're coming now.' Trish hung up the phone and looked straight at Mum and said, 'Steve's had an accident and we have to go now.' Mum went into an immediate panic and assumed the worst: 'Is he dead?' Is he dead? What sort of a question is that? Of course he wasn't dead. It was just like Mum to immediately think the worst, and it was just like Steven to have another accident and get a few days off school. Trish didn't reply to Mum's comment, but gave Kel a look as they scrambled for the car. Graham jumped into the back seat and Trish told him to get out and for all of us to go back to my house, get Trevor and bring him back here.

So off we went. We took the short cut through the bush, across the park, past Wayne's house to my house. Trevor wasn't doing much and I just said that we had to go to Shane and Graham's house because Steven had had an accident. On the walk back we talked about what might have happened, but never linked the ambulance we saw with the accident. We decided that it sounded pretty serious, so he must have broken his leg or something like that. A year before, Allan had told me after school that Steven had had an accident and had been taken to hospital. Mum and Steven arrived home that night at about 7.00 pm — Steven had broken his collar bone. I didn't even know we had a collar bone, but assumed it was located somewhere near where the shirt collar sits. We guessed it was going to be like that. When we arrived back at Shane and Graham's house, the parents still hadn't returned, so we just sat at the kitchen table and waited. About an hour later, Kel walked in and said, 'Alright, do you know what's happened?'

'No,' I said.

'Okay, Steven's been killed.'

I felt as if someone had hit me in the chest with a sledgehammer and I wanted to scream, 'bullshit!' But I could barely breathe, let alone scream. I knew it was true, so I bowed my head and the tears started to pour out of me. I didn't know what else to do. Kel tried to get us to stop and said that Mum was coming in and we should give her a big hug and that she really needed our support. Mum came in looking absolutely destroyed and broken. She could barely put one foot in front of the other and was supported by Trish. This was really happening. We moved to Shane and Graham's bedroom where we just sat and cried while holding each other. We seemed to sit there for hours crying. I was destroyed, this couldn't be happening. Poor Mum, she'd already been through so much and now this. She was crying so much and couldn't really talk. Eventually we broke apart and Trevor and I went and sat in the lounge room and kept crying, as did Shane and Graham. Trish, who had already contacted Lex with the news, comforted Mum. I learnt that Steven had skidded on his bike on some spilt gravel and had gone under one of those semi-trailers that carry cars. It was Friday night and the time seemed to pass very slowly as an intense pain settled deeply into every fibre of my body.

We spent the weekend at Trish's house while Mum insisted on going home. She collapsed in the hallway outside Steven's bedroom and a doctor was called to sedate her. I went home the next day to see Mum, but she wasn't much better and I knew it was going to be a long time before she would recover. For me, it was still surreal. Shane, Graham and I visited friends to talk about what had happened, but we were just kids struggling to decipher what it all meant. The tears had stopped momentarily, but came back the next evening when Trish took us to the cathedral in the city to light a candle for Steven; but again, I really didn't know what this all meant. Trish described the usual routine in the church and, after lighting the candle, we all dropped to our knees in pews and prayed for Steven's soul. But again, we were just kids and had no real idea what was going on. Frankly I was expecting Steven to just walk into the house at any time.

Trish was a solid friend and leader throughout all this and all but adopted Trevor and me while Mum struggled to maintain some sanity. Trish took us to church, she organised fundraising at the football club to help Mum pay for the funeral and basically kept us kids occupied while she helped Mum to cope. To my surprise, Shane and Graham spent our saved golf ball money buying Trevor and me silver and gold necklaces with a small crucifix with our names engraved on them. It was a damned nice thing to do.

The funeral was on Wednesday at the Albany Creek Crematorium. Most of the year 6 and 7 students from school were there, along with most of the football club. In all, about 300 people were present. Mum sat up the front while Trevor and I sat a few aisles back with friends. It was strange that we didn't stay with Mum — I don't know why we didn't. We even arrived at the crematorium at different times. I cried some more and wondered if I would ever run out of tears. I learnt on this day that funerals seem to be about everyone else rather than the person who'd died. Everyone wants to be associated with the family and be part of the drama and loss. But when it's all over you're left with only your true friends, incredible loss, heartache and absence. This day was no different; the surreal experience continued, as if I was living someone else's life for a while. I wasn't sure what we were doing and expected Steven to be dropped off any minute so we could all get back to normal.

After the funeral I spent a lot of time thinking and continued to struggle to accept that Steven was gone, but realised soon enough that he wasn't coming home. What sort of god takes a child so violently? A religious friend explained that it was 'God's way'. Well, I decided, if that's how God worked, I wanted nothing further to do with Him. I gave up trying to understand why Steven was dead; the only way I could cope with what had happened was to forget about it. And that's what I did. If the topic was raised at the dinner table, I walked away. If I was asked a question about the accident, I pretended not to hear and walked away. I was 11 years old and didn't shed another tear for more than 30 years. What else could there possibly be to cry about after losing a brother? Only in the last year or so have I been comfortable talking about Steven's death. I missed him then and still do now.

14.
NIGHTMARE DAYS SEVEN AND EIGHT

Sudoku and *Primal Fear* were not enough to distract my mind, so I decided to go for a walk and try to think about something else for a while. But it was pointless. I felt my eyes starting to moisten again when I thought about my kids and Sallie. I had to force myself to remove these thoughts, as I couldn't afford to have my fellow prisoners see me as a sook. Instead I thought about what I should be doing right now. I should be at Kathmandu airport waiting for the plane to take me home and on holiday to Fiji with Sallie. Instead I was stuck in the oversized toilet that was now home and all because of the angry man, the SP and my damned stupidity. For the hundredth time I asked myself, how the bloody hell did I end up here? I decided I couldn't think about this any more, so I went back to the cage and read for a while.

The loud-talking guard visited my cell and offered nice words of encouragement. He told me he could see that I was an important man and well educated and that, with prayer, I would be released very soon. Bloody hell, had this guy got me wrong — or maybe I'd fooled him. Apparently one of his brothers was a professor at a university in Mumbai and another was a financial director of an international company in Delhi. I wanted to ask what had happened to him and how he got it so wrong. But he seemed happy with his lot and obviously had no regrets. When he left, the old man returned and delivered one of his sermons and we finished with a biscuit each.

An hour later, my new mattress arrived in my cage. It was an old, thin mattress so I folded it in half for additional cushioning, but it was 100 times better than the hessian sack on the ground. The old man nagged me to have my bucket bath and then the politician and I went for our nightly walk around this shit pit. Thankfully we didn't talk much; I just didn't think I could've handled any of his 'deep' questions today. We sat on the planter box and watched the lock-up process. He introduced me to a young lad and I suspected there might have been some after-hours activity going on there.

After lock-down, the Warden visited and offered words of encouragement. I thanked him for his support and for tolerating all my visitors. He said he didn't mind and only wanted the best for me. Manish brought some food; well, I think it was food. It looked more like baby shit in a bowl. He offered me his phone if I promised to eat the meal. I agreed and quickly called Sallie and asked her to call back on this number. It was great to have a quick chat with her. Then I threw the food in my rubbish bag. Manish took his phone and I was left in peace and on my own for the next 10 hours.

My nights were now routine: I set up my mosquito net, I worked out in darkness for an hour doing push-ups and sit-ups until exhaustion set in and then I read or did Sudoku for two or three hours while eating a biscuit or two. I usually tried to sleep at around midnight and hoped for dreams so I could escape the thought of the rats chewing on my body during the night. But the sleep was too short and not deep enough for the dreams to take hold. So I was well awake by the time the caveman grunted at 5.00 the next morning.

Saturday 31 May

This morning I decided to remain where I was under the mosquito net for a while longer. When I first arrived at the gaol I assumed that I had to be out of bed at 5.00 am, but quickly discovered that others just stayed where they were. Now that I was resigned to the fact that I was going to be there for a while, I realised that I had no real need to spring out of bed. So I stayed where I was, still under my mosquito net which became my shield from the outside world. I thought about the day before and felt like a fool for being so emotional. I was in prison and needed to toughen up if I was going to survive this experience. If I cried like a woman again, one of these dirty bastards might try to treat me like his woman and then I'd be up on a murder charge. Now I felt more content with my situation. I knew I was going to be here for a few more days. This realisation allowed me to forget about being released and start thinking about adapting to this shitty experience.

Ujwal visited at 11.00 am and told me that the petition submitted by the angry man had been thrown out, and that the angry man would be no more trouble. Apparently the angry man had another wife living just over the Nepali border and frequently visited her. The Nepali police visited the angry man when he was at his wife's house and told him that, if I wasn't released soon, and they saw him in Nepal again, they'd kill him. The angry man assured Ujwal that he wouldn't cause any more trouble as long as the Nepali police didn't hurt him. Ujwal agreed to talk to the Nepali police. It would have been easier for all if the angry man had just left me alone in the first place. I'd almost be back in Australia by now and would have nothing more on my mind than my holiday in Fiji. Damn that old prick; I'd love to see him again somewhere.

Ujwal had to return to Kathmandu to apply for more leave and to stir up some government action. 'Okay mate,' I said, accepting that I'd be by myself for a few days without a visitor. 'Have you got my cell phone with you?' I asked.

'No, it is in the car,' Ujwal said with little interest.

'Go and get it and give it to me,' I said as Ujwal nearly fell over.

'No, this is impossible; I don't think you can do this.'

'I can, Ujwal. Half the population of the prison has a bloody cell phone. Please get it for me.'

Ujwal returned to the car as I waited on the other side of the barred gate. When Ujwal visited on his own he wasn't allowed into the gaol. He returned and passed my phone through the bars and I immediately put it down the front of my underwear.

'Thanks mate, I'll see you in a few days.' We shook hands and he was gone. I returned to the cage, but then became concerned that Ujwal probably hadn't silenced the phone. I hoped it wouldn't ring while I was en route.

Back in my cage I couldn't wait to read the history of text messages and see who had called, but Ugly Guard was sitting on my mattress enjoying my fan. I willed the ugly bastard to piss off, but he didn't go anywhere. The other problem was that I still didn't know whether the phone was on silent so it could ring at any minute. I had to somehow get him to leave. I decided to lie down and pretend to sleep, but he didn't budge, and just sat there staring out the front of the cell. Then the loud-talking guard walked past and saw Ugly Guard resting in my cage. He ran into my cage and raised his beating stick as though he was going to belt me with it. Instead he brought the stick down on Ugly Guard's back and there was an almighty crack, quickly followed by a torrent of abuse. I rolled off the mattress into the corner out of the way as Ugly Guard ran out the front of the cage with Loud Talker chasing him with more swings of his stick and abuse. As quickly as it started, it was over. I remained in the corner for a moment wondering what the hell had just happened. Holy shit, that was interesting. I didn't think Ugly Guard would be back again, but one thing was for sure, he was going to be really pissed off with me.

I was now by myself so I rolled over and checked my phone. Thankfully the phone was turned off, so I turned it on and put it under my mattress while it made its turning-on noises. I gave it a few minutes then went berserk sending text messages to everyone letting them know I had my phone with me. I even lay on my side and placed the phone under my ear risking a short call to Sallie. It was difficult; I had to whisper the words. Sallie told me she was leaving on Monday and would go to New Delhi first then come to me by Wednesday. I was pissed off that I'd even be here on Wednesday. When I was done with my phone, I turned it off and stashed it in a small plastic bag that held my socks, jocks and money. I put the money on top of the bag so a potential thief would take the notes and leave the rest.

I slid my mattress to the back wall of the cage and sat against the wall reading more *Primal Fear*. I was approaching the end of this book so I had to slow down a bit. As I settled into the pages, Loud-Talking Guard came into my cage, but this time he approached quietly and sat at the end of the mattress. He said nothing about his efforts a few hours ago, but told me the Nepali journalists were protesting at the border today over my arrest.

In the afternoon I felt a little desperate, so I went to the office to talk to the Warden. He was busy and told me to wait. When he was free I asked if he could pass a message to the kind man who had visited me the other day. The Warden had no idea who I was talking about so I pushed on with more descriptions. I figured I needed help and there didn't seem to be much happening. That man had been kind enough to bring me a mosquito net, he spoke excellent English and he did say to contact him if I ever needed anything, so I thought I'd ask the Warden to please do just that. But the Warden had no idea who I was talking about so, after a few minutes, I let it go.

At 6.30 pm, I was sitting on the planter box with the politician discussing the complex issues of life and watching the day come to a close at the camp — another day in hell. Thankfully the politician didn't interrogate me with too many complex questions tonight; I don't think I could have handled it. But at least today I had scored a tiny victory: my smuggled cell phone had become a lifeline to the outside world.

15.

NIGHTMARE DAYS
NINE AND TEN

Sunday 1 June

At 11.00 am I had just finished a quick, covert chat with Sallie when Manish came to the cage and told me to go the office. The new High Commission guy had arrived. His name was Rajeesh and he seemed to be a nice guy. Like the angry man, Rajeesh suffered from terrible vitiligo. He asked the Warden if I could make a quick call to my wife, so I called Sallie. Sallie was delighted that we could have a conversation that was more than just whispers. I asked the guys whether they had spoken to the kind man who brought me the mosquito net. They said they were going to see the Sub-District Magistrate following this meeting. I asked them to explain to the Warden who the Sub-District Magistrate was. The penny dropped with the Warden and he laughed; of course he knew the Sub-District Magistrate and they agreed to ask him to visit.

Back in the yard I decided to walk laps and I seemed to walk for bloody miles. As I walked past one of the cell blocks for what seemed like the fiftieth time, I could hear a TV running, so had a peek through the barred window. An old black and white TV with massive knobs to change the channel was mounted in the corner of the dormitory-style building. Something that resembled the Sunday matinee was playing and the movie looked old, although it could have been the effect of the black and white TV. A crowd of around 50 prisoners sat in front watching the movie and I found myself becoming absorbed by the show as well. I couldn't understand what was happening because it was in Hindi, but it was something different to do. Then, inevitably, there was a blackout and, since the generators weren't used during the day, that was the end of the program. The prisoners protested loudly and, if it hadn't been for Loud Talker swinging his stick, there would have been a riot. Loud Talker pulled out his long stick, yelled a pile of abuse at everyone and then started to swing, which seemed to quiet everyone down. That was my cue to continue my Sunday afternoon stroll.

That afternoon I was summoned to the Warden's office where the Sub-District Magistrate was waiting. He said the High Commission guys had visited and passed on my message. He asked what I needed and said I should feel free to ask him — as a friend — for anything. I explained that I'd run out of soap and needed shampoo. He agreed to buy these things for me. I went to get the money, but he refused and sent his lackey to buy lemonade for us. The door to the Warden's office was closed and the Sub-District Magistrate poured a glass of lemonade for us both. It was cold and I could see the beads starting to form on the outside of the glass as the bubbles rose to the surface. Finally, he handed it to me. I raised my glass in appreciation and took a little sip. I was certain that my mouth had an orgasm — bloody hell that lemonade tasted good. I finished the glass too quickly and the Sub-District Magistrate asked if I'd like more.

'Sure, perhaps just a little,' I said. In reality, I wanted to grab the bottle and run to my cage and scull the lot, but of course I played it cool. The Sub-District Magistrate insisted that I stop calling him 'Sir' and use his first name — Bala. Bala was younger than I was, possibly in his early thirties or late twenties. You'd probably describe him as handsome with a very gentle nature. We sat chatting about life and global politics for 20 minutes or so and then he was off and I wandered back to my cage.

The old man was waiting for me back at the cage and started nagging me about the time and my bucket bath. I decided not to argue because the old man was so good to me and I had a soft spot for him. The old bastard washed my back again. I bloody hated it and could just imagine the shit I'd cop if any of my mates saw me, but frankly I was over fighting the issue. I missed the walk with the politician and just decided to relax and listen to the Hari Krishnas. The old man had taken to dropping rose petals all over my old mattress — fuck me, this was getting crazy. I had to say something and, just before the cage was locked, he placed a woven bouquet of flowers on my cage door.

'Thanks,' I said, and mumbled, 'oh God, please kill me.'

As it got dark, I removed my light, stashed the globe into the Calvins and began a quiet work-out. I could now manage 50 push-ups without a problem and then continue in smaller sets until I'd done 100. Sit-ups were the same and, by the time I'd finished, my abs were screaming at me for a rest. That was it; I put the light back in and finished *Primal Fear*.

Monday 2 June

Dreams are freedom in gaol. This night I was blessed with a relaxing, sensual dream. I was on my back in Sallie's bed and the feel of the soft bed and clean sheets were paradise against my body. I felt so relaxed and relieved to be out of gaol. Sallie was giving me a soft and tender massage after a long day of training. Her fingers were light on my body and seemed to be all over the place at once. I asked for a little more pressure and felt the sudden change. All her fingers were dancing up my legs towards my thighs and I relaxed further with anticipation. Then she was on my chest. Her fingers just seemed to be everywhere and it felt so good. One hand swept around the back of my head and then Sallie placed small tender kisses against my ear. I looked down at my beautiful Sallie as her fingers continued their gentle touching of my body. She wasn't rubbing, just touching with her fingertips. Then I felt her bite, but I didn't see her doing it. The bite was so small yet fucking painful. The pain dragged me from the image of my beautiful Sallie. The colours and warmth disappeared into the darkness and cold and, moments later, my eyes were open and I was back in the cage. Then the pain hit again, but I could still feel Sallie's fingers on me and, for a moment, I thought Sallie was with me. I looked down trying to see her in the dark and saw a cat on my chest. Still half-asleep, I tried to pat the cat. As my hand got close to the cat, I suddenly realised that it was not a cat but a rat, and that there were about five of them on me. Repulsed,

I sat up and the rats leapt for safety and scrambled out of the cage as the caveman appeared with a torch.

'Shine that torch down here,' I called to him.

He grunted and left.

'Fuck it, dirty horrible bastards.'

I got up and dug into the Calvins for the light. On inspection, the bite was minor and only drew a little blood, but the thought ensured I didn't sleep again. This was fucked, and what the hell was kissing my ear?

My thin mattress supplied by the High Commission guys was great and made sleeping easier (or it would have if I could have kept the rats away) and my old bones didn't hurt as much when I got up. I knew the day was going to be quiet so I didn't spring off the mattress when the caveman grunted and unlocked the door.

No visitors came today, so I spent the day very much on my own. I still had the usual morning routine to get through before I could relax. As usual, I emptied my pee bottle into the garden and then ran the gauntlet as I made my way to the drain for a pee. I walked with the politician, took my cold bucket bath, then relaxed with my book. The High Commission guys also brought me some additional food for which I had no appetite, so I gave it to the old man and the sick guys next door. They were rapt when they got more chocolate.

I was slowly acquiring more and more possessions, so the politician told me to watch my belongings and ensure I always closed my cage door when I left. On one occasion he even told the old man to stand at the gate as we walked. I felt terrible for my old mate, but he didn't seem to mind. I think my presence had taken the old man from a life of boredom to a life of purpose. He had gone from sweeping my floor to being my personal assistant. He did everything for me; it kept him occupied and he made a few bucks on the side and certainly made my life easier.

There was a Hindu temple in the middle of the yard with a series of tiles depicting various Gods cemented to the side, and a bell suspended from the mango tree adjacent to the temple. The prisoners rang the bell at the start and at the finish of their prayer sessions. The politician told me that the prisoners rang the bell to wake the gods so they'd be alert when the prayer was said; then they rang the bell so the gods would know they'd come to the end.

'I think the gods must be bloody pissed off because that bell rings every five minutes so the gods aren't getting any sleep.'

'Yes, you are for sure very correct. This is why all these people are here because the gods are tired and grumpy all the time.'

Others prayed while they took a bucket bath. Apparently they worshipped a water god and uttered prayers as they poured water over their heads. Clearly they were not in drought.

The police brought in a very old man who could barely walk. He moved along very slowly, was all bent over and used an old stick to avoid collapsing onto the ground. I wondered why the police had him in chains. He wasn't going anywhere and if he did try to make a run for it, you could have put the kettle on, made a cup of tea, cooked a batch of Anzac biscuits and apprehended the guy before he got five metres away. He wore spectacles with one side shattered as if the lens had been hit with a rock. He was dressed in a filthy old sarong and nothing else. I later learnt that his family had him arrested because of dowry issues. He'd refused to pay a daughter's dowry, so they had him arrested. Unbelievable! That old guy should have been in a nursing home, not in the prison. But they wouldn't know what a nursing home was in Bihar Province.

There was always some excitement in the yard when an interesting prisoner arrived. It certainly happened in my case — and I was generally still a curiosity — but the bloody old bloke created a stir and certainly some comment, and then a kid of about 15 years old arrived. He looked like I probably did, despite trying to look tough. He was clearly shitting himself and had a crowd of a few hundred milling around him. The poor little bastard was almost in a state of shock and I knew that this was going to be compounded after lock-in when some of these long-term prisoners got hold of him.

Next door, the lunatic was at it again. He obviously had some severe mental issues going on and, like the kid and the old bloke, should never have been in the prison. Had he been diagnosed correctly, he could probably have been medicated and lived a relatively normal life. But this was India, and Bihar, so the chances of there being a psychologist close by were next to zero. He decided to take his pants off in front of my cage and go nude for a while. The old man, realising the guards would not be happy, pleaded with him to behave himself and put his clothes back on, but the lunatic seemed to have no idea what was coming and continued to enjoy the freedom of nudity. The other prisoners weren't as kind as the old man. They yelled abuse and moved away. Nudity is a strange thing in India and is not culturally acceptable. The men bathe, as I did, in underwear, so having the lunatic prance around with all his kit hanging out wasn't on as far as they were concerned. I just shrugged my shoulders and felt for the poor bastard as I knew he was in for it when the guards saw him. Sure enough, Ugly arrived and attempted to shackle the lunatic. The lunatic resisted, so Ugly let fly with a pretty solid short drive with his right fist into the lunatic's solar plexus. This certainly confirmed that the lunatic was a bit slow, because the punch came from way back behind Ugly's back and any normal boxer with very little training could have landed three straight jabs on Ugly's chin in the time it took for his low punch to connect with the lunatic. The lunatic let out an almost silent noise as all the air in his lungs was abruptly forced out of his mouth, and he went down in a gasping heap. Then Ugly dragged his sorry arse to the front of his cage and shackled his hands to the bars on the gate. The poor bloody lunatic stayed on the ground struggling to find his breath after Ugly's cheap shot had winded him so badly. He then proceeded to cry for the next few hours. Great. That was all I needed. Here I was just minding my own business trying to relax on a Monday afternoon with my book for company, and Ugly goes and destroys that by belting the only person in the place he stands a chance of beating in a fight. Now I had to listen to this crying. What was the world coming to?

I grabbed my cream biscuits from my stash and walked to the cell next door. The lunatic looked pretty pathetic. He was still nude, but had a filthy old sarong thrown on him. Snot ran from his nose taking the short cut straight across his mouth rather than going around it. Tears ran from his eyes following the paths laid by the litres of previous tears. He looked up at me and seemed a little frightened. I suddenly realised that I was probably doing the wrong thing. You know what it's like when you feed a stray dog — not that I'm comparing the lunatic to a dog — but when you feed a stray dog it decides you are now its best friend and hangs around for attention and more food. What if I gave the lunatic these biscuits and he decided to harass me for more? Ah, bugger it. Should have thought about that and asked the old man to give him the biscuits. But I was already there and the lunatic had seen the biscuits in my hand, so I placed the biscuits in his manacled hands. But the way Ugly had shackled his hands, he couldn't bring them to his mouth, so he dropped his mouth to his hands and shoved the biscuits in, all the while keeping a watchful eye on me — I suppose just the way a stray dog might.

Another new arrival was in the sick cell next door. He had a fresh bandage around his head, arm and shoulder. In fact he looked as if he should still be in hospital receiving ongoing treatment. But this being India, he was thrown in the slammer. He looked as if he was in constant pain and the medic in me wanted to help this guy with some Panadol Forte. He looked pretty sad and sorry for himself. As well as the bandage wrapped around his head, he had burn marks over his body. That afternoon, as I strolled the yard with the politician, I asked what had happened to the injured bloke. The politician looked at me, then walked up to the injured guy, pointed and said, 'This boy?'
Embarrassed, I replied, 'Yes.'
The politician spoke to the man for a while and I listened to the Hindi conversation as it went back and forth. Finally the politician turned to me and, momentarily gathering his thoughts said, 'This man is a thief. He was caught stealing and the village people beat him before calling the police.' He related the man's tale without accusation or emotion.
'Oh, right,' I said, immediately regretting any feelings of pity I had for the dirty, thieving prick and wanting to add my contribution to his injuries. I hate thieves. If you want something, work for it, but don't steal what some other bloke has worked hard to get.

Sallie left for New Delhi today. What a mess this was that she had to go to all that effort to come and rescue me. To say that I felt like a fool would have been an understatement. I couldn't wait to see her though, but would rather she didn't see me like this. My dream was that she would arrive and the Magistrate would agree to release me at the same time and we would go home together. Sallie has a wealthy friend in the USA who was incarcerated in New Zealand when he was caught with a very small amount of personal-use marijuana in his pocket at the airport. He spent two days in the lock-up with members of the notorious New Zealand Mongrel Mob. He had some idea what I was going through and told Sallie he'd fly me home first class — bloody nice of him. Frankly, I'd be happy to get a third class bus home if they let me out now. But if we could leave together we could enjoy first class and maybe a day or two off in Bangkok on the way home. It was just a dream, but all I had for now.

I could feel myself developing a cold — excellent and just what I needed. Normally, when I get the first indications of a cold approaching, I start to overdose on vitamin C tablets and start drinking calcium ascorbate powder. This rapid intervention has, in 95% of cases, crippled the cold and sent it on its merry way. But I didn't have these drugs on me and, even if I wasn't in the big house, Bihar didn't look like the sort of town that had a local Terry White chemist. These people weren't big on tissues either, but I refused to lower myself to their filthy behaviour. They spat everywhere and then lay around all day on the ground in that spit — repulsive. Every morning, 580 prisoners went through a routine of clearing their throats. It's a cultural thing that everyone seemed to do. This activity continued through to about 7.00 am when they all tried their hardest to cough up some lung tissue or spew out their stomachs. I remained in my cage while this was going on because I just couldn't stand it. Then, when I did walk, I found myself dodging oysters everywhere. The contrast is that they are personally clean people. They washed every day and sometimes twice a day. They washed their bedding and clothes regularly and no-one smelt of body odour. But I wasn't going to start spitting on the ground.

Another habit these guys had was to chew this pre-packaged betel nut. It came in a little foil packet and they thumbed the contents in their palm before throwing it into their mouths and chewing on it. The content turns red and they start spitting the residue into a bucket or on the ground. Talking to people who are chewing on this stuff was not an attractive process as they invariably tried to store it in one part of their mouth while attempting to string some words together. I couldn't stand it and, on a few occasions, told Manish to go and spit. The first time he spat a great gob of chunky red shit in front of my gate. I made it very clear that I'd rather he didn't do that. In fact, I said, 'Are you fucking right? Spit that horrible shit over there somewhere.'

'Sorry, okay, sorry.'

Dotted around the yard were five old-fashioned water pumps used for drinking, washing and cooking. The water from the pumps flowed into a system of drains that ran around the yard. The drains were made of concrete 'U' channel, were about 250 millimetres wide and were also used for pissing into. The end result was a very long urinal that stank of stale urine like an old, seldom-cleaned public toilet. But I suppose that smell was better than the general smell of shit that emanated from the very soil in the yard. The place was simply a toilet. I was living in a fucking toilet, sleeping on a floor of ancient turds.

The place was also a huge rubbish dump. There was rubbish everywhere. Again, I refused to be drawn into this bad behaviour that seemed to be a cultural thing. The people just threw rubbish on the ground where they stood. I was sure they weren't even aware they were doing it. Before I was arrested, I drove to Biratnagar from the eastern side of Nepal with Ujwal and a few of the students. We stopped to grab a drink and some chocolate to snack on as we kept driving. As these guys finished their drinks and chocolate, it was like a continuous delivery of litter out the window. When I finished mine, Ujwal grabbed my litter and, thinking he was helping, went to throw it out the window as well. 'No,' I said, grabbing my rubbish, 'I'll find a bin later.' But there were no bins. I had to take my rubbish to my room where there was a small bin. In the cage, I put all my rubbish into a plastic bag and the old man emptied it for me every day. This all sounded good until one day I happened to see the old man disposing of my rubbish. He found a spot in the yard, emptied my rubbish on the ground and returned the bag to my cell. Periodically, a guard would force a prisoner to sweep the compound and all the rubbish would end up in the drains causing the piss and water to overflow into the yard where people walked and sat. Oh, life was good.

The guards were generally good to me. They would come to my cell after lock-up and try to be friendly, but knew I couldn't speak Hindi. Ugly would come to my cell during the day. He was supposed to be posted at the entrance, but had become lazy and taken to sitting on my mattress with my fan turned to face him instead of me. When Ugly was in my cell, the old man would come in and Ugly would start to order him around. It pissed me off a bit and I wanted to take charge and tell Ugly to go fuck himself, but obviously couldn't. One day the old man brought a plastic seat into the cage for me to sit on. It was great, but short-lived when Ugly came looking for his stolen seat and I was unceremoniously told in Hindi to 'move arsehole'. On one occasion Ugly told the old man to get him some water, so the old man picked up one of my small buckets and went to fetch the water. Ugly didn't thank the old man when he returned with the water and gave it to the guard who took a good, long drink. The old man gave me a sideways glance and I detected a hint of a smile as we both watched with some satisfaction as Ugly sculled water from my arse-wiping bucket.

I was really getting bored, so decided to walk to the prison office where Manish worked. The Chief Clerk told me to sit and sent someone to buy Sprite. We had a glass each and it tasted so good and I could feel the sugar give my energy level a slight lift. While in the office I found two old newspapers with a Sudoku puzzle in each. Sudoku gave me something to do at night, so I asked if I could take the puzzles. The Chief Clerk happily agreed. I sat there for a while and watched the activity in this very small office happen around me. It soon became apparent that there just wasn't room for me, the Chief Clerk, Manish and Gaz, so I told them I would return to the cage. But they wouldn't hear of it and insisted that I sit.

The Chief Clerk and the Warden were the only prison employees working in the office, all the others were prisoners working for extra privileges. Gaz worked alongside Manish with the Chief Clerk. He and Manish were arrested together for the same offence, but both declared their innocence. Gaz had some long Indian name that I couldn't pronounce, so I shortened it to 'Gaz'. After a day the name stuck and I heard the Chief Clerk refer to him as 'Gaz'.

Chapter 15

So, on orders to stay, I watched as the prisoners who had been to court during the day were processed back into the prison. I also noticed the prison guards outside as they patrolled with their old, rusted weapons. It reminded me of the time I spent in the Highlands of Papua New Guinea (PNG) working at a gold mine. It was like another life …

16.
THE LAST FRONTIER

I had been out of the army for six months and was working as a security supervisor at a gold mine in the Highlands of PNG. I hated the job and couldn't relate to the people; I really missed the army. I was on night shift this night and doing security guard work at the sag mill. The sag mill is the place where they sent all the big rocks to be ground down to a thick paste. The thick paste was full of gold dust and the locals knew this. So there I was sitting on the awning that covered the massive generator, reading a book, with my Mossberg shotgun by my side. The awning gave me a good view over one side of the compound, but in reality it was a lazy option to sit somewhere out of the way. Next to the awning was a staircase that led to the first floor of the building. A mill worker was driving the bobcat around the yard moving dirt from one place to another and I was so bored that I was entertained by his skill on the machine. Suddenly a man ran from the doorway next to the awning. He was a PNG national and he ran down the stairs and across the yard. The mill worker stopped the bobcat and watched the man run in panic. I grabbed my Mossberg, jumped off the awning, ran down the stairs and chased the man across the yard thinking he'd stolen something.

The man stopped in the corner of the yard and pointed frantically back towards the staircase we'd both just run down. I turned around and saw two men appear in the doorway. The man in the rear had a pistol to the head of the man in front of him. I cocked my Mossberg and saw another man appear behind the two. He had a shotgun and appeared shocked that I wasn't still on the roof of the awning. I reached for my hand-held radio and raised the alarm in the security control room where I knew I could find some reinforcements. My message was clear and understood and I had a sense of confidence that assistance was on the way. The bobcat driver was still sitting frozen in the bobcat, so I told him to get out, which he did and ran underneath the building.

Talking on the radio created some tension between the criminals and me. They were yelling at me to drop my gun. I aimed my weapon at the head of the man restraining the hostage, who I now identified as the security guard from the front gate, and knew I could hit him, but at this point in time a lot of 'what ifs' entered my mind. Like, what if the man pulls the trigger of his pistol as he falls and kills the hostage? What if I miss and hit the hostage? And let's not forget that, at that point in time, I had a shotgun pointed at my head too. I decided to take cover behind a pile of rocks, but the two men and hostage kept walking towards me. Suddenly, the police were blurting out instructions on the radio which, at this time, was located in my pocket. I couldn't grab it, to do so would mean letting go of my weapon.

The criminals became alarmed, realising that their plan had gone to shit, so they began to back up. Now it was my turn to follow. I decided the best thing to do was to contain the incident until help arrived, which would hopefully be soon.

Phil and Darren were having a break in the security control room when they heard my garbled call over the radio. Darren grabbed a Mossberg from the armoury, a 25-round belt of ammunition and ran for the vehicle. On his way to the incident, a faster vehicle passed him from the security office, which was also responding. As the response crews arrived, they were confronted by a locked gate. Meanwhile, the reserve police elements had arrived at the front gate and were directed by Darren to move down behind the fence line in an attempt to cut off the criminals' escape route.

I followed the three towards the corner of the fence line. I knew they were trapped; there was no way out except over the fence which was covered in razor wire. As I backed them up, to my horror, I saw two more men jump the fence and another five or six running around on the other side of the fence, all with weapons. The men were climbing up onto the roof of the toilet block located along the fence line and were jumping off the roof into the compound. I decided to take some cover and see where that fucking support was.

The group of three continued pacing back and forth along the fence line looking for a way out. The other men behind the fence were trying unsuccessfully to cut into it with machetes. I decided to throw a gas grenade to break up this activity. Unfortunately, I've never had a good throwing arm and the grenade landed short and blew back into me, causing my eyes to water and to continue watering while I remained in this position. I started laughing at the stupidity of the situation. There were about 10 men with guns and a hostage only a short distance away and only me in their way and I had added to their arsenal by gassing myself — classic. I felt comfortable that no shots had been fired at this stage and I thought that the criminals just wanted out, so I decided to move across the yard to another covered position away from the gas. As I moved, I was pursued by a volley of shots; this changed everything. No longer was this a stand-off, it was now a gunfight. My new position was about 10 metres from the hostage and the criminal. The third man had joined two other men behind a pipe and continued to fire in my direction. They weren't very good shots though, and their rounds were well off target.

The police were now down behind the criminal gang and were located on the other side of a creek. They were lying low in an attempt to ambush the criminals when they withdrew. I heard them tell Darren on the radio that they were in position. I wondered where the hell Darren was.

At the gate, Darren tried to squeeze through the two steel gates, but the gap wasn't wide enough, so he directed a vehicle to nudge up against the fence and continue moving forward. Eventually the lock snapped open and the response force was in. When Darren entered the yard, he could see the hostage and criminal walking back and forth along the fence line, but couldn't see me. At this stage the incident was contained, but we still had a jittery criminal holding a hostage with the odd round coming in. I could see a local security guard near some old drums, so I ran over to him and asked if he'd seen Darren.

'Yes, he's down between the drums.'

I moved to Darren and briefed him on what had happened and the situation at hand. We decided to call for the Sig Sauer 5.56 semi-automatic assault rifle to be brought up to us. If we had to take out the criminal, this weapon would be far more accurate than the Mossberg. I moved back to my position to give us a better coverage of the incident. I could see men crawling around on the other side of the fence trying to get a better shot at me, so I had to watch them as well as keep an eye on the hostage and the criminal. They were now near the toilet block and some men were jumping onto the toilet block and were escaping. They'd given up on their mate who was still caught inside with the hostage. I tried to warn the police that the group was on its way down towards them, but a group of locals had assembled on the other side of the creek on the high ground and was warning the criminals to go up the creek because a trap had been set. I then tried to tell the police to move up towards the toilet block, but the battery on my radio had gone flat — isn't that always the way? So Darren passed the message.

The lone criminal was still located at the toilet. Every time he let go of the hostage to attempt to jump onto the toilet roof, I called out to him and he grabbed the hostage again. This happened four or five times until I decided to move closer to the two of them — I really wanted to arrest one of them. At this, the criminal decided to just go for it and off he went, leaving the hostage behind. Darren moved up to me and we both watched for any further movement, but saw nothing. Up until this time I hadn't fired any rounds, but Darren had fired a few suppressive rounds. We had ample opportunity to fire and hit the criminals, but there was no justification. A number of times the criminals stood up behind the corrugated iron and fired at us, we could have fired a solid round (a solid is a single ball of lead fired from the shotgun) straight through the iron and into one of them, and believe me we were tempted, but there was no justification to do this, so we didn't. We secured the hostage and told him to report to the front gate where a group of security guards was waiting to be deployed. The police were now at the fence line, but hadn't made any arrests. The Mill Foreman contacted Darren and I and told us that one of his men was missing. Darren and I realised that we had no choice but to go and get him. We jumped the fence and, with the police and a dog and handler, we moved forward. We'd moved about five metres when Darren and I realised we were on our own. We tried to call the police forward into an extended line, but they were reluctant, so off we went, essentially on our own.

We climbed a small rise, one man moving at a time while the other covered. I moved with my weapon on fire, a solid in the chamber, the butt in my shoulder and my finger lightly on the trigger. We reached the top of the rise and moved down the other side trying to get out of the silhouette as quickly as possible. We found the bottom of the five-metre descent and began to climb again. To the front of us, about five metres away, was a patch of thick grass and weeds standing about a metre high. I was concerned about the covered area and strained my eyes to see into it, when I saw a flash erupt from the bush and then heard the crack. Darren yelled that he had been hit in the shoulder and I could see a lot of movement in the grass. A man stood up out of the grass and pointed his weapon directly at me. I raised my weapon and instinctively fired. The man fell and his limp body rolled back down the rise. I quickly moved to him and felt his carotid pulse for any sign of life — there was none. The man had died instantly. As Darren was hit, another man had appeared to the left, a bit further off. Darren fired the Sig and the figure jumped clear and ran away under cover of darkness. The years of training as an infantry soldier kept me from dwelling on the life I'd just taken and I continued forward to a covered position and asked if Darren was okay — he seemed to be coping. We continued to move forward in turn, clearing as we went. My pulse was racing now, let me tell you.

Behind us, the police were moving through the grass when the dog started to bark. A man was trying to crawl away from the scene, but had made enough noise for the dog to detect him. The police moved in and jumped on the man who happened to be the criminal who had held the hostage in the yard. They took the pistol from him and then dished out a little PNG justice, which included picking up rocks and driving them into his head. The man tried to cover himself by putting his hands over his face, but they just continued to smash rocks into his face, splitting his fingers open like squashed bananas in the process. By the time they were finished, the man was a bleeding mess. Darren and I saw this, but kept moving forward.

After moving about 15 metres beyond the grass area, we received word that the person who was missing had been located. Darren and I stopped and I told him that I'd killed one. He hadn't realised and was surprised. We moved back to the compound and called in the civilian police who began an investigation.

The next few days proved eventful. Darren and I had to write statements and brief the rest of the security department on what had occurred at the mill. The man who was arrested and beaten by the police escaped from prison and is still on the run. Security was boosted with the expectation of a reprisal. The body went for a post-mortem that consisted of the doctor removing a solid slug from the chest of the deceased and nothing more. Death was said to have occurred because all of the major internal organs were destroyed; that'll do it. No action was taken against me — the shot was deemed to be legal and justified.

But that was then and this is now and I was bored and wanted to stroll the yard with the politician before lock-down; I also knew that the old man would be pissed if I didn't get back in time for my evening bath. So I got up and simply said I had to go, ignoring their pleas to stay. These three guys were good people and they broke up my very long days and stopped me thinking about my crap situation.

That night the Hari Krishnas let rip again, then the Warden came by for his usual evening chat. He was a very kind man and told me not despair, but to pray to God and everything would be okay. I wondered whether he would be so kind to me if the police Inspector hadn't asked for special treatment, or the Nepali Police Superintendent hadn't been supporting me or, importantly, the Mayor, Bala, hadn't insisted he be called if I needed anything. Whatever, I was glad he seemed to be on my team. In fact, I was damned fortunate to have all that support.

Manish came by around 9.00 pm. Manish was allowed extra privileges because he worked in the prison. He wasn't paid for this, but the extra privileges would certainly make his 20 years in gaol a little easier to bear. Manish kindly brought me four cold rotis and a cup of lukewarm vomit in which to dip my roti. I thanked him and discarded both once he had left. It was a quiet night of thinking, Sudoku and more thinking. I spent a lot of time thinking about the kids and our future. I was also worried about my dear old dad.

Dad hadn't really been there for Steven, Trevor and me when we were growing up. He had left when I was young, which broke my mother's heart. Mum, being the champion she was, never ever let her emotions show so, as kids, we never really felt the impact of Dad's departure and I didn't give it much thought. Dad was a soldier, so was rarely around anyway and, one day, he just seemed to go and never came back. I know that Mum decided to make life a little difficult for Dad if he ever asked to take us out, so he gave up and was posted to another state with the army. But when I was 17 Dad left the army and returned to our lives. It took me a long time to accept Dad back into my life and, in reality, this had only occurred in the last two or three years. He was a good man and did his best but, like me, wasn't really cut out to be a father. Now Dad was ill and didn't have a great deal of time left in this world and I wanted to spend some time with him before he died. Being in this shithouse looked set to prevent that.

I munched on three biscuits and a mouthful of bottled water and waited for the activity outside to slow down before getting stuck into my nightly work-out. By now I was struggling with my work-out and had started to feel the effects of the poor diet catching up with me. Working out each night wasn't enough to maintain my fitness; I also needed to eat well, but this was all I had for now. I had two mosquito coils burning in my cage, one in the top corner near my head and the other at my feet. I just didn't think I could handle a case of malaria right now.

I then spent a lot of time (which I seemed to have plenty of) rat-proofing my mosquito net. As I now had 12 bottles of water, I was able to position them all round the base of the net to try to dissuade the rats from forcing themselves under the barrier. On my left side I lined up some bottles so that, once I finished reading, put the light into the Calvins and had a pee, I could get back under the net and line these up along the bottom to complete the barrier. It was a complicated procedure, but it promised a rat-free night, so it was well worth the hassle.

17.
NIGHTMARE DAY ELEVEN

Tuesday 3 June

I can happily report that my fortress kept the rats out last night despite their visit at around 2.00 this morning. I didn't know why they entered my cage because I was careful not to leave any scraps of biscuit lying around and the biscuit packets were in a plastic bag hanging on a nail on the wall. Perhaps they had a taste for my feet, the filthy bastards. I was reminded of a scene from the movie *Pulp Fiction* in which John Travolta and Samuel Jackson are in a diner and Travolta orders bacon, but Jackson refuses. Travolta asks whether this is a religious thing and Jackson says, 'No, I just don't dine on swine, that's all.'

'Yeh, but bacon tastes good; pork chops taste good.'

'Hey, a sewer rat might taste like pumpkin pie, but I'd never know because I wouldn't eat the filthy motherfucker. Pigs eat and root and shit. That's a filthy animal. I don't eat nothing that ain't got sense enough to disregard its own faeces.'

'A dog eats its own faeces.'

'I don't eat dog either.'

'But do you regard a dog as a filthy animal?'

'I wouldn't go as far as calling a dog filthy, they're definitely dirty. But a dog's got personality.'

'Ah yes, but by that rationale, if a pig had a better personality it would cease to be a filthy animal.'

'Well, we'd have to be talking about one charming mother fucking pig. He'd have to be 10 times more charming than that Arnold from *Green Acres*.'

I started laughing and felt the need to watch the movie again. It was just classic writing; I loved the dialogue in that movie and it confirmed Tarantino as a genius.

As I lay on my mattress under the mozzie net enjoying the cool morning, I sensed something in the back of my mind that wasn't quite right. Sometimes when my stars weren't lined up I got a light feeling in my gut that told me to watch my arcs — I'm not sure where that sense disappeared to when I crossed the fucking border. I tried to dissect the previous day, but couldn't think of anything and nothing happened last night to knock the stars from alignment. Maybe it was just me being a dick, but I normally had good senses and had learnt over the years to trust them. So I relaxed and thought about the random dream I had last night of a dear old friend of the family called Vicky.

I had known Vicky since I first joined the army as a 19-year-old when her son and Colin, my half-brother, started playing football in the same team as seven-year-olds. Vicky was a large woman with a happy personality and beautiful spirit. She was indeed a lifelong friend of the family; Mum regarded Vicky as her best friend. It was huge shock to us all when Vicky died last year and it certainly left a gap in the lives of everyone she came in contact with. Vicky had one request for her funeral; her favourite colour was pink, so she wanted everyone to wear something pink. I can comfortably confirm that I didn't have any item of clothing that was pink, so I bought a pink tie. The crowd at Vicky's funeral was a testament to the person she was and the number of lives she touched and it was fantastic to see all the pink flowers, dresses, shirts and ties.

It was strange that Vicky would talk to me the way she did. It wasn't like a normal dream that's mixed with the unreal and absurd. I didn't know whether we were sitting or standing, but Vicky was holding my hand as I looked down and she just said, 'Don't worry, this will all turn out okay.' That was it, nothing more, but it was so real — almost not a dream.

Even though the caveman had opened the cage and delivered his morning grunt, I just wanted to stay where I was a little longer. It was going to be another beautiful day and the temperature still had

Chapter 17

an edge to it, so I tried as best I could under the circumstances to curl up under my thin sheet. But then my incredibly friendly neighbour, Sanjay, walked into my cage. I lay still, hoping he'd think that I was still asleep and go away. Oh no, not Sanjay. It wouldn't even occur to Sanjay that a motionless person under a mozzie net might still be sleeping.

'Morning, Sir.'

I grunt.

'Sir, morning,' he persists.

'For fuck's sake,' I mumble.

'Sir, good morning.'

'Are you kidding?'

'Good morning, Sir.'

'Yeh, good morning,' I mumbled.

'Sir, Sir, present for you.'

I prop up on one elbow and Sanjay hands me a pink rose under my mosquito net. Oh shit, I'd heard this sort of stuff goes on in prison, and thought I'd be safe in here, but now it has started. I sat up in bed and contemplated my next move, smelling the rose. It smelt good, with a strong perfume.

'Thanks Sanjay, very kind of you.'

'No problem, Sir,' he said as he pranced out the door.

Bloody hell, I thought.

This flower reminded me of Vicki. What a strange coincidence. I dreamt of Vicky talking to me last night and today Sanjay handed me a pink flower. This was too much, so I checked the date on my G Shock and it suddenly dawned on me that Vicky died a year ago today. Wow — this was a little spooky. Whatever it was, I needed all the help I could get, so I urged Vicky to 'go for your life'.

I eventually got up, but I wanted to spend another day hiding in my cell. I just didn't want to do anything or talk to anyone. I wished I could just go to sleep or slip into a coma, or place my body into a cryogenic state until the day I would be released. This was taking far too long for something so bloody benign.

The old man came in and I got the hint that I needed to move so he could clean my cell. He was a great guy and I knew I was lucky to have him. I wished I could take him home with me. He had to be in his mid-sixties. He had a great head of flowing grey hair and a beard to match. He was about 5 feet 3 inches (160 centimetres) and must have weighed only 45 kilograms. His dark brown skin was stretched tightly over his rib cage and stomach and he carried absolutely no fat at all. He rarely wore a shirt and the only time I saw him wearing thongs was when he went to court. At night he would put on an old tracksuit top, but generally only wore a green sarong. He seemed to still have most of his teeth as I was certain a dentist wouldn't make a set of teeth that looked that bad. He had too many teeth in the top row and his right front tooth was very prominent. He had been convicted of robbery and sentenced to a year in prison. He'd done five months but insisted that he didn't do it, but couldn't afford a lawyer to plead his innocence. His home town was near the border with Pakistan and, given that he and his family were very poor, he had never had a family member visit him.

Mid-morning I was lying down with my legs crossed when the old man came in to preach to me. This wasn't as torturous as it sounds; in fact, it was quite entertaining. I'd just lie and listen to him as he threw his arms around and went on and on about something. Then it would all stop, just when I'd had about enough of the sermon. This time when he stopped, I closed my eyes, but they smashed open when the old man suddenly grabbed my legs and straightened them and, before I could protest (as I'd done every other time he suggested a massage), he was kneading my legs with his grip of steel using those calloused old hands of his. I started laughing at the sight of this and could imagine telling Sallie. The old bugger had the roughest and strongest hands and was actually inflicting pain on me. I went with it for about 30 seconds before finally putting a stop to it. He told me to turn over, but that wasn't happening. Washing my back was enough. This was a line we weren't stepping over. The reality was that the old man made life a lot easier for me and I valued his friendship and assistance, but I just can't handle a man touching me in any way. I remember once doing some bodyguard work for an American actor who was rumoured to be gay. When the gig was over, the actor gave me the man hug and the other lads told me later how funny it looked because, when the actor came in for the hug, my hips immediately withdrew, so there was plenty of air between our groins. Stupid, I know, and I can just hear my gay friends laughing at me, but that's the way it was. The old man realised I wasn't going to weaken, so he gave up and decided to leave.

My cold was getting worse, which was just what I needed; frankly, I was surprised I hadn't contracted hepatitis, scurvy, malaria and Ebola in this shit hole. It was now 1.10 pm and, aside from the bucket bath this morning and a slow walk to the piss drain, I hadn't left the cage. I wished I could sleep more. I'd had no visitors so that meant I would be here for another night — excellent. I knew people were working very hard for me on the outside, but I had no visibility of any of that so felt quite helpless and, worst of all, had no control over events.

Sallie was in New Delhi meeting the Australian High Commissioner, John McCarthy. I hoped she'd be okay. She was certainly the right person to have running this because her instincts were generally very good; although I was sure she would let the High Commission guys have a mouthful if things weren't moving quickly enough.

It was getting late in the day so I thought I'd go and visit Manish, Gaz and the Chief Clerk. I needed to ask Manish to organise more mosquito coils for me. The mozzie net was good, but the coils also helped to keep the little bastards at bay. Manish was happy to help and mentioned to the Chief Clerk that I needed more mozzie coils. The Chief Clerk stood at the barred gate and yelled to a young bloke who ran over. Apparently the young bloke was the Chief Clerk's cook. Some notes were exchanged and the young bloke bolted towards the entrance to the prison, turned left and disappeared.

After a bucket bath and a walk with the politician, the caveman locked the cage and I used this time to check and clear my text messages. I was very careful when I used the phone and only kept it turned on for short periods so it didn't go flat. I got some nice messages from the kids, my brother Trevor and my mate, Dave. With an eye on the door, I placed the phone back in its hiding place.

The old man was trying to be helpful and placed my water bottles in a large bucket of water to try to keep them cool through the night. It wasn't really necessary as the water didn't get too hot and I decided to tell him tomorrow not to worry about it. Then, as I was standing at the gate wondering once again whether I should grab a tin cup and start dragging it along the bars the way they did in the movies, I picked up the bucket and started doing arm curls. After three sets of 10, my arms were screaming for mercy, so I let a little water out of the bucket and continued with three sets of 10 lateral shoulder raises. I was well and truly knackered after that and had changed my mind about the bucket staying in the cage at night. I rested for an hour or so then completed my usual routine of sit-ups and push-ups. I then spent about 30 minutes getting the mozzie net right and got two coils burning before relaxing on my mattress with Sudoku. I managed to stay awake until 1.00 am, which pleased me no end. It would mean I'd be tired during the day tomorrow and sleep would come easily.

18.
NIGHTMARE DAY TWELVE

Wednesday 4 June

It was nice to wake up this morning to the yelling and screaming coming from the sick cell next door. There was a pretty good chance the lunatic had done something to piss the others off. The yelling and commotion hadn't really woken me; I had woken quite early and read some more. It was nice being on my own and the chill in the early morning air meant I could curl up under the sheet. I then realised that it was the old man yelling, with the periodic support of Sanjay, and others would join in when there was a gap in the tirade. When Ugly unlocked the gates, the yelling got worse as my neighbours poured out of the cell. I decided to get away from it all and go for my morning pee in the drain. When I returned to the cage I walked past my neighbour's cell to see the lunatic throwing buckets of water through the cell and the section in front. I later learnt that the lunatic had shat in the cell through the night and they were, justifiably, pretty pissed off. They made him carry bucket after bucket to clean the mess, which he did without complaint. I was glad I wasn't in with those poor buggers.

My walking mate (Satya the politician) had to go to court today, so I walked alone. It was a relief not to have to think so hard first thing in the morning when responding to his deep questions like the one about childbirth in Australia. With Satya off to make his court appearance today, I was happy to have another quiet one knowing I'd be getting no visitors. As I slowly strolled around the yard, other prisoners were preparing for their day. Some were getting the fires burning in their makeshift stoves so they could build up a nice pile of hot coals, while others prepared chai for the morning. I received plenty of invites to sit and drink chai, but I respectfully declined and continued on my walk.

Before my friend Satya went to court he came to my cell and the old man also came in. We talked for a while, then Satya mentioned that the old man was a great singer and asked him to sing sweet songs for us. Oh God, no. So the old man started singing and, after two minutes, he stopped and told the story, then let rip with some more singing. I sat there with a smile on my face while considering how I might kill Satya for suggesting something so bloody torturous, and at the same time wondering when the old man would stop. The other thing that occurred to me was that I now thought it was the old man who had been singing at 3.00 in the morning, but couldn't have been the one taking the beating!

Then Satya said he had to go to court, but this didn't perturb the old man; he just kept on singing and explaining like I had a clue what he was on about. I was dying a slow and horrible death and was relieved when, after about 30 minutes, the old man finally stopped. I seized the moment and offered him a biscuit hoping that he couldn't sing while chewing on biscuits. Then he got angry with me for not eating enough, so I had a biscuit as well. Finally, the old man decided he had things to do and left me in peace. Fucking Satya, I vowed I'd kill him.

I was desperate for some drugs to sort out this cold. It seemed to be getting worse every day. My nose was running like a tap, the headaches were crushing and my joints ached. I hoped desperately that I didn't have malaria. I decided to try to sleep through it. Sallie was coming tomorrow. She was travelling to Katmandu today and Biratnagar this afternoon. I was worried about her, but I was sure Ujwal would look after her.

At about 1.00 pm, Sanjay and the old man came into my cell as I was resting on my back reading my book. Then they attacked me. Both of them grabbed a leg each and started massaging. The old man had fingers like steel rods covered in very course sandpaper. I started laughing again. 'What the hell are you blokes doing?'
'Massage, Sir,' replied Sanjay.

Chapter 18

'Oh, really, I hadn't noticed, mate.'

'Yes, massage.'

I let it go for a few minutes but couldn't handle it so, when the old man had almost removed my calf muscle, I put a stop to it. They were just killing time and I'd become their pet project — someone or something different to fill their days. How could this be happening to me — I'm in prison in northern Indian being massaged by fellow prisoners! How had this become my life?

I had a visit from Rajeesh, the new High Commission guy. Rajeesh is a local Indian, so he could stay in Biratnagar and cross the border daily if necessary. He proved quite ineffectual. I don't blame the High Commission guys for their inaction — their hands were tied in what they could and couldn't do and they wouldn't bend the rules at all. The fact that they had taken an interest and made some calls helped, although word from New Delhi never seemed to reach the local government officers here. Rajeesh brought five bottles of water and some biscuits which was very kind of him, but I hated it because it meant that I'd be here for a while longer, particularly as Rajeesh told me that I should stockpile the water for the future. That meeting ended with me feeling depressed over my future and, returning to my cage, I just waited for lock-down.

That afternoon I took the long way to the piss drain and passed the really old man who was just slumped on the ground wearing his filthy, tattered clothes. When I got back to my cage I grabbed a packet of biscuits and gave them to him. I felt sorry for the old bugger. He should have been in hospital or at home being looked after by his family, not stuck in here living like a pig. It was interesting the way the other prisoners helped him with a mat to sit on and bits and pieces of food. I suppose, like me, they were trying for some nice return karma.

My old man was really throwing himself into his role as my helper. At night, after my bucket bath, he would roll out my bedding, set up my mosquito net, then throw flowers and flower petals around my cell. It may sound nice if you're that way inclined, but it was bloody annoying for me because I always ended up with flowers stuck to my face in the morning and, frankly, I'm not a flower sort of guy.

I stayed up late worrying about tomorrow and Sallie's visit. I wished she didn't have to see me like this and I hated the idea of her being in the hotel in Biratnagar by herself. I knew she could handle herself, but I was still worried. The reality was that she shouldn't have had to be doing this. Fuck that crazy prick at the border.

I decided to organise my mozzie coils which always took some time because the matches were cheap and always seemed to be a little damp. Every coil took about 10 matches to light. Then, in true male fashion, I decided it was time to scratch my crutch. It felt good, so instinctively I scratched again, but it was feeling too good, so I had to investigate. I adjusted the light globe and had a look in and around my kit and was shocked and repulsed by my condition. I clearly had developed a hideous fungal infection. The insides of both thighs were covered in horrible welts or slightly raised, red skin. 'Arrrh, for fuck's sake,' I spat. Bloody disgusting and there was nothing I could do about it. I had no medicines and wasn't about to mention this to the Chief Clerk. I'd seen the doctor's sick call in the afternoons. Anyone who reported sick got a needle resembling a four-inch nail shoved into their arse. I just had to forget about it and try to sleep.

19.
NIGHTMARE DAY THIRTEEN

Thursday 5 June

As usual, I slept poorly. Next door, the lunatic had decided to make an arse of himself last night, got a couple of punches for his trouble and then cried for two hours. So I decided to read some more *Primal Fear*. I'd read this book before and had seen the movie, with Richard Gere playing the lawyer. The book's an average read, but it passed the time. I dozed off again and woke at 4.00 am to enjoy the quiet and the cool morning air. I left the fan on all night as it only cooled down in the early hours of the morning and it kept the mosquitoes somewhat at bay. During the day the fan kept the flies off me.

I rolled over and noticed a pile of dirt about 20 centimetres from my head. A rat had come into my cage during the night and dug a hole where a piece of concrete had been removed. At least the filthy thing hadn't come inside my mozzie net for a visit. I wasn't sure I could handle that again. Rats and a fungal growth that had set up camp way too close to my kit just might have been too much at this time.

I found myself singing the theme song to the old TV series *Prisoner*:

She used to give me roses
I wish she could again
But that was on the outside
And things were different then

THE EASY DAY WAS YESTERDAY

On the inside the sun still shines
And the rain falls down
But the sun and rains on our Christmas to
When morning comes around

Last night I dreamed we were together
Sharing all the love we'd known
Till I had to face the nightmare
Of waking up alone

On the inside the roses grow
They don't mind the stony ground
But the roses here are Christmas to
When morning comes around

I remembered as a kid lying in bed after watching the weekly episode of *Prisoner*. While the closing song was playing, the guard wandered the corridors of the gaol locking the gates for the night. It always depressed me and I used to think how bloody awful it would be in prison — yep!

Freedom is a luxury we don't realise we have until it's gone. Like most modern-day luxuries, we take it for granted and don't really acknowledge its existence until we don't have it any more — and then it becomes priceless. I knew what it was like to have no control over what I did, where I went, who I talked to, what I ate and drank, what time I went to bed, what time I got up — it just continued in an endless list. The list of things you lost in prison was as long as the days spent there and suddenly you started to prioritise things differently. My kids and my relationship with Sallie became more important to me than anything else.

Ugly opened the gate with his usual pleasantries, but I didn't want to get up straight away — my time hidden under my mosquito net away from the never-ending stares was precious. Finally, Sanjay decided I needed help to get up.

'Morning Sir … Sir, good morning … Sir, I have a gift … Sir.'

Oh for fuck's sake. 'Morning, Sanjay, thanks for the flower.'

Delighted, Sanjay bounced away humming some tune. How the hell could he be happy? Is he gay? He seems gay. But I don't think he's gay. Is it a bit gay that I accept the flowers? What else can I do? He's a big bugger, but if he decided to go gay on me I reckoned I could sort him out — I'd certainly go out fighting, that was for sure. No. He wouldn't do that. He was harmless and only meant to be nice and gain some points with the Hindu gods.

So, I was up now and decided I might as well get into it. I rolled out from under my mosquito net, boots on, shirt on, sarong wrapped tightly and stumbled to the drain located 20 metres away. The section of drain that I used was between two concrete barriers about one metre square and 10 centimetres wide. The barriers offered some privacy, but the technique for peeing meant that privacy really wasn't a problem. I balanced on the edge of the drain, slowly squatted down trying not to touch anything, carefully unleashed the beast, peed, put the beast back in the cage, stood slowly, careful again not to touch anything and backed away to the water pump where a fellow inmate pumped water so I could wash my hands. 'Thanks, mate.'

Then I walked for 30 minutes with Satya and endured a series of intense questions — it was just too early in the morning to have to think so hard. Once I realised that he didn't understand most of what I said, I sometimes just responded randomly. Satya would ask, 'Is there corruption in politics in Australia? This I would want to know about.' 'Well, the difference between the Christians and the Muslims runs deep and goes all the way back to the Crusades.'

'Yes, yes, yes,' he'd reply earnestly.

I decided to mention to Satya that my girlfriend was coming today.

'This is good news. Please allow me to meet your wife.'

'Okay, sure.' It was easier to let people call Sallie my wife, which also allowed her a greater voice in the efforts for my release.

The old man ended the morning walk by insisting that it was time for my morning bucket bath. He had the water ready, so I said goodbye to Satya and prepared myself for my wash. I changed into the massive underpants that I always used for washing, wrapped a towel around myself, slipped on my thongs and headed to the bucket which the old man had positioned on a clean section of concrete near the water pump. I removed my towel and draped it over a bush to keep it off the ground and out of the water. I knelt down and scooped the first load of water and poured it over my head. The first one was always a shock as it was bloody cold, and I hoped every time that this would be the last time I did this. I used most of the bucket to wet my whole body then stood to soap myself up. The old man made a move to wash my back, but I stopped him just in time. He cursed me then refilled the bucket. I poured two loads on my head to wash off all the soap and then the old man poured the remains of the bucket on me. I nearly drowned every time as about 20 litres was dropped on me. I stood and dried myself with my towel before slipping on my thongs and returning to my cage. In my cage I hid in the corner to remove my wet underpants and put on a dry pair. I still had the constant gallery of fellow prisons with bugger all else to do but come and stare at the white man, so I had to hide to change. Nudity is not acceptable in India and certainly not in prison. No-one in the prison bathed naked; it was a lesson I was taught very early on.

When my dry sarong was wrapped around me, the old man took my wet underwear and washed it before hanging it to dry on a line in front of my cage. I always tried to prevent the old man washing my jocks, but he wouldn't hear of it, so it became just a show I performed every time he asked for them. I decided that I would shave today and I knew Sanjay had a razor because he'd been at me for days to shave, but I'd always told him that I'd wait until I got back to the hotel in Nepal. I thought this would be better because I could use my own razor in front of a decent-sized mirror. So I walked into the medical cell next door to speak to Sanjay and got my first look at their cage. Immediately I felt like a shit because I had the same sized cage to myself and there were eight of them cramped into their cage. Where my cage enjoyed some light, theirs was dark and had that all-too-familiar smell. It reminded me of some point in my past, but I couldn't think when ... oh, that's it, Rwanda. No, Kibeho with its smell of vomit, faeces, fear and death.

20.
DEPLOYED TO HELL

In 1995 I was deployed with my patrol to Rwanda as part of Australia's second contingent in support of the United Nations Assistance Mission for Rwanda (UNAMIR). We joined 300 other medics, doctors, infantrymen, drivers, cooks, engineers and signallers who were tasked with providing the UN medical support. Being the only SAS guys, we were given some autonomy, but reported to the medical company and took responsibility for the ambulances and evacuations. It was an interesting way to employ SAS soldiers, but we were just happy to get a gig and, besides, being in evac meant that we had our own room in the headquarters building while most of the others were jammed into dormitory-style accommodation for the six-month deployment.

About six weeks into the deployment, with not much in the way of excitement going on, people were starting to go on their first short leave to Nairobi. You'd get three days' break in which people basically relaxed, drank, ate and, for the younger men, screwed the local girls. The nightclubs in Nairobi were full of young, attractive women who were looking for a white man to marry them, so sex wasn't a hard thing to find for those in need. One place everyone would go was a restaurant called Carnivores. Basically, you'd pay US$20 and eat giraffe, ostrich, zebra, antelope and whatever else was in season. You pretty much threw about three kilograms of meat into your guts, then went on your way feeling shithouse and as though you needed to give birth to a brick.

Jon Church and I were all set to go on leave and were on the standby team when I was told that we might be deployed to an IDP (internally displaced persons) camp. The Operations Officer asked if I'd been told about it.

'No, Sir, news to me.'

Jon and I decided to pack the ambulance anyway, just in case we were going somewhere. We put two plastic jerry cans of water into the compartment on the roof along with our packs, two foldaway chairs, a bucket for washing, a heap of spare rations, two dumb-bells so we could continue our training, and two stretchers to sleep on. Being vehicle-mounted soldiers we knew exactly how to deploy in vehicles. If there was a chance we might have needed something and we had room, we took it.

That night, Tuesday 18 April 1995, at 5.00 pm, 32 members of the Australian Medical Support Force (AUSMED) were given orders to provide medical assistance to IDPs at the largest camp, close to the small town of Kibeho. We were told that the RPA (Rwandan Patriotic Army) was going to close all the camps starting with Kibeho, and would do so by force if necessary. I suspected they would have to use force, because the IDPs were being looked after in the camps with food, water and shelter and had no reason to leave. There was also an element of fear because the majority of the IDPs were Hutus, while the RPA was predominantly Tutsi. The Hutus had been the aggressors during the genocide 12 months earlier in which almost a million Tutsis had died. Kibeho camp was situated five hours' drive south-west of Kigali, and was reported to contain 120,000 IDPs.

After orders, Jon and I returned to the Swamp (the evac room, named in honour of the *MASH* series) to sort out any last minute bits and pieces. I also ran into Terry Pickard. Terry was a good soldier and 2IC of the Casualty Clearing Post (CCP). I asked Terry if they were all packed. 'Hell, no, mate, we've got miles to go.'

'Do you need help? We're done here.'

'Nah, we're good, thanks Jordo.'

'Righto, see you in a few hours.'

The force, commanded by Major Steve McCrowin, comprised two infantry sections commanded by Lieutenant Steve Tilbrook; the CCP commanded by Captain Carol Vaughan-Evans (an army doctor); one evacuation crew which I commanded; and a signals detachment which was to be located at the Zambian Headquarters at Gikongoro. The force departed Kigali at 3.00 am on Wednesday morning and headed west to Butare. At the UN Headquarters in Butare we turned right and continued on to Gikongoro. A two-minute drive out of Gikongoro had us at the Zambian Headquarters at 7.30 am where we set up a base camp.

This was a very long drive for that hour of the morning. After orders the night before, Jon and I had decided to have a few beers to help us get to sleep. We got our heads down at about 9.00 pm and, ten minutes later, we were called out on an evacuation task. We were told to go to the MP (Military Police) compound where a prisoner had been beaten. Realising that we smelt of beer, we threw half a dozen minties into our mouths so we wouldn't get our arses kicked by the MPs for driving around half-pissed. As it turned out, there was nothing wrong with the prisoner, so we went back to the hospital to see how things were going down there. The poor bastards were still at it, loading shit into the truck. We hung around for a while, but given that they were nearly done, we went back to bed, happy that we had pre-empted the move and packed the moment we had got wind of the deployment. We were back in the compound and in bed by 12.30 am. So, when we got up two hours later, we weren't quite ready for an outing to a massacre.

I'm buggered if I know how Jon drove for the five hours without falling asleep and killing both of us, but he managed to get us there without any drama while I slept my lazy arse off next to him. Occasionally, I asked Jon if he wanted a spell, but he always said that he was okay, which was a good thing because, the way I felt, I'd have driven about 300 metres before I'd have fallen asleep and driven the ambo off a cliff. It was great when the sun came up because we got to see some more of this country and, while it was still recovering from the genocide that had taken place a year before, it was a beautiful country with a great climate. I pulled out some of our French rations and made myself useful by making some snacks for Jon to keep him going. I also had the map laid out so I could work out where we were and where we were going.

At 7.45 am, I left the ambulance with Jon at the Zambian Battalion Headquarters with one infantry section and, under command of Major McCrowin, the remaining section, the CCP and I continued on to Kibeho. The drive to Kibeho was interesting. Gikongoro was surrounded by a mountain range and the best way for the kids to get into town was to scream down these hills on home-made wooden scooters. The scooters were fashioned from old bits of wood, but were quite well put together. The wheels were made of wood as were the axles. The forks sat over the axle without anything to lock them in. The riders of these scooters had to dodge the holes in the road because to hit one would see the axle jump out of the forks and some poor kid doing cartwheels down the hill.

We left the solid road and hit the dirt road that would take us all the way into Kibeho. On the way we were surprised to see some quite large IDP camps, although the occupants seemed to be doing okay. We drove through coffee plantations and small villages. We passed a number of small children walking along the roads and they gave us the usual greeting by calling for 'bisquee'. During the French occupation they had obviously given the kids biscuits, so now they demanded them every time we saw them. After a while the infantry lads got sick of this, so they'd hold a biscuit out the back of the rover and tease the kids into chasing after them. The kids would run flat out trying to get the biscuit while the infantry soldier took a bite from it. Finally, after three kilometres or so when the kids would start to slow, the infantry lad would drop the biscuit. Bloody cruel, but they were bored.

We arrived at the outskirts of the camp at 9.30 am. The place looked like a ghost town and we all assumed that we'd missed the IDPs. We were told that the RPA were going to clear the camp and we thought that they had already done so. As we continued through the camp I could see that it had been cleared very quickly because most of the IDPs' belongings had been left behind. We continued on towards the buildings of Kibeho and, as we rounded the corner to the centre of the community, we were confronted by a sea of humanity. It's difficult to describe the sight of 120,000 people all herded together like sheep. There were so many of them it was overwhelming. Later, we found out that the RPA had used gunfire to round up all the IDPs and, in the rush, 10 children had been trampled to death. As we drove through the camp, the crowd parted and began to clap and cheer as if we were their saviours. I wasn't sure what they thought we could do for them.

The Zambian company located at Kibeho had set up a watering point and, beyond that, was the documentation point where the identification of all IDPs was being checked by the RPA before they were loaded onto trucks to be transported back to their communities. We tried to set up the CCP but were twice told that our location wasn't satisfactory and eventually we set up beyond the documentation point. While the RPA were not happy with us being in the camp, they put up with us. We spent the whole day there and saw only one casualty, a Zambian soldier with a minor injury. We left the camp that Wednesday with the feeling that we were not really required and should return to Kigali.

Back at the Zambian compound, Jon and I had a work-out using the dumb-bells and then got cleaned up for dinner. We were invited to have dinner in the respective messes with the Zambians, and the food was quite good — certainly better than the French rations we had. The French ration packs made a change from the Aussie packs, but were good for only one day, and then we'd have been happy with an Aussie rat pack again. The French rations were full of lollies and biscuits. The lollies consisted of a bag of caramel bits which, due to my love of caramel, I managed to shove into my mouth all at once, and a piece of sugar-covered jelly which I also liked. The quantity of lollies and biscuits contained in the rat packs told us why they were thrown to the kids — there were just so many.

The Zambian camp was surrounded with concertina wire and, beyond that, there was always a local or two asking for food. The kids openly asked for food, but the adults just stood there looking at us until we could stand it no longer and gave them a tin or two. Jon and I did a lot of our eating while on the move; I'd pull out a rat pack and start making cheese and pâté biscuits. We did this because we were dog tired, and the eating gave us something to take our minds off sleeping. It also took some time to put these culinary delights together and therefore gave us something to occupy our time.

THE EASY DAY WAS YESTERDAY

On Thursday 20 April, we arrived at Kibeho at 8.30 am and entered the Zambian Charlie Company compound. This time I had Jon and the ambulance with me. The Charlie Company compound was located in the middle of all the IDPs. We were told by the Zambians that they had a woman who had given birth the night before and still had a child inside her. She also had a three-year-old daughter who, at the time, was with an old woman who had two children herself. Carol spoke to one of the specialists back at AUSMED and explained the situation to him. This took some time because a driver had to go to the hospital to collect the specialist and take him to the communications centre. The specialist recommended evacuating the lady back to AUSMED, so Carol prepared the woman for the flight. We argued the point with our headquarters in Kigali that the woman's young daughter should travel back to AUSMED with her. However the headquarters said no, so we felt as though we had broken up another family. AUSMED insisted they didn't have the manpower to babysit a child while her mother was recovering. We had her aeromedically evacuated (AME) to Kigali and it was later discovered in theatre that all she had was a swollen bladder. Once again, we set up the CCP at the documentation point and this time we went 'shopping' for casualties.

The RPA soldiers would fire their weapons into the air to control the IDPs. At around 1.00 pm we heard sporadic fire, so three infantry soldiers, Jon and I moved off towards the fire to look for casualties, although we didn't manage to locate anyone who needed our help. Tension was mounting in the camp and, as we left that night, we heard more firing from inside the camp. We had difficulty leaving the camp that day as the RPA had set up roadblocks. We decided to follow a convoy carrying IDPs when one truck slid in the mud and went off the bank, so every other truck stopped and blocked the road. We turned around to find another way out and, as we passed Kibeho, we again heard the crackle of gunfire.

We eventually found a secure route out and were 30 minutes from the camp when we spoke to a man from UNICEF (United Nations International Children's Emergency Fund). He told us that he'd heard over the radio that 10 IDPs had been shot dead in the camp. Due to restrictions we were not permitted to stay in the camp overnight, so we continued back to the Zambian Headquarters.

Chapter 20

Once back at the Zambian Headquarters we showered in a bucket of cold water and went to the Zambian mess for some dinner. Inside the mess, the fire they used to cook the dinner was like a bushfire and was smoking terribly. This didn't seem to worry the Zambians and they chatted happily to us in the smoke-filled room. But in the end I had to get out of there because I was starting to drown in my tears — it was horrendous. Jon and I slept in the back of the ambulance because it offered the best bed in the area.

On Friday 20 April, we arrived at Kibeho at 8.30 am and were told that there were 30 dead from the night before and that the Médecins Sans Frontières (MSF) hospital was busy, but at this stage required no help. When the Kibeho camp was initially established, MSF moved into the camp to set up a small hospital which was kept very busy. We set up the CCP at the documentation point and saw a few patients who were suffering from colds and basic infections. For most, it was a case of giving them antibiotics and sending them on their way. A number of children came into the CCP and, if there were no RPA around, we gave them dry clothes and pushed some lollies into their mouths. Towards the afternoon we picked up an IDP with a broken femur whom we planned to drive back to the hospital in Butare that evening.

There was a group of IDPs sitting on some high ground near the documentation point awaiting transport, so some of us went over to look through the crowd for wounded. As we did this, an RPA soldier started to tell me to leave the area. I approached him and, even though he wasn't speaking English, I knew exactly what he wanted. I basically told him to shove it up his arse and, even though I couldn't speak Rwandan, he knew what I meant and didn't trouble us any more. Sometimes the bluff worked, most times it didn't. That morning, an RPA Corporal tried to make us leave the documentation point and set up somewhere else. Major McCrowin told the Corporal that we were not moving and that he would not speak to him, reminding the Corporal that he was a Major. He told the Corporal to go and get his CO as he was the only person he would speak to. The Corporal left and we never heard any more about it. In the early afternoon, Major McCrowin left Kibeho to return to Kigali and placed Lieutenant

Steve Tilbrook in command. Tilbrook was a young infantry platoon commander with a couple of years' experience up his sleeve and, by all accounts, a pretty good officer.

Eating became a bit of a problem. I mean, there were thousands of starving IDPs walking past us the whole time; we couldn't just rip out a bar of chocolate and start feeding our faces in front of these people. Jon and I took it in turns getting into the back of the ambulance and eating a cold meal. We always waited till we got back to the Zambian Battalion compound to have a decent feed. Another problem was the call of nature. For most, it was a case of not going. The Zambian company at Kibeho had three toilets dug next to its compound, but you'd have to be pretty desperate to hang your arse over them. The dug toilets at the Zambian Headquarters weren't too bad, so we went in the morning or at night. But, right now, we were down at the documentation point where a toilet had yet to be dug. Before the good old Infantry had it dug, Jon felt the need, so he found a nice little secluded spot next to an abandoned hut, dug himself a hole and went for it. Just as he was settling in and starting to enjoy himself, he heard some laughter and swivelled around to notice a group of RPA soldiers behind him giggling. It was probably the first white arse they had seen. Needless to say, Jon finished up and got the hell out of there. Jon couldn't wait to tell me about it. I always knew when he had a good story to tell. Jon was one of those blokes who had trouble getting words out when telling a funny story because he laughed so much during the telling.

As we packed up that evening, we were told that the MSF hospital had six priority one patients and needed assistance to get them out. Carol Vaughan-Evans, Terry Pickard, Jon and I went down to the hospital and identified those patients requiring AME by helicopter. As an MSF nurse identified the patients to Carol, I followed, recording the patient's state and location within the maze of hospital rooms and patients. At one stage we all walked into a small theatre where a young boy was having his calf muscle sewn back on. The boy was conscious and the doctor, wearing a pair of shorts and a singlet, told the nurse which patients to evacuate. This was unusual for us to see because, back at AUSMED, you were lucky to get anywhere near the theatre, let alone wander in and see a doctor in shorts and singlet. One patient had recently been struck with a machete across her arm, so Jon stayed with her to get her ready for AME. Once all the patients had been identified, Carol, Terry and Jon returned to the compound to prepare a CCP to stabilise the patients before the AME arrived. I stayed at the hospital ready to identify the patients to the infantry. The infantry came to the hospital with stretchers and we transported the patients to the compound where we prepared them for AME. This involved inserting an intravenous (IV) drip, stopping any bleeding and bandaging their wounds. Then we put the patients into the ambulance and drove them to the helipad.

The helo landed at 5.00 pm and we loaded the patients on board. One patient had been shot through the bladder and bowel and could not sit up, but it was a case of either sit up or stay here, so Jon and I forced him to sit up. Once we had him on the helo we noticed a lot of blood coming from the bullet hole in his backside. We checked the stretcher and saw that the bandage had fallen off. The end result was we simply pretended that we hadn't seen it. We could not evacuate the man with the broken femur because there was no way we could get him to sit up, so we decided to take him with us to the Butare hospital.

The RPA were not happy that people were being evacuated by helo and wanted to inspect every wound to be sure we were not smuggling people out of the camp. This delayed the AME by 20 minutes, but it eventually took off. This was my first experience in negotiating with the RPA Major (who spoke good English) and was certainly not to be my last.

We moved from the helipad back to the Charlie Company compound and were told that we had another wounded IDP. This one had been shot in the lung and had a sucking chest wound. He was in a bad way and, as it was getting dark, we decided to take him with us in the ambulance. Carol and Jon stabilised the man for travel. The military treatment for a sucking chest wound is to stick the outer wrapper of a field dressing over the hole and, using sticking plaster, stick three sides down. This creates a valve, stopping air from going in, but letting air out. This bloke was covered in blood and sweat; there was no way that plaster was going to stick. Jon had to hold the wrapper firmly over the hole and try to judge when he was breathing out so he could release the wrapper to let the trapped air out. We were then faced with the problem of getting through the RPA checkpoints. Carol and Jon sat in the rear of the ambulance and continually worked on the patient as we talked our way through each checkpoint. At the checkpoints we were forced to open the ambulance and the patients were checked to ensure there was no faking of injuries.

After two hours of travelling through rough terrain, the convoy (which consisted of two military observers from Uruguay driving a Pathfinder, the infantry 6 x 6 troop carrier with the infantry section and Lieutenant Tilbrook on board, the ambo with the two casualties and Jon and Carol in the back, and the CCP land rover) came across a muddy section of road. The Pathfinder driven by the military observers drove straight through the bog without hesitation as the other three vehicles prepared to negotiate it. The 6 x 6 troop carrier took off up the right-hand side of the bog with the driver giving her all she had. Soldiers bounced around the back as the 6 x 6 slowed down and stopped right in the middle of the bog and wasn't going anywhere in a hurry. I decided there was bugger all we could do from the back so put the ambo into 6-wheel drive, threw her into second gear, told Jon and Carol to hang on, and gave her a solid kick in the guts. We took off up the left-hand side of the troop carrier with the old ambo, being top heavy, bouncing all over the place. As I came level with the stranded 6 x 6, the bog began to direct me towards the rear of it. There was no way I was going to take my foot of the accelerator, momentum was the only way to get through areas like this. If the back of the ambo connected with the front of the 6 x 6, so be it. Fortunately, the ambo didn't connect and I could feel the wheels start to grip the road under the mud and we drove through the bog. I pulled over behind the Pathfinder and had a look at the situation, watching the CCP vehicle also become hopelessly bogged. The only thing we could do was to try to winch them out using my winch. There were no trees around so, for a quick recovery, the winch on the 6 x 6 was useless. I opened the back of the ambo to give Jon and Carol some fresh air and told them what we were doing. Carol was concerned about the sucking chest wound and said that we couldn't stop for long. I turned the ambo around, parked it, pulled the winch out, and attached it to the bull bar on the 6 x 6. Jon operated the winch from the front of the vehicle as I operated the gears and accelerator while, at the same time, the driver of the 6 x 6 tried to drive forward. All we did was buckle the bull bar and drag the ambo back towards the bog. The 6 x 6 was so heavily bogged that we couldn't get a chain around the chassis so the bull bar was as good as it was going to get, and we'd just about stuffed that. Again Carol told me we had to go. 'One more go,' I told her, 'one more go.' I backed up the ambo and attached the chain lower down on the bull bar of the 6 x 6. Once again, with Jon on the winch and me behind the wheel, we tried to recover the 6 x 6, but once again the ambo was being dragged towards the bog. I told Lieutenant Tilbrook that we couldn't help any more and that we had to go because the sucking chest wound was getting worse. Tilbrook and I made arrangements to marry up at the UN Headquarters in Butare.

Once again we were on the move towards Butare following the military observer blokes. Thank God they were with us; I had no idea where the hell we were. The observer guys drove fast in their Pathfinder while I pretended to be in the Paris to Dakar rally, throwing the ambo into every corner trying to make some ground on the observers, but they always seemed to be waiting for me. This went on for another hour when Jon put his head through the adjoining window and asked how long it would be until we got there. I told him another half an hour and he informed me that they were both suffering from motion sickness in the back, and were preparing to open the hatch on the floor to vomit through. Any wonder, the way I was driving, but while I felt for them, I couldn't stop laughing. Neither of them did vomit, but both looked like shit (and probably felt the same) once we arrived in Butare.

When we arrived at the hospital we were told that there were no doctors on duty and that one would have to be called in. In the meantime, with some assistance from three nurses from Care Australia, we moved the sucking chest wound to a theatre we'd located. We put the bloke on the operating table and attached his drip to the drip stand — he was into his fourth litre of fluid. Jon and I went scavenging for more fluid and anything that could help this bloke, but found nothing; this hospital was worse off than we were. The patient was still bleeding quite badly when we were told that no doctor was coming, so we carried him back to the ambulance. Just as we were putting him in the ambulance, a doctor arrived, much to our relief. We got the sucking chest wound out of the ambo again and put him onto a trolley so Carol could do a proper handover to the doctor. The doctor, a Tutsi, took one look at the sucking chest wound, a Hutu, then got back into his car and drove away. We threw a few mouthfuls of abuse at this prick. After all we had been through to get this bloke to some proper medical care, our efforts were being rejected. We were at a loss. We thought of driving the bloke back to Kigali, but we wouldn't get there until 4.00 or 5.00 in the morning. By then he'd be dead and we wouldn't be back in time to return to Kibeho first thing in the morning. We thought of keeping him until morning and calling for a helicopter, but again he would be dead by then. All seemed lost.

The nurses from Care saved the day by organising for the sucking chest to go to another hospital at a school called Groupe Scolaire. In the meantime, we had found a ward for the broken femur. The nurse there wanted some morphine for the patient so, while Carol organised that, Jon and I got the patient back into the ambulance. We moved off again towards Groupe Scolaire. The nurses from Care had arranged for us to be met at the front gate because the RPA providing security for the place wouldn't allow us entry. Groupe Scolaire was only a 10-minute drive and we soon arrived at the front gate with the Care Australia nurses in front and the observers bringing up the rear. We were met at the front gate by a foreign aid worker driving a ute. We collected the sucking chest wound and loaded him into the back of the ute. There was no official handover — Carol gave the aid worker some hastily drawn-up notes and that was it. We made arrangements with Care Australia to return our stretcher to us at Kigali. The ute drove off and we never saw the sucking chest wound again. He probably died.

I only had a general idea where I was so, once again, I was glad the observers were around as they knew the area well and took us back to the UN compound where they lived. The infantry and CCP vehicles had arrived there after being recovered from the bog and, best of all, they had a crate of coke with them. I managed to get a couple of bottles which I shared with Carol and Jon. It was a well-deserved coke that tasted bloody good; what a day! The time was 11.00 pm and we were all exhausted, totally rooted, and we still had to drive to the Zambian Headquarters. I didn't realise how exhausted I was or how great the pressure was to get these guys to some aid, but once we had freed ourselves and had a drink of coke, I just felt like lying down and slipping into a coma. The drive back to the Zambian Headquarters took 30 minutes but seemed to take two hours. As we drove along the winding road I began to hallucinate that the road was going straight ahead. I could see the road quite clearly going straight and then I'd shake my head and realise that the road wasn't going that way, it was going the other way. Had I not shaken myself out of this dream, I'd have driven the ambo off a cliff face. At the time, as my mind played tricks on me, I wasn't concerned and the hallucinations attacked me the whole way back. I couldn't ask Jon or Carol to drive; they had been working their arses off the whole way in the back of the ambo while battling motion sickness. I was so relieved to see the Zambian Headquarters gates appear in front of me.

When we arrived back at the Headquarters we couldn't go to sleep because the back of the ambulance looked like a butcher's shop. There was blood and old bandages everywhere. It took an hour to clean up and disinfect the back of the ambulance so we could sleep in there and be ready to go again first thing in the morning. We'd used some of our medical supplies from the ambo so we restocked with IV bags, giving sets (used to deliver the IV fluid from the bag to the IV needle), IV needles (cannulas) and bandages. Throughout the afternoon we had used the patrol medical kits that we brought with us from the SAS, and these were open with the contents lying all over the place, so we refurbished these as well. We couldn't wait to sleep and got our heads down as soon as the nightly brief was over. Thank Christ Lieutenant Tilbrook's briefs were short and to the point. Jon was usually asleep when I got back to the ambo so I updated him in the morning.

On Saturday we arrived at Kibeho at 7.45 am and were informed by a Jordanian UNICEF worker that the hospital was overrun with patients and that the MSF workers were not there. At this stage the UNICEF worker was the only foreigner in the camp. Carol, Jon, Rob Lucas (a nurse) and I went down to the hospital and saw about 100 IDPs who had either been shot or macheted or both. It was absolute chaos. I'd never seen anything like it in my life. There were bleeding IDPs all over the place. Their wounds were horrific. The first woman I saw had been hit in the face with a machete. The machete had gone through the bridge of her nose down through to her bottom jaw and all of this was resting on her chest, and she just sat there and looked at us with desperate eyes. 'Fuck me,' was all Jon and I kept saying to ourselves. There were people with massive cuts to their heads, to their arms and all over their bodies. One man had been hit across the head and his brain was clearly visible, yet not damaged. Later I saw a local nurse just fold the skullcap and skin over and sew it up. There were people with bullet wounds to various parts of their bodies, some with several bullet wounds and some just lying on the ground in a huge puddle of blood in the last stages of life. I saw a large box of bandages sitting alongside the IDPs and started to hand them out in an attempt to get them treating themselves. We just didn't have the numbers to treat them all. The situation was just beyond huge, beyond anything I could ever have imagined. Yesterday we had nothing; today we were overwhelmed.

Most of the patients were located in an area between two wings of the hospital, and we were pretty much covered from view and from the gunfire which we could hear coming from the other side of the hospital. Carol and I had a talk about the situation and agreed that she would return to the compound to prepare the CCP, and we'd triage the worst of them and send them to her on stretchers carried by the ever-faithful infantry. Jon, Rob and I started the triage process. But where were we to start? In the end we just grabbed the nearest patient who looked bad and gave him/her a priority of one, two or three — one being the worst. But we'd start on one person then another would appear in far worse condition. At times we were called on to play

That bloody rickshaw ride.

Saying thanks to the Nepali Police after my release. Ujwal, me, Nepali Police.

Dragged to the hospital.

Hallway to my cell at the hospital. My cell is on the immediate right.

The veiw from my hospital cell.

Bala and Sallie in discussions with the Deputy Superintendant of Police.

Prison water pump.

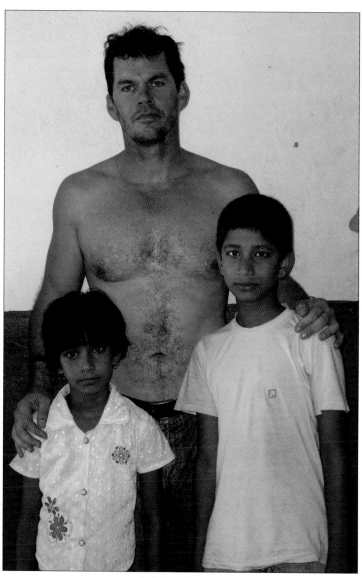

The kids at the hospital.

Rwanda - Carol, me, Rob Lucas wearing the baseball cap and Terry Pickard in the background preparing a victim for evacuation. Photo: George Gittoes.

Rwanda - waiting for the medical evacuation helicopter. Left to right: Signaller Quinn, Trooper Jon Church, Private Paul Price and me. Photo: George Gittoes.

Rwanda - me carrying a victim away from the line of fire of a recoilless weapon. Photo: George Gittoes.

Rwanda - uncovering a victim, unfortunately he was dead. Photo: George Gittoes.

Rwanda - pretending to be a doctor, but really not having a clue. This is Maria who was shot through the hand and into her chest. She had a classic sucking chest wound. Photo: George Gittoes.

Old Betsy with Walter, Charlie and me at the wheel. Iraq war, 2003. Photo: Jeff Barwise.

*Looking through the windscreen as we approach Baghdad on the
final push north. Iraq war, 2003. Photo: Jeff Barwise.*

Me in 2003 during the Iraq war.

An Iraqi Republican Guard Major we found and assumed to be dead. This photo was taken moments before he sat up. Iraq war, 2003. Photo: Jeff Barwise.

Aceh - a boat in the main street.

Aceh.

Negotiations with local police to get to a polling booth - Baghdad 2005.

*Sallie's daughters, Poppy and Lucy. They both wrote me a
beautiful card which Sallie delivered to me in gaol.*

Dad and Trevor.

Zac, Sayge and Sam.

Colin and mum in New York.

Steven - my brother a few months before he was killed.

*My dad, Warrant Officer Class 1 William Jordan (left) on
the day he retired after 25 years in the Army.*

God and put people to one side whom we thought wouldn't survive or would take too much time to save when that time could be better spent saving two or three other IDPs.

Back in the compound, Lieutenant Tilbrook had organised his defences around the compound itself and had also established communications with AUSMED Headquarters. At this stage a mass casualty evacuation was declared.

The Jordanian UNICEF guy wanted to point out some more casualties outside the hospital in the town courtyard. I saw about 30 people there; some were dead, but most were in the final stages of life. So I rolled them onto their sides to improve their airways and at least give them some chance. It had rained through the night and all the bodies were lying in pools of muddy, bloody water. Large numbers of IDPs began approaching me at this time with freshly inflicted injuries. This concerned Jon and me. It meant that the gunfire we could hear close by was directed at these people. People were being shot and killed in our vicinity, so we decided to re-enter the hospital and work on what we could manage for now. The Jordanian kept saying, 'What about this one?' and 'What about that one?'

'Yeh, wait on mate, there's only three of us,' I yelled over the sound of gunfire. 'Here, grab one of these and start bandaging someone.'

Jon and I continued triaging patients. I was treating a woman by the name of Maria (I remember her name because she was in the back of the ambulance all day) who had been shot through the hand and into her right lung. Her hand was quite a mess, but she only had a small hole in her chest about the size of a 20 cent coin. My first response was to treat her hand, but soon remembered the priority of treatment and began to treat her sucking chest wound, although there wasn't a lot of air or blood coming from her chest. I listened to her chest with my stethoscope, and even though I really had no idea what I was doing, I knew the lung wasn't working properly — this made her a priority one.

Jon drew my attention to the patient he was treating. He had a very deep cut across his eye and through his face and another very deep cut through his chin and into his throat. Jon completely bandaged his face and had no fear of not maintaining an airway because the man was breathing through the slice in his throat. The man was fighting Jon the whole time and became difficult to manage, so he left him and moved on to another who wanted help.

Jon, Rob and I continued to prioritise patients when the infantry arrived and stretchered the indicated patients back to the Zambian compound where Carol had prepared the CCP to handle the incoming patients. Most of the infantry had never seen a dead person before and certainly had never seen such ruthless carnage but, just like everyone else, they drew down the emotional curtain and got on with their business. The Infantry (in true grunt style) were tireless in their efforts stretchering the patients back. Quinny, the communications guru, managed to establish communications with AUSMED Headquarters and began the lengthy and tiring process of trying to get an immediate AME. But, with the gunfire and mortar fire in the background, the UN refused to allow one of its helicopters to land at a hot landing zone.

Jon continued to process patients for the infantry lads to carry back. I took a moment and watched him work. He was moving through the injured, rapidly identifying those who needed immediate help, patching them very quickly, pointing them out to the infantry lads and then moving on to the next unfortunate. He was like a machine — it was unbelievable how quickly he adapted to the situation. This playing medic stuff wasn't our core skill. We were SAS operators filling a gap that needed filling. We were using this opportunity to improve our medical skills which were just a small part of the expertise required of each SAS soldier, and Jon was doing some really great stuff this morning. He was smooth, calculated and compassionate when required.

Meanwhile, in the courtyard and around the hospital, the firing escalated and we were ordered to return to the compound. We left the hospital, informing the MSF workers who had finally shown up, that we were leaving to work on the casualties we had. The MSF workers decided to stay and were subsequently caught in the battle and couldn't leave the hospital. Once again, it was the under-appreciated infantry who had to go and pull the MSF from the hospital. In doing so,

Lieutenant Tilbrook took fire from a sniper. Corporal Brian Buskell was quick to take a sight picture on the sniper, but to take the shot would have endangered the lives of further IDPs and the sniper slipped back into the crowd.

The work continued in the compound with many casualties walking in themselves. At about 10.00 am, some of the IDPs made a run for it through the re-entrants surrounding the compound. We watched (and could do little more) as these people were hunted down and shot. The RPA were terrible shots and, at times, were within 10 metres of the running IDPs and were still missing their targets. If the RPA managed to wound an IDP, they would save their bullets and bayonet the IDP to death. The RPA had RPGs (recoilless rockets) sited up on the next ridgeline which they were also firing into the IDPs. This went on for two hours until all the IDPs who'd made the break were either dead or dying. This was all happening about 300 metres away from us which was, unfortunately, too far for us to go and help them. As I watched the IDPs being bayoneted to death, I could only imagine how much it would have hurt having a bayonet continually thrust into your body — not to mention the fact that you were dying at the time. It was a slow, painful, horrible death that the young infantry guys were forced to watch as, under the UN mandate, they could not intervene. I say 'forced' because it was happening right in their line of sight.

As patients were stabilised, they were loaded onto the Unimog truck where Nico the medic was looking after them; those deemed critical were loaded into the ambulance which, by now, had become a makeshift intensive care unit. The treatment was quick; we went from one patient to another. If someone was having trouble, another person would come and help or, if it was serious enough, Carol would come and help. But she was in great demand, so it was a matter of doing our best without her.

It was now about 10.00 am, the firing had intensified and it had begun to rain. But the work continued, with the infantry providing and holding a secure perimeter. Everybody was either behind a truck or a sandbag wall working. We strung up hutchies to keep the rain off the patients and, if we needed to clean their arms for an IV line, we simply hung the arm out in the rain. I moved to a position behind a sandbag wall to see what was going on when I noticed the Zambians trying to tell a young boy to get down to the ground. I could see the boy about 50 metres away. He was frightened and confused with everyone yelling at him and the bullets flying all around him. So, with my weapon in my right hand, I bolted out of the compound, grabbed the boy around his waist with my left arm and ran back. All the while, some pricks continued to take pot-shots at us. I tried to get him to lie down, but he kept babbling something to me, so I kicked his legs out from under him, motioned that he should stay there, and went back to see if the infantry needed any help. Damn, that was a pretty crazy thing to do, but if the UN wouldn't let me use my weapon to protect these people, then I was determined to use my body. I returned to the boy after five minutes and saw him flat out on the ground with a glazed look in his eyes. Nico said, 'He's dead, Jordo, leave him.'

'What? How can that be?'

Terry came over and we both saw him move and that was good enough for us. We started to work on him and were later assisted by Carol. We could see blood in his mouth and eventually found a small piece of shrapnel in his right lung. I put a mask on his face and forced air into his lungs with the attached bag, while Carol managed to get a cannula into his femoral vein to provide him with more fluids — his other veins had shut down, so the femoral vein was the best access to the circulatory system. We got him breathing again and then put him into the ambulance where he was watched closely until he was evacuated that afternoon. Later we found that his mother had told him that, if they should be separated, he should run to the *mazungus* (white people) which he had tried to do.

As the work continued, an IDP ran into the compound with no apparent injuries. I was walking across the compound to assist the infantry on the perimeter when this IDP ran straight at me. I raised my weapon to fend him off, but he grabbed it and I found myself wrestling with him. His eyes caught mine as we wrestled with my weapon. He had a look I will never forget: a look of true and absolute terror. It was an alarming thing to see in the eyes of a grown man. I tried to pacify the man as I knew he didn't mean any harm. I could have rammed my size 11 boot straight into his chest, but I didn't want the other IDPs seeing an Australian soldier assaulting an IDP. The Zambians, however, do things a little differently. A Zambian soldier decided to help me by kicking the IDP in the head. It was good kick, plenty of height and nice momentum, and connected with a horrible thud. The IDP's eyes rolled back in his head, he let go and collapsed to the ground unconscious. The Zambian gave me a big toothy grin. What could I do? 'Thanks, mate,' I said and continued on my way after rolling my unconscious friend onto his side. The Zambians didn't piss around with these people; they had been in Kibeho for six months and knew them better than we did.

Everyone was flat out. We had no time to eat or drink all day. Those who managed to pick up a water bottle went around and poured water into the mouths of everyone else who had blood up to their elbows. We drank water periodically, but no-one ate at all during the day. There was no time and I don't think any of us noticed our hunger anyway.

The technique of putting in IV cannulas had to change a little from the way we'd learnt on medical courses. Basically, a cannula was only thrown away if it was broken. On one occasion, Nico and I were working on a boy trying to get an IV in. The boy had lost a lot of blood and his veins had shrunk until they were barely noticeable, which didn't help. Nico had one arm and I had the other. I'd have a go and miss, then I'd hand the cannula to Nico. As Nico was having a go, I'd be getting another vein ready and when Nico blew it, I'd have a go. Eventually I got it into the back of the boy's hand. It was amazing that the cannula even went in because, after nine or ten attempts, it would have been very blunt.

The firing continued with more IDPs shot all over the camp, but it wasn't only the RPA doing the killing. The IDPs were doing their fair share of killing their own as well. The RPA had demanded the handing over of the Interahamwe elements among the IDPs. The Interahamwe were the militia elements of the Hutu population who'd been involved in the genocide the year before. There'd been a lot of finger-pointing which obviously the Interahamwe resented, so they were resorting to killing as well. They used machetes and guns, and the injuries they inflicted were always horrific. We worked flat out all day with the continuous gunfire in the background and with barely enough time to scratch ourselves. Time flew by and, before we realised, it was mid-afternoon.

Lieutenant Tilbrook spent most of his time negotiating with the RPA to allow him to bring in helicopters to evacuate the wounded. Obviously he did a great job, because the AMEs went ahead. However, the mortars continued to fall around the camp and the rifle fire wouldn't let up, so the helicopters still couldn't land. Lieutenant Tilbrook was the tactical commander all throughout the time we were in Kibeho and certainly had his work cut out for him. When all was said and done, he had total control of the Australians at all times and did a bloody good job.

By the time we'd gathered 25 casualties in the Unimog and the ambulance, Quinny the Sig had managed to organise an AME, so we moved out of the compound to the helo landing place. On the way there a large formation of RPA soldiers, possibly company strength, marched down the road towards the IDPs. The soldiers were singing in hushed tones and morale seemed to be through the roof. Jon and I just looked on and wondered what they were up to — it couldn't be good.

Jon and I sat in the ambulance with our feet on the dash waiting for the helo when a lone IDP ran down the road towards us. An RPA soldier was chasing the runaway IDP and firing wildly at him. No rounds hit the IDP, again they were crap shots, but every burst landed around the ambulance. There's nothing like a few bullets landing around you to wake you up, and Jon and I quickly bailed out and took shelter behind the ambulance. Some of the bullets came very close to a group of RPA officers standing near the front of the ambulance. When the IDP arrived at the ambo, he threw himself at the feet of the RPA officers and begged for mercy. The officers barely acknowledged him and nodded to the pursuing RPA solder who dragged the IDP behind the nearest building and shot him in the head. We always cringed when this sort of shit was happening. The IDP kicked and screamed for our help the whole way to his execution point. We should have done something for the poor bastard.

Chapter 20

At about 4.00 pm the helos arrived and, once again, I was forced to argue with the RPA Major about the evacuation. I could see he didn't really care; he just didn't want to make life too easy for me. Again he insisted that one of his officers inspect each patient to ensure we weren't trying to smuggle people out of the camp, or that the IDPs were not faking injuries to get evacuated. The helos brought in a load of journalists to make a quick report on the situation. They raced around snapping photos and trying to secure interviews. Sergeant Brett Dick and WO2 Scott (Scotty) were also on the helicopter. They'd come in to lend a hand.

Rob Lucas accompanied Burageya on the flight back to Kigali. Burageya was the boy we'd worked on earlier and thought was dead. Rob had to carry the boy and, as we were getting the boy settled on Rob's lap, a female journalist pointed to a lot of blood coming from the bottom of the blanket wrapped around the boy. We couldn't work out where it was coming from. I thought we had missed a substantial injury. On closer inspection I realised that the femoral IV cannula had come out. I pulled it all the way out, much to Carol's annoyance, and Rob put pressure on it during the trip back. Jon was sitting in the back of the ambo waiting to stretcher his mate with the cut throat when some journos started asking him some questions. Jon answered diplomatically, without giving too much away, when one of them shoved a microphone into his face. This was the end, and he simply told the journo to 'fuck off' in his drawn-out way. After the RPA Major's display of power, he eventually allowed me to evacuate all the injured IDPs and journos in three helicopters and, by 5.00 pm, the job was complete. The journos couldn't wait to get out and tell their stories to the world.

At the same time the IDPs ran through the wire into the compound and the infantry found themselves alongside the Zambians pushing the IDPs back over the wire. Some IDPs had grenades, which caused some concern to the infantry soldiers. Lieutenant Tilbrook told me over the radio to stay at the helipad a bit longer because they were still fighting off the IDPs. The infantry lads had fixed their bayonets in order to push the panicked IDPs out of the compound.

As the last helicopter took off, the RPA company which we'd earlier seen walking down the road, began firing into the crowd. This caused about 2000 IDPs to stampede down the re-entrant away from the camp — they were running for their lives. The RPA had anticipated this and had pre-positioned themselves up on the high ground around the re-entrant where they fired rifles, machine-guns, rockets and mortars onto and into the fleeing IDPs. It was a massacre, absolute carnage. We watched hundreds of people fall under the hail of fire, mortars and rockets and decided it would be best to get back inside the compound given that the helipad was so open. Jon and I loaded everyone into the back of the ambulance, made a hasty trip back to the compound and took cover behind the sandbag walls.

From behind the sandbag walls, we watched everything, and could do little more. Fortunately for the IDPs, it had started to rain and it really came down, which provided some cover for the IDPs to escape. RPG rockets landed among the stampeding crowd and 10 people would fall and not get up again. Mortars continued to fall and there were dead and wounded all over the place. The noise of the barrage and machine-gun fire was unbelievable. It was just a constant roar of explosions and gunfire as the death toll rapidly climbed.

An old woman stood up 50 metres to our front; an RPA soldier was the same distance beyond her. We yelled and pleaded with the woman to come to us for safety, but she just stood there looking at us, then at the RPA soldier. We thought the soldier was going to shoot the old woman right in front of us and, given the poor marksmanship of the RPA, the bullets would miss and travel in our direction. Instead, the RPA soldier called the woman over to him as we did the same thing trying to get her to come to us. But, to our astonishment, she went to him. He put his arm around her shoulders and walked up the hill towards the helipad. He got to the top of the rise where the road bent towards the helipad and turned and looked at us; then he threw the woman to the ground and shot her. This was the RPA at its finest. Basically this was a sign that the UN forces had no power and couldn't do anything to stop them. Unfortunately, they were right.

As the rain died off, so did the firing. There was no-one running down the re-entrant anymore; they were all either dead or dying. I moved to the other side of the compound to help the infantry lads hold the perimeter. I was standing alongside the building watching the crowd when I heard a loud crack above me and felt the crumbled brickwork fall onto my head. My natural reaction was to duck, but it would obviously have been far too late. I looked up and saw that the brick on the corner of the building about 10 centimetres above my head had disintegrated. The RPA soldiers standing nearby thought the incident was hilarious. I felt like showing them something funny by shooting their kneecaps. I wondered who had taken a shot at me — the RPA or an IDP. I moved to a different spot and looked for the prick who had shot at me when I saw a young boy walk through the barbed wire, straight past the RPA and towards me. I thought this kid was showing some real balls; the RPA saw his wounds and let him continue. He was wearing a blood-soaked T-shirt and had an obvious facial injury. I put on my gloves and, as the boy approached me, he extended his hand. I shook it and he pointed to where a bullet had entered his left nostril and was sitting in his upper jaw. I took the boy to the ambulance and, given that it was getting dark and all the firing was directed in the opposite direction to the way we were going, we decided to make a break for it. At the same time, a man was brought in with an abdominal injury. He'd been shot through the abdomen and his small intestine was exposed. If we had stayed in the camp we would have been working for the next 24 hours straight, there were so many wounded who needed the medics' care. But we had to go and go now.

Jon drove this time and I got in the back with Carol. Nico jumped in the front with Jon. As we left the camp, Jon and Nico saw a little girl who was about two years old clinging to the body of her dead mother. Jon opened the driver's door of the moving ambo, grabbed the kid by the shirt and threw her through the window joining the driver's compartment and the back of the ambo. This presented a couple of problems for Carol and me; we were busy working on two serious patients and didn't have time to deal with a screaming kid who smelt strongly of urine. The kid had no injuries and we knew that when the RPA did their search, any IDP who wasn't injured would be returned to the camp or killed. If this happened, the RPA wouldn't allow us to take any more injured IDPs out of the camp and possibly not even let us back in. So saving this little orphaned, uninjured girl from this nightmarish place was bloody risky — but worth it. I decided to bandage the girl's arm and slide the end of an IV line under the bandage. Despite her appearance and smell she was a sweet little girl. She stared at both Carol and me not knowing what the hell was happening or who we were. I gave her the sweet sugar-coated jelly from the French ration pack and she forced a weak smile. Then it hit me; this kid wasn't just another patient. She was a little girl who had sat with her mother while she was murdered. She probably expected her mother to get up and look after her. What must her mother have thought when she died? She would have been so concerned for her little girl. Now this poor little thing, who hadn't seen soap and water for maybe a month and hadn't eaten real food for more than a week, was sitting in the back of an ambulance with two white people. Actually, compared to the others in the camp, she was pretty lucky. She would go to the orphanage and wait for the unlikely event of a distant relative arriving to save her when all this was over.

As I got her settled and Carol worked on the boy with the bullet in the nose and the man with the bullet in the guts, I got a call from Jon up front and stuck my head through the window. Jon motioned with his head to the scene in front. I think he just couldn't find the words to describe the scene. Dead bodies littered the road. They were everywhere. Jon negotiated as best he could and was forced on a number of occasions to reverse and manoeuvre the ambo so he didn't run over arms or legs. It was now dark and we were still trying to get out of Kibeho.

The first time we were searched, the girl spoke and waved to the RPA while Carol and I tried to drown her voice out with stories of the terrible injuries she had suffered. The RPA accepted this and off we went to the next roadblock. We couldn't risk this girl talking to the RPA again, so we put her up in the blanket rack and strapped her in. Carol gave her an injection to make her sleep and she screamed her head off, so we gave her a biscuit and, when we were next searched, the girl just stayed still and the RPA never knew she was there. The girl slept the whole way to Butare and I would say that it was probably the best sleep she'd had in 12 months.

After being held up at one of the roadblocks for an hour the convoy, including all the NGO people, made its way out of Kibeho and went to another Zambian company compound. This one was three-quarters of the way back to the Zambian Headquarters location near Gikongoro. The boy who'd been shot in the nose was simply incredible. He knew just how serious his injuries were. Carol had me doing suction on him to clear all the blood from his mouth. When I'd done this twice he knew what was going on and decided to do it himself. After each suction, he'd pull out different pieces of his upper jawbone and put them in the contaminated waste bag (a large yellow plastic bag). Then he'd lie down and rest until he needed suction again.

When we arrived at the Zambian company position, we met the second CCP which had come from Kigali to help. Jon pulled up in front of one of the buildings and Nico opened the back of the ambo. Kathleen Pyne, a RAAF Nursing Officer, got into the ambulance to lend a hand while we took the opportunity to eat for the first time since breakfast. Jon and I grabbed a handful of rations from the bin over the cabin, gave some to Carol, and went inside to eat. Suddenly I felt the desperate need to piss, realising that I hadn't pissed all day. I had a quick look for a toilet, but couldn't find one, so I found a suitable tree in the darkness. The feeling amongst everyone as we ate inside the building was euphoric. Secretly, I think we were all happy to have left Kibeho so we could breathe easier for a few hours. Once we'd finished eating we continued on to the headquarters location. Carol and I climbed back into the ambo and I told Kathleen to stay as well. Before we left, the boy with the bullet in the nostril surprised Kath by getting up. I said, 'It's okay, he just wants to use the suction,' but he didn't. The boy indicated that he wanted to get out of the ambo. So I unhooked the drip and followed him. All he wanted was to have a piss.

Kath continued to ride in the back of the ambulance for the rest of the trip and we laughed at everything, which was a great tension release. I stood up at one stage to get some water and knocked the giving set out of the boy's IV. We reconnected it, but it continued to fall out of the drip and would always end up in the contaminated waste bag, which looked like we'd just killed a sheep in it. We'd simply reconnect because we had no other giving sets to replace it with. Kath was initially shocked by it all, but quickly understood the situation and laughed along with Carol and me. She probably thought we'd lost it — maybe we had. I'd always imagined Kath to be a bit soft, but during the next few days I realised that she could handle any situation and could tough it out as much as the rest of us — a good officer.

The boy was the ideal patient, he never complained once. It was truly amazing. He had shown enormous bravado by walking past the RPA and straight through the perimeter in the first place. Then, in the ambo, he handled himself with what I can only describe as extraordinary determination to survive. I admired him. The bloke with the abdominal wound bitched the whole time about his pain despite the fact that we'd given him enough morphine to drop an elephant. In the end we told him that, if he didn't stop whinging, we'd take him back to Kibeho — after that we didn't hear a word out of him. Imagine doing all that complaining just because half your gut is resting on the outside of your body, what a wimp! Poor bastard. The little girl continued to sleep peacefully with a biscuit tightly clutched in her hand.

Once we'd arrived at the Zambian Headquarters, the second CCP took the ambo with the casualties to the Butare hospital (good luck) and the little girl to the CARE Australia orphanage. Before the ambo left, Jon and I grabbed our sleeping gear from the bin over the cabin and moved in with the infantry section in one of the buildings. We assembled our stretchers and found a small space near the door. We finally managed to get our heads down at around 11.00 pm. We were totally shattered. I'm sure I fell asleep while I was putting my stretcher together. I lay down and dreamed ...

Chapter 20

My lungs scream for more air as I sprint down the hill. There isn't enough air at this altitude. I have to keep going hard and fast to survive. One mortar lands just to my left and a family of four goes down and doesn't move again, their bodies violently ripped to pieces by the flying pieces of serrated metal. The explosive wave carries pieces of hacked flesh and bone in each direction. A small brown hand that only moments before had been attached to a living, breathing child, slaps my leg with such force that my leg is thrown out from under me and I fall. I stand quickly and notice the bloody stain left by the hand on my right trouser leg.

There are hundreds of people fleeing the attack. Mortars slam into the earth every few seconds and the fertile brown soil is thrown into the air. The noise is indescribable. Every mortar is like a bowling ball getting a strike as the people drop like pins. But they don't drop — they're ripped into unrecognisable pieces. There are mutilated bodies everywhere. Some bodies still have some life in them and they grab at my legs as I run past — a pitiful, last-ditch grasp for survival. I hear their screams and cries, but I can't help them, there are too many. I hear more mortars being given their wings. They are being fired by an unseen aggressor, but they're hitting their marks with certain accuracy.

Mortars drop like hail in a storm and more people collapse onto the blood-soaked ground. I jump bodies as I run, but the sheer number of bleeding piles of butchered meat makes it difficult to continue at a fast pace. A 50 calibre machine-gun set on fixed lines opens up from the high ground and begins to sweep across the stampeding mass as if waving a wand of death over all in its path, until only the stragglers remain. The 50 cal stops and I can hear the small arms begin to pick off the targets that remain.

I continue racing down the re-entrant dodging the shocking remains of people, wondering if my bullet has been fired and anticipating the impact. I am trying to run faster, but the bodies on the ground continue to slow me down. Twice I fall onto and into a pile of bloodied appendages and twice I struggle to my feet and continue my sprint for life. I know I'm not safe yet because the ground is still far too open. I still have a good 300 metres to sprint before I hit the safety of the tree line. I'm starting to tire and I pump my legs harder. I'm grateful to be running down the re-entrant and not up it.

I see a small baby girl clinging to a pile of red meat that was clearly her mother only moments before. As I continue my run, I make a snap decision and I bend down and scoop up the girl. She screams with fright and then clings to me, tighter and tighter, as if the closeness would somehow protect her. Her grip on me tightens even more as the blast wave from each mortar slaps her face. The blast waves carry dirt and rock and pieces of metal that seemed to be continually fired into our bodies. I look into her face and she has tears forging rivers through her blood and mud-caked cheeks and there is nothing I can do. I feel helpless.

I hear the salvo of mortars being fired and I fall as one lands too close. I get up and scoop the girl up in my arms. I stop running because the mortars are landing all around me. My path is blocked, I can't move, there's no-one left but me and the little nameless girl. I realise I've put the girl in danger; I wish I had left her where she was. Now she will die with me. The soldiers make themselves visible and take aim at me. I tell the girl I'm sorry, but she only looks at me with terror mixed with confusion in her eyes. What have I done? I can't save anyone and manage only to get another person killed. 'Fuck off,' I yell at the soldiers, 'you don't need to do this!'

'Jordo, wake up! Jordo, you've got an orders group in 10 minutes.'

'Huh, what?'

'Mate, you've been dreaming, you've got orders in 10 minutes.'

I sat up and looked at the signaller who'd woken me.

'What time is it?'

'Ten to three.'

'Shit, all right, I'll be there,' I mumbled.

The Sig wandered off to wake someone else as I sat in the dark trying to get my bearings. I looked at my watch: 2.55 am. Three hours' sleep, excellent. That'll have to do, I suppose. I hadn't had a nightmare like that before. After the day's delightful performance, it's no wonder I was becoming a nutcase. While the nightmare was bad, the fact that one of these people had seen me during a weakened moment pissed me off more. I looked around as my vision improved in the darkness. Most people still slept, some stirred, and one or two were doing the same as me. I hoped I hadn't yelled and carried on so that others could hear me. Jon was next to me, and he looked to be sleeping soundly and undisturbed; perhaps the demons hadn't visited him yet, but if I hadn't woken him perhaps I hadn't been that loud after all.

Captain McMahon had taken over now and told us that we were going back to Kibeho and were leaving at 5.00 am. I woke Jon at 4.00 am and we quickly refurbished the ambulance with IV fluid, giving sets, cannulas, bandages and, of course, gloves. Yesterday we were using the same set of gloves on as many people as possible. It wouldn't matter if the gloves were covered in someone else's blood —they'd only be thrown away when they were holed. The second CCP, commanded by George Donalec, was to go into the camp first today and Carol's CCP was to arrive a few hours later.

On Sunday 23 April, we re-entered the camp at around 6.30 am with the initial mission of counting the dead. As usual, we parked the vehicles in the compound and some members of the new infantry section (the infantry sections were taking turns at going into the camp) indicated to me a lot of dead just beyond the concertina wire. Jon and I stepped over the wire and approached a woman who was in the last stages of dying. There was nothing we could do for her, but she had a baby strapped to her back who was still alive. We released the baby, but she'd been caught underneath her mum all night and couldn't walk. We gave the baby to a young woman standing nearby. The strange thing was that there were a lot of people standing around this woman, but no-one had helped. Most of the people were in a state of shock. We released a lot of babies that morning who were in a similar state. I found another baby attached to her mother's back. I rolled mum over — she was clearly dead and had been so for several hours. I unwrapped the cloth around mum's waist. There was a lot of blood. Maybe the baby was injured? I grabbed the kid and immediately dropped it again. The baby had been decapitated while strapped to her mother's back; possibly a wild swing from a machete. I couldn't believe what I'd just seen. The image of that baby still visits me.

Before the count started, I took Scotty down to have a look at the hospital. Inside there were about 15 dead. We entered one room and a pregnant woman was lying on a mattress with a young boy at the foot of the bed. As we walked in, the young boy smiled and waved at us. After all this kid had been through, he was still able to smile. We couldn't take him at that stage, but decided we would come back to get him and his mother later. We then went up the hill to look at the woman we'd seen executed the day before. She'd been shot through the chest and probably would have survived if we'd gone to get her. We continued on to have a look at the area around the helipad when an IDP jumped out of the long grass at us. He scared the shit out of me and I nearly shot the prick. This bloke kept grabbing us and mumbling something — he was shitting himself, poor bastard. Jon and I pushed him back into the long grass and indicated that he should stay there. We couldn't take him with us. If the RPA had seen us walking with him they'd have taken him and shot him, so it was a case of 'stay there dopey, until after dark'.

Scotty took half a section and I took another and we walked each side of the road that divided the camp and counted the dead and wounded. On my side of the road I had the hospital that contained 15 dead, and then out in the courtyard there were 100 dead. There were a lot of children just sitting on piles of rubbish; some were sitting next to dead bodies. The Zambians were collecting all the live babies and children and handing them over to the Red Cross who had now arrived. The area was covered in rubbish and, quite often as I walked, I'd disturb some rubbish and find a dead baby. I counted 20 such babies, but obviously I couldn't check under acres of rubbish. Every time one of the young soldiers called that they'd found another dead person I added another click to my pace counter. I came across another woman with a baby strapped to her back. I could see that the woman was dead, but hoped that the baby was still alive. I rolled Mum over and realised I had found another decapitated baby strapped to Mum's back. I walked on; click, click.

Along the road near the documentation point there were about 200 bodies lined up for burial. For some of the dead it was difficult, at a glance, to determine the cause of death. The blood had dried and was difficult to see against their black skin, or in their matted hair, but then I'd notice brain matter exposed, or ribs protruding, all caused by savage blows from a machete. The half-section and I saw a number of casualties lying and sitting inside some small huts that were being protected by the RPA. I told the infantry to watch my back and I walked down the small decline and approached the huts. My intention was to count the bodies and to get an idea of the casualties inside. The RPA soldier defending the group of dead waved his finger at me indicating that he wanted me to leave and leave now. I had a look at him and realised that he was actually about 13 years old. His uniform was too big and the AK47 hung very heavily in his hands. I waved off the soldier and stepped around him and, at the same time, heard the soldiers behind me remove the safety catches on their weapons. I turned around to see what the problem was and found myself looking straight down the barrel of the kid's AK47. The child soldier had the weapon's barrel about an inch away from the bridge of my nose. As I looked down the barrel I saw that the end was full of mud. I later wondered whether he had used it the day before in the massacre or whether he had dropped it in the mud overnight. I protested for a minute, but he held his ground, so I left it. Most times the RPA gave in if you pushed them, but with an AK47 in your face, you tend to leave well enough alone. I mentioned before that the RPA were terrible shots, but at a range of two centimetres, it's hard to miss.

We continued on and married up with Scotty's party on the road. They'd counted many more dead than we had. Jon was with this other party and, as I approached him, I saw that he was carrying a very small baby. During the count, Jon caught sight of the baby in the corner of his eye in a puddle of mud. I had a look at the little fellow and saw that he was very small; in fact the little bloke looked as if he was an hour or so old, and still had a long length of umbilical cord attached. I had an image of a poor woman delivering this baby while on the run. Jon and I wandered over to the Red Cross guys and handed them the baby. They'd set up a small tarpaulin off the side of their Nissan 4 x 4 to shelter the 15 or so babies and children they already had.

Scotty and I met and agreed the total count was about 4000 dead and 650 wounded, but we knew we hadn't counted them all. Neither group went down the re-entrant where so many were mowed down the day before for fear of unexploded ordnance or mines. We returned to the compound and set about helping the medics treat the casualties. Carol's CCP had arrived, so we had the two doctors and more medics. This time, due to the limited gunfire, the medics set up the CCP outside the Zambian compound. We'd really gone from the shithouse to the penthouse: it was luxurious. We had the Unimog to work from which was loaded with medical stores and we had heaps of stretchers. The need for security wasn't as paramount as it was the previous day, so the infantry were also assisting with treatment. This certainly beat working from the medical packs with our helmets and flak jackets on. With the manpower and trucks we managed to clear 85 patients.

More and more NGOs started to fill the camp as well as military observers from various countries and, of course, the media. A Ghanaian Major asked Scotty and I to go to another area, not far from the documentation point, to collect some more injured. We collected two patients. One was a small boy of about 10 years of age who was lying under a tarp and, as I lifted the tarp, he looked at us and pulled it back down over his face. He looked as if he just wanted to curl up and die. He was laying in filth, had his year-old tattered shorts and torn shirt on and had a look in his eyes that just said, 'Leave me alone, I'm done.' I felt for the poor bloke — what an existence for a young lad. I just couldn't image what he'd seen and been through or where his parents were. I lifted the tarp again and smiled at the young bloke. He stared at me and didn't attempt to cover himself again. Maybe he thought that I couldn't do any more to him than had already been done. I reached out and picked up his hand, patted it and nodded to him. I was trying to let him know that I was going to help him. I scanned his body looking for injuries and quickly saw the problem. He had an open fracture of the femur; the bone was clearly visible protruding beneath his shorts. We had to get him to the Major's Hilux, so we used his tarp to make a stretcher and carried him. Obviously, when you've got a broken femur, any movement is excruciatingly painful and, quite understandably, he screamed in pain.

The other patient was inside a small shelter and also had a broken femur. Scotty and I just picked him up and put him in the back of the Hilux. As expected, the man screamed the whole way. We took the two back to the CCP to be treated and loaded onto the truck. As I was driving back, I saw the RPA burying a lot of the dead, possibly to reduce the count. The Zambians also buried some of the dead, but at this stage it was only those around their compound.

Brett Dick and Terry Pickard were tasked with collecting casualties from around the camp. They would identify the casualties and the infantry would deliver them to the CCP on stretchers, or they'd be brought in on trucks. A truck arrived and Jon and I jumped on the truck first to triage the patients. We found that two casualties had died in transit to the CCP and had been left on the truck. By that stage we had both, in our own way, learnt to live with the constant death and continued to triage those still alive with little concern for the dead. We even started to struggle to empathise with those badly injured. When you are constantly exposed to brutal death and horrible injuries by the thousands you tend to become less sensitive; you tend to pull the shutters down and block out the fact that these are real people. They had injuries varying from broken bones, to internal injuries, to gunshot and machete wounds, and they'd been delivered to us on the back of a truck. The pain alone probably killed the two already dead in the back of the truck.

When the casualties on the truck were cleared, Jon and I went back into the hospital to collect the pregnant woman and her boy. She had a hard time walking and I thought she was going to deliver right then and there. She didn't, and was lucky enough to be evacuated, with her son, by helo to Butare that day.

Jon and I made only two trips to the helipad that morning. Shortly after the second helo landed, the pilot handed something to a journalist and received something in return (probably film). My RPA Major friend saw this and went off. He called me over as we were loading the casualties on board and said, 'The helicopter will not leave until the pilot gives me the package he was handed.' I thought he was playing with me, so I started to go through my now well-rehearsed banter, but he just looked at me and repeated, 'The helicopter will not leave until the pilot gives me the package he was handed.' I knew he meant business and I needed some new lines. I approached the helicopter pilot as Jon continued with the loading. 'What the fuck have you got on board that you're not supposed to have?'

'Nothing.'

'What did the journo give you?'

'Nothing. He's a UN photographer. I gave him some film, but he didn't give me anything.'

'I hope that's the truth, mate, because they will want to search the helo.'

'No problem, they can search.'

I returned to the Major who was now inspecting the wounded. 'Sir [I was starting to suck up], the pilot has nothing on board that he shouldn't have, and invites you to search the helicopter if you want.'

Three RPA officers checked every compartment in the helicopter. They opened boxes and packages, which were mostly survival packages, and found nothing — thank Christ. Finally, the Major gave the pilot permission to leave, and Jon and I headed back to the CCP.

During the morning the RPA shot an IDP very close to where we were. They'd shot him in the leg and then played with him. Lieutenant Tilbrook and a couple of soldiers stood over the bloke preventing the RPA from doing any more damage, and then carried him over to the CCP. He was losing a lot of blood. He wasn't yelling and screaming as he had been initially, but had begun to drift into a semi-conscious state. Carol and George worked on him, but the blood loss through the femoral artery was too great. We filled him up with morphine and put him behind the Unimog, which was a quiet spot. He was dead inside five minutes.

The CO and RSM arrived in the early afternoon by helo, and we arranged to AME our four worst casualties on the helicopter that had brought them in. As Jon and I waited at the helipad for the helo, the RPA Major once again turned up to inspect the casualties. I had got to know the Major quite well by this stage, but I never let my guard down. That cowboy hat made him looked relaxed, but he was a crafty, ruthless bastard. He was in control of this camp and therefore responsible for the massacre the day before and for the shit that was continuing. This time the Major went through the four patients very carefully, then pointed to one casualty, a man about 30 years old, and said that we couldn't take him. I argued and pointed to his horrendous injuries, but it didn't do any good. The Major explained that the man was a criminal and could only go on the trucks. I explained that the long trip on the truck would be too much for the man and that whether he went out by helo or truck he would still end up at the same place and his men could find him there. But the Major would not change his mind.

While I was arguing with the Major, a Zambian soldier handed Jon a small boy about 18 months old. He'd been shot in the backside, but there was no visible exit wound and the young boy seemed happy enough. The kid was amazing. He was playing around our feet and getting in the way as any young boy does. He was just like any other kid; only he had a bullet in his butt. What this kid was doing at the helipad I'll never know, but it probably saved his life. Kids are so resilient. The RPA Major said to take the young boy instead of the man, which we ended up doing. The RPA Major then told me that one of his men was being brought up. He arrived shortly after on an old mattress carried by four of his colleagues. He'd been shot through the right lung and the Major insisted that I hold the helo for his man. I argued that if he wanted me to do him a favour, then he must do one for me and let the other man go as well.

'Either my man goes or no-one goes, you decide.'

I thought it best to stop arguing. Jon and I patched him up as best we could, but he was in a bad way. A bullet had hit him in right lung and exited just below his shoulder blade taking with it a piece of his lung. The Major wanted to send another one of his soldiers on the helo to accompany his wounded man. I told the Major that it wasn't appropriate to send an armed soldier on the AME helo (I made that up on the spot) and that the space would be required for wounded. He said his man was going and that he would unload his weapon and give the bullets and weapon to the pilot. The pilot agreed with this and the AME went ahead.

A convoy of trucks driven by soldiers from India showed up and evacuated the majority of the patients. This meant a two-hour journey (if they made good time which was unlikely) along a bumpy dirt road that was in such a poor state that constant four-wheel drive was required to get from Kibeho to Butare. It would have been incredibly painful for the patients who were sitting or lying on the bare boards of the trucks. Each truck travelled without a medic on board — we simply couldn't afford the manpower. Given this, drips were turned down so they would last the journey, but no morphine was given because we just didn't have the stocks. The patients would have been bouncing all over the back of the trucks — most with broken bones. The trucks took all those on board to a stadium in Butare. A C130 Hercules aircraft with a medical team on board was deployed to Butare to load up with priority one and two patients to deliver them to AUSMED in Kigali. Later, we discovered the C130 couldn't get in and had been forced to return to Kigali.

Another helo came in to take the RSM and CO back to AUSMED and was to take a load of casualties as well. Jon and I loaded up the ambulance and drove back to the helipad, a distance of 300 metres. The CO and RSM arrived and we sat there talking for a few minutes when I was called on the radio to bring the patients back as they were now going out on the truck. I was starting to get pissed off with this. We had so many people involved in this now that we were slipping into the quagmire of bureaucracy. When I got back to the CCP, I was told that room had to be made on the helo to get the journalists out. Okay, now the fuse was getting short. Fuck the damn journos, let them get into the back of the truck. Jon and I were filthy. Later, we realised that this story needed to be told to the world as soon as possible, so it probably wasn't a bad idea to get these leeches out of here quickly. But maybe it would have given them something additional to write about if they had travelled with the wounded in the trucks for a few hours.

Just before leaving the camp, Jon and I went to have a look at a man who was trying to hide in the Zambian long drop toilet. It is a clear indication of how bad things are when you need to drop yourself three metres down into a metre of piss and shit. He must have been petrified. I guess he thought that this was the safest place to hide.

We left the camp at around 5.00 pm and spent the night at the Bravo Company position (the same place we'd met the second CCP the night before) which was only half an hour away. It almost felt like an early knock-off. We arrived at the Bravo Company position at 5.30 pm and were allocated a room where we could spend the night. The Bravo Company Commander was a big fellow with a massive fat arse that caused him to waddle like a duck. Jon and I retrieved our packs and food from the bin above the cabin and found ourselves a spot in the room. We made some chow with the bits and pieces from the French ration packs. After that, there wasn't much conversation happening, everyone was just happy to get some sleep.

On Monday 24 April we went back to Kibeho. Carol's CCP was told to stay back at the Bravo Company position which understandably upset her, and George Donalec took his CCP into Kibeho. When we arrived at Kibeho, the CCP started to set up, and we saw the RPA carrying a recoilless rifle past our position in the compound. This thing was huge and was a clear indicator that we were in for an interesting day. Jon and I went to the hospital to gather some injured when we saw the recoilless rifle on its tripod pointing at one of the buildings which was said to house armed Hutu criminals. We later confirmed that there were armed Hutus in the building. We stopped and watched as RPA soldiers busied themselves siting the rifle. There were a number of UN observers at the rifle site trying to persuade the RPA to dismantle the gun. Captain McMahon was also involved in the negotiations. He told us the RPA had given us until 12.00 noon to clear the camp because they were going to fire the rifle into the building to kill all the criminals. The building was located in the courtyard and obviously the rocket would kill a lot of other people as well as destroying the building.

Jon and I moved back to the CCP. They were setting up in the same place as the day before, but I told them to pack up because they and all the vehicles were in the line of fire. I thought the Zambians should have cleared the building days ago. The buildings clearly held members of the Interahamwe militia and should have been removed. The RPA was afraid to enter the courtyard for fear of being shot and was using the recoilless rifle as a weak way of clearing the building.

Meanwhile, back at the Zambian compound, the Zambians pulled out two men who had been trying to hide in the shit pit all night. They were quite a sight. They had shit up to their ears, and toilet paper on their heads. What could Jon and I do but laugh — poor buggers.

The Zambian Company Commander wanted to sweep through and force the IDPS out with the Australians alongside to assist, but we had to get permission from AUSMED Headquarters and, because everyone wanted to be in charge, we were 10 minutes late in helping the Zambians, which was embarrassing. The infantry spread out and Lieutenant Tilbrook tasked Jon and me to watch for snipers in the buildings. The infantry started to clear the rooms where the wounded were housed. The wounded were the only ones to be evacuated because the other IDPs had been told by the Interahamwe that, if they went with the white people, they would be killed when they reached their destination, and they thought it better to die where they were. We all tried to talk them into coming with us, but to no avail. We were all bloody frustrated that we couldn't do anything for them because we couldn't communicate our intentions clearly. The Interahamwe had themselves a human shield of frightened-for their-lives IDPs.

At this stage about 20 reporters showed up to record what was happening. They were basically a pain in the arse. We'd be running towards the trucks with a kid slung over each shoulder and a fool photographer would step in front to slow you down so he could get his photo. We started to get aggressive towards them and, if they got in the way, we'd push, shoulder charge or kick them out of the way. In retrospect I realise the importance of their presence in reporting this so all the world would know about this barbaric massacre, but at the time we just trying to get as many kids out as quickly as we could.

'Gun!' Jon screamed for all to hear. A Hutu pointed an AK47 at us and he, in return, had ten weapons pointed at him. He quickly dropped his weapon and hid in the building. All the IDPs in the courtyard hit the deck screaming, which didn't help our cause in persuading them that we were the good guys. I don't know how the others felt, but I was tempted to shoot that bastard. I wanted someone to pay for what had happened here. I wanted to feel some revenge. These Interahamwe militants were just as responsible for the Kibeho massacre as the RPA soldiers. The militants had hacked their people with machetes and shot them with their AK47s and now ensured their protective shield remained around them. On two occasions we saw IDPs jumping down from the roof with weapons in their hands, but they weren't being pointed at us any more. Why the fuck didn't we just go in and kill them all? Jon and I with a couple of infantry lads could have quietly sorted this drama without too much fuss, and then gone back to the task at hand — saving lives. Fuck the UN and their rules of engagement!

The IDPs handed us a lot of children, but they wouldn't come themselves. I suppose they thought we would spare the children a horrible white-person death. I managed to convince a group of very frightened ladies to leave the camp, and I agreed to walk with them to a waiting UN truck. As I walked them slowly through the remaining people towards the trucks, another IDP approached them and convinced them that I was taking them away to be killed. I pushed this guy away, but he was persistent, so I punched him in the side of his head. Unfortunately, this confirmed for the ladies that I wasn't the nice guy I was trying to pretend to be. The once saved turned around and went back into the courtyard. It was so frustrating. I just stood there in despair when two children ran to me, held my hands, and I walked them out to the Red Cross trucks. This gave me some hope in what seemed to be a hopeless situation. Others were standing around and listening to someone read from the Bible, or they were reading the Bible themselves. The only possession most IDPs still retained was an old Bible. Their faith was incredible, but then again what else did they have but some hope there might be a better life after their imminent death? How could this be? What greater being would ever allow people to be treated this badly? This was beyond inhuman and I can't find a word to depict such indiscriminate, sadistic horror. Where was God in all this? I've seen thousands of people executed, butchered, mutilated and all said, 'Please God, don't.' But God never intervened.

At some stage before the deadline, I got a bottle of water and jumped into the back of the truck that held the IDPs who wanted to leave the camp. I passed the water around and nearly caused a riot. I had to get violent with some of the adults so the children could have a drink first. These people had not been given water for two days and had been drinking from water collected in tarps or off the ground. For food, some still had a little grain; others were digging non-digested corn from shit lying all over the place. They washed the corn in the muddy water on the ground and re-ate it. That's hunger! That's how desperate these souls were. I found more water and they drank their fill.

I took a group of infantry and we went to the hospital to see if any IDPs had gone there. We found two very pregnant women, some children and two injured men — one of whom could not walk. We found an old stretcher and the infantry stretchered the man out. I got the women walking and, even though they were having a lot of trouble, they made it out. The other injured man had been lying down for so long he had trouble getting up. I didn't have the manpower to carry him, so I indicated that he had to walk. He pleaded with me with his eyes and hand gestures, but I just shrugged and we walked away. As I walked out the door, I turned and saw the old guy struggle to get to his feet and begin shuffling after us. He saw me looking on and smiled, so we waited until he caught up with us and together we all made our way to the trucks.

The deadline to fire the recoilless rifle was getting close, so Captain McMahon told me to tell everyone to stay in the courtyard and within sight. He wanted everyone visible for a quick evacuation if necessary. However, the deadline came and went with the UN observers persuading the RPA not to fire the recoilless rifle.

By now it was almost 1.00 pm, so Jon and I went to prepare the ambo for the trip back to Kigali. Our time in Kibeho was almost complete. The replacement crew was on its way and was only half an hour from Kibeho. To be honest, I was shattered. I'd had enough, but the job wasn't finished yet. I never really understood how badly run the UN was. It is a dysfunctional organisation with no power. It's directed by the Security Council, a group of old politicians from various countries who have no idea what really happens to defenceless people all over the world every day — the same defenceless people the UN is supposed to protect and help, but doesn't. The UN didn't help in Cambodia and the killing fields and last year they sat on their hands while almost a million people were murdered and wouldn't give us the power to defend the people in this massacre; it's a useless machine that's nothing more than a waste of money.

At 1.30 pm Dominic, George, Shane, and Col arrived at Kibeho wide-eyed and ready to get their hands dirty. Jon and I showed them around and explained what had occurred. I was glad the entire evac crew had made it to Kibeho. The experience would be good for them, as it had been for Jon and me. Jon and I took a walk down to the documentation point to see how George, Kath and the new CCP were getting on. They had a lot of kids with them and appeared to be assisting the Red Cross. They had a few patients, but nothing serious. We said our goodbyes and, under command of Lieutenant Tilbrook, we rotated out of the camp. Lieutenant Tilbrook and his two infantry sections were relieved by Lieutenant White and his two infantry sections. There was a lot of resentment at leaving the camp because the job was incomplete, but we knew when we deployed to Kibeho that, if required, we'd be replaced on Monday, and so we were. Clearly, the command element of AUSMED wanted to get everyone through Kibeho to experience another side to their Rwandan deployment. Having said this, we certainly didn't want to give Kibeho over to someone else. She was ours; we'd been through so much together, nobody could possibly know her like we did.

We estimated that 4000 people had been killed over the weekend, probably — no, certainly — more; we didn't count all those shot in the re-entrants. There was very little we could have done about that, but had we not been there to witness the massacre, then I believe the RPA would have continued with the killing until all the IDPs were dead. The RPA Major had a job to do in clearing the camp and killing them all probably seemed like the easiest way of completing the job. It must be remembered that, while the predominantly Tutsi RPA did kill thousands of people, 12 months before, the Hutus had killed almost a million Tutsi civilians. Today the Butare stadium had become an emergency treatment area full of Hutus, while 12 months previously, the same stadium had been full of terrified Tutsis. Maybe the RPA thought it was payback time. Who knows, and who are we to question this? Our job was to clean up the mess. It's the UN Security Council's job to question this, but they have no voice and this will eventually be forgotten.

As we drove back to Kigali, with Jon driving and Carol in the back getting some well-earned rest, I reflected on what had happened to us. Where had the time gone? From Friday afternoon until now seemed like a blur. All of a sudden we were out of Kibeho and going home. I could only imagine how this would be reported to the world. Jon and I decided to record everything that had happened during our six days in Kibeho so we could send something home to the Regiment. We wanted them to have a clear picture of what had transpired. I pulled out my army notebook and started writing immediately. If I forgot something, Jon reminded me. 'Don't forget this; don't forget that,' he kept saying. The days seemed to blend together; it took both of us and Carol to place everything in order. After three hours, we had enough to type up when we got the chance back at the hospital — then it was time for some biscuits and pâté. Obviously we could only report what had happened to us and those nearest to us. So much had happened to each of the 32 people deployed — but that's their story.

Many people will ask why we didn't stop the killings. To them I say that there were 32 of us and a battalion's worth of RPA soldiers. We were good, but not that good. Had we shot an RPA soldier, the RPA would have eventually killed all of us, and then had a go at those still in Kigali. Believe me when I say that we all wanted to take action, and many times the RPA tempted us, hoping that one of us would shoot so they had an excuse to shoot back at us. We had to restrain ourselves to preserve our own lives and the lives of those around us. It was a decision easily made at the time, but one we will all live with for the rest of our lives.

The 22nd of April 1995 will be a day that none of the original 32 people deployed to Kibeho will ever forget. We saw things that most people will never see, and should never see. We witnessed the brutal deaths of more than 4000 people, but continued to protect the medics so they could save those they could without faltering. The relationship established by those 32 members is one that will last a long time, and one that could not be explained to anyone and certainly not in this chapter.

Many of those Kibeho Originals continue to suffer from the horrible memories of the massacre. These are professional warriors who left part of themselves in that camp that will remain there forever. Terry Pickard was one of those warriors. Terry penned an excellent account of Kibeho and the effect on him of the whole incident. Terry's account is much more about what the group was doing, whereas my words centre on my own little world — what was happening around me. Terry's problems are similar to many. In his book, he observes that I survived Kibeho because I was in the SAS. I would argue that it's the other way around. I was in the SAS because I had the ability to survive Kibeho. That ability comes from a challenging upbringing, a strong influence from my mother and her survival genetics and superlative training at Campbell Barracks.

21.
NIGHTMARE DAY
FOURTEEN

I snapped out of that memory and asked Sanjay if I could borrow his razor. Sanjay's face lit up as he replied, 'Yyyeeeesss, Sir.' But he insisted on shaving me, so he and the old man prepared things in front of my cage. Sanjay had a very old razor just like the one I was issued in the army. The safety razor blade sits on top of the handle and a top piece is screwed into place. Sanjay lathered my face perfectly then started. Oh fuck, I thought, but he seemed to be doing okay. He asked me to hold the mirror, but I said I didn't need to. I just didn't want to see myself as a caged man — strange, I know, but I just couldn't look at myself. But Sanjay was struggling because my whiskers were now ten days long, so he removed the top piece of metal and turned the razor into a cut-throat. Oh God, here we go, this should be big. I insisted that I now take over and Sanjay reluctantly agreed, but when I mentioned that I'd never done this before, he insisted that he take over again. I let him do it and he did a great job. The only cut I got was from when I insisted on doing my upper lip. Sanjay was pissed off that I had used the razor myself and really filthy with me when some blood appeared from the small shaving cut on my upper lip.

The old man cleaned all the excess cream off my face and that was the end of that mission. It was probably one of my best shaves in years. I've had a smoother feel to my face though, but that was after having my face threaded in Iraq. I was on the job with Nicholas Rothwell, a great journalist from *The Australian* newspaper, in Baghdad and we went to the local barber shop to get an interview with some local people. I took an interest in this bizarre thing the barber was doing to this guy's face and was invited to give it a go. I sat in the next chair and, when the barber was done with the customer, he rubbed some gel into my face. Nicholas picked up the tube and I asked what it was. 'Lidnocaine,' he replied in his usual articulate way.

'Lignocaine, local anaesthetic?' I asked.

'Yes, it seems that way.'

'Oh shit, this could be big.'

And it bloody was. The barber took two pieces of thread that looked like dental floss, and rolled them over areas of my face snaring small hair follicles, then violently pulled backwards, plucking about 200 small hairs in one go. Under my breath I was fucking screaming and wondered what the use-by date on the lignocaine was because it wasn't working. After about five minutes Nicholas asked how it was going and, when I turned to look at him, the moisture building in my eyes was enough for him to get the idea and start laughing. But I tell you this; I didn't need to shave again for about five days. It was the smoothest shave I have ever had, but hell will freeze over before I'll do that again.

Back in the cage I decided I needed a post-shave rest. The old man and Sanjay came into the cell for a chat. Sanjay decided to read my palm. Read away mate, as long as I don't have to get up. His technique was to simply grab my hand and start examining it — I had little choice in the matter. I'm very sceptical about such things. My former wife convinced me to see a tarot card reader just after I left the army. This woman, dressed like someone who should have been reading a crystal ball, told me my life would settle down very soon after years of frequently changing jobs.

'I've just resigned from the army after 10 years of service and the last eight years were in the same place in Perth,' I said.

'Oh.'

And that was the end of that. So, when Sanjay wanted to read my palm I was understandably sceptical, but decided to go through with it, if only for the entertainment value — oh yes, I was bored.

Sanjay declared that I would have a long, adventurous life. I'm forthright and will be married twice — this bloke might be onto something here: I have already been through one disastrous marriage and have entered another relationship. Then he told me I should stay away from the ocean as it is dangerous for me. That's weird, I love the ocean; I wish he hadn't told me that bit. I'll be expecting to be eaten by a great white shark every time I go body surfing now. After they left I tried to sleep for an hour, but couldn't as I was too anxious — Sallie was coming today.

By 11.00 am Sallie had yet to arrive. Maybe she was visiting others first. I didn't mind. I'd rather she worked on everyone before coming to me if it meant I could get out of here and hold her as a free man. It would be great if she could take me home with her in the next few days.

I decided I needed to do number twos and dreaded the idea. It's bloody disgusting and the whole prison smells like a toilet, but the squatters smell a hundred times worse, and the idea of using a bucket of water for toilet paper makes me dry retch every time. No matter how many times I do it, I manage to get shit all over the place.

At 11.20, Sanjay rushed into my cage all excited.

'Sir, Sir, a white lady at the gate! Sir, your wife is here!'

I sat up with some interest.

'Did you see her, Sanjay?'

'Yyyyyyeeeess, Sir,' he replied, barely able to contain himself as he pranced away.

Man, he has got to be gay, I thought as I watched him leave my cage.

I got dressed in my Calvins and T-shirt. My jeans were very baggy on me due to the weight I'd lost. I walked to the administration building and picked a rose on the way. I expected to see Sallie straight away, but she was having her photo taken by the guards prior to entering the prison. I periodically caught a glimpse of her and started to become emotional, but quickly controlled that feeling because my fellow prisoners, who were also excited to see a pretty white woman in the prison, had surrounded me. Manish, the prison clerk, told me to sit and be patient, but I couldn't and responded forcefully to his repeated attempts to tell me to sit. It was unworthy of me as Manish had been good while I'd been in this shit heap, but I was overwhelmed with emotion — a combination of feeling like a dickhead for being in this predicament and wanting to see a familiar face.

The waiting lasted an eternity. I later discovered that the guards took a few more photos than they really needed to — they didn't have the opportunity to photograph too many white women so they grabbed the moment. Finally I saw her, she looked great and in total control. She was dressed discreetly, covered from neck to wrist to ankle and was wearing a headscarf. Good girl, she knew how to travel and dress appropriately. The scarf covered her blonde hair and the loose-fitting clothes concealed her neat figure. I moved out of the way as her approach created some commotion. The guards were at the gate waiting for her and pushed people aside so they could open the gate. She entered the prison gate and looked around. She saw me and we hugged until we were told to separate by a prison guard and ushered into the Warden's office. We spent an hour together. She had already seen the Magistrate and begged and cried for my release. She had seen Bala and, like me, immediately liked him. She had seen my lawyer, Debu-San, and confirmed the brief that he needed to drop all other cases and just work on mine. Next she planned to visit the SP (Siddiqui) and told me she would offer money for a favourable statement if necessary.

It was so good to see her that I almost ignored all the others with her — there seemed to be quite an entourage. There was the High Commission guy, Rajeesh; Ujwal, back from Kathmandu, who had escorted Sallie to Biratnagar; and Martin, one of the senior managers with my company and formerly a colonel in the Australian Army. I could see Martin through the bars wandering around just in front of the office block. He approached Loud Talker, stopped and delivered a perfectly executed salute which I knew would greatly impress and flatter Loud Talker. The Nepali SP was here as well — it was so good of him to go out of his way for me. He also told me he would go with Sallie and the entourage to see Siddiqui.

Sallie brought me a heap of supplies including vitamins, antibiotics, ear ointment, eye cream and antiseptic hand gel. She brought magazines, a skipping rope, tennis balls to throw against the prison wall like Steve McQueen in *The Great Escape*, photos of my family and of us together. The Warden needed to clear all this stuff for the prison and immediately refused to allow the skipping rope, which I could understand; everything else was permitted. The Warden told us that it was normal procedure for prisoners to be allowed only one visitor every two weeks but, given the distances and the fact that Bala had made the request, Sallie could visit every day. I thanked him profusely and then told Sallie how good the Warden had been to me. I was well and truly kissing arse which would have seen me getting the shit kicked out of me in an Australian prison. The visit was over quickly. I didn't want her to go, but I did want her to visit these people and try to get me out of here as soon as possible. I said goodbye to Rajeesh who reminded me that I was going to court tomorrow.

'I'll be ready Rajeesh, don't worry.'

I was on my own again, but on a slight high having seen Sallie. Now I had to go back to waiting to see what tomorrow would bring. Sallie had brought me so much stuff which generated a lot of interest from my fellow prisoners, so I tried to stash as much as possible out of sight. As I went through it all I found a Sudoku book, pens, food, chocolate and juice as well as all those items previously mentioned. I couldn't believe she had brought all this stuff. She had been so very thoughtful and considerate. As I went through all the different drugs she brought I saw two boxes of sleeping pills.

The old man and Sanjay came into my cell so I showed them the photos of my family and Sallie. They become very excited and the old man rushed next door to his cell and returned with passport-type photos of his wife and children. He was so proud of them, so I dropped all my stuff and spent the right amount of time asking questions about his family and the people in the photos. He was a good guy who clearly missed his family and I noticed a tear forming in his eyes. I couldn't get a straight answer on how long he'd been here, but it seemed to be anywhere between three months and six months and in that time he hadn't had a visitor. I quickly changed the subject and pulled out some of the Cadbury's chocolate Sallie brought and we all shared it. Sanjay and the old man were delighted.

I decided to read the *Who* magazine first so I could give it away to the prisoners waiting outside my cell. Now I just wanted everyone to get out of my cell so I could go through my goodies in peace, but I had to be patient as these guys rarely received anything and were excited by what I'd been given. Satya joined the old man and Sanjay reading a magazine — *Men's Health* I think. The group to whom I gave the *Who* magazine debated the meaning of an advertisement. There was a picture of a woman sleeping on her side wearing only underwear in a comfortable bed with the caption '*Sleep tight with Stayfree*'. They called me over and asked, 'What is Stayfree?'

I started to laugh, but then saw the serious looks on their faces. Wow, this could be big. If I got this wrong, maybe we'd have an international incident.

'It's a pillow and it comes in that box,' I said, pointing to the small pads box. 'Oh yes. It must be expensive,' one prisoner said and they all agreed. Content with that answer, they read on.

The Nepali SP returned to the prison and I was summoned to the administration building. The SP told me that the meeting had gone very well, but the Indian SP had kept them all waiting in the sun for three hours — some power play I suppose. He told me not to worry as the Indian SP had assured him he'd write a very positive report and I'd probably be released tomorrow. He could only stay a very short time as it was 6.00 pm and he had to get back across the border before it closed. I got his phone number and thanked him for all his help. His generosity and the lengths to which he'd gone to help me were not lost on me. My morale was high as I was now certain I'd be released tomorrow.

Sallie and I spoke briefly on my phone. She said the police report was okay, but it still said that I had committed a crime. She wasn't able to read the report, as this was illegal. One of the strange laws they have in India is that no statements can be made available to the defence team — all the defence is entitled to are the names of the witnesses, which begs the question of how you can mount a defence when you don't know what you been accused of. Sallie thought I had an 85% chance of being released tomorrow. She also passed on a message from Colin Rigby who advised me not to get my hopes up for release. This was good advice and I knew this was how I was supposed to think — I teach this lesson on my training courses, but it's almost impossible to the point that it can't be done.

I returned to my cell thinking this was my last night in this hell hole. Sallie had also brought some Australia souvenirs to give to the guards and fellow prisoners, so I clipped one of the koalas to the bars of my gate. The photos from home were precious; I couldn't stop looking at the kids and Sallie. I couldn't imagine any other woman doing what she had done so far. She was beyond amazing. She had a gold ring that I sometimes wore as I could slip it on my little finger. This was another thing she had brought me and I wore it as I sat and looked at those precious photos. It was such a thoughtful thing to do; just a small thing, but it meant so much to me and reminded me of home. The caveman came by to close and lock the cage and saw the koala on the bar. He unclipped it as I got up and approached. He looked at it then played with it by clipping it to his finger. Then a miracle happened and he smiled and I was certain his face was going to fall off. Using hand motions I told him that he could have the koala. He realised what I was saying and re-clipped the koala to the bar and walked away. No problem, my pleasure, you grumpy old sour prick. Obviously this was a thought and not something I said. He wouldn't have understood the words but would have heard the tone. Loud and clear.

22.

NIGHTMARE DAY FIFTEEN

Friday 6 June

For the first time, I slept for five hours straight and woke up a bit stiff, but grateful for the sleep. I woke at 3.00 am and crawled out from under my mosquito net and screwed in the light bulb so I could read for a while. At 5.00 am the cage was opened by Mr Personality, better known as the caveman, so I got up and started to pack those things that I wanted to take out of here and set aside those things that I never wanted to see again — like my sarong, thongs, my boots that have walked daily through this toilet and other bits that I wanted to give to the old man.

I shaved myself with my razor — another thing Sallie had brought me. The old man and Sanjay were disappointed, as they seemed to like shaving me. They had given me a good shave, but I didn't like the idea of another bloke shaving my face. The old man and Sanjay were impressed with my Gillette triple blade razor with the pivot head and I made a mental note to give it to Sanjay when I left.

I dug out a pair of clean trousers that I'd been saving for a special occasion, and the only other pair I had apart from my Calvins, and also put on a clean T-shirt that Sallie had brought me. I found a clean pair of socks and, by 6.30 am, I was ready for court. At 7.00 am Satya came to my cell and told me it was time, so I walked to the administration office. There was some murmuring among the prisoners as they saw me in my good clothes. At the administration office I approached Manish and told him that I was here and ready for court. He told me that my day for court was tomorrow.

'Yeh, right, stop bullshitting me.'

'No, Mr Paul, you go to court tomorrow, not today.'

'Are you fucking kidding?' I replied, ready to blow.

'No, Mr Paul, you go to court tomorrow, see it is written,' he said and showed me my file with a court date written on the front.

'Okay, thanks mate,' I said as calmly as I could and wanted to fucking kill someone. On the way back to my cage to get out of my good clothes, a prisoner stepped in my path and, using a hand motion, asked what was happening to me. I made that same motion back to him and said, 'What the fuck does this mean, mate?' and walked around him to my cage.

I was totally deflated and wanted to kill Rajeesh, the High Commission guy. Clearly they had no idea what was going on. Back in the cage I decided to stay dressed as somewhere deep inside me I believed the clerk had made a mistake. But by 10.00 am I realised that I was not going to court and the poor clerk that I gave a mouthful to was right and bloody Rajeesh had got the wrong date. All I wanted to do now was sleep. I just wanted time to disappear. I couldn't do anything to help myself in here so I might as well just slip into a coma until I was released. Maybe it would be six months. I supposed that would have me out by Christmas. I hoped Dad could hang on that long. I wondered if the kids would still think about me or whether they would take to my ex-wife's new partner. Would the company still be generous if this dragged on that long? How would I pay the bills with no income? Would I lose the house? Where would the kids live? How could I have cocked this up so much?

At 1.30 pm, Sallie and Ujwal visited. I didn't feel so good now — in fact I was suddenly very weak. I was not sure what had happened to me as I had trouble standing and walking — but it was still great to see Sallie and Ujwal. I told them about this morning and they were as annoyed with Rajeesh as I was. I'd settled down a bit as I knew Rajeesh hadn't meant to get it wrong and he probably didn't appreciate the mental let-down such misinformation could cause. Sallie told me they had been forced to wait in the hot sun yesterday by Siddiqui. When they asked if they could wait inside a room they were told that this was not allowed. This included the Nepali SP, which clearly indicated

Chapter 22

the level of hostility the Indian SP had for me. He told Sallie that, as a journalist, I should have known better. Sallie told him that I'm not a journalist, just a trainer, but he waved her off. Now I was worried.

They only stayed a short time. I hugged Sallie and they both left. Sallie lingered at the gate. I knew she was worried about my health, so I started singing the theme to the movie *Love Actually*:

You know I love you
I always will
My mind's made up
By the way that I feel
There's no beginning
There'll be no end
You're all I'll love
I can't pretend

Well, that drew some attention from the prisoners and the prison staff and gave them a topic of conversation for a while.

I returned to my cell to watch the curry-eating goose walk past my cage and the smart arse bloody thing gave me a mouthful as it went past. I tried to sleep the afternoon away, but woke up to see Sanjay at my gate staring at me.

'Sir, this man wants to talk to you.'

Fuck me. 'What does he want?'

Sanjay pushed the old prisoner forward and he said, 'Hello mister.'

'Yeh, hello mate, what's up?'

'Hello mister.'

Oh God, kill me. 'Yes hello, how can I help you, my friend?'

Then just staring.

'What do you want, mate?'

Nothing, just staring.

'Okay, goodbye.'

As I rolled over to sleep some more, Sanjay started on me.

'Sir, Sir.'

For fuck's sake. 'What, Sanjay?'

'Everything okay, Sir?'

'Everything is fine. I just want to rest, please leave me be.'

'You want to be not disturb Sir?'

'Yes, Sanjay.'

That was that sorted. Sanjay was a good guy, but could be fucking painful at times.

Satya and I walked that night, but I wasn't up to his questions, so we sat on the wall and watched prison life slow down and get ready for lock-down. People cooked all day on stoves made from cement and mud using coal and ingredients delivered to them by family members. The food smelt good and I was often invited to share a meal, but politely refused. There was a group just outside my cell and when they started their cooking every morning, my cell would fill with smoke. It could be a bit suffocating at times, but at least the smoke cleared the mosquitoes and flies. I gave these guys excess biscuits when I had them for two reasons: first, I had too many packets and could never eat them; second, these guys never bothered me or walked into my cell or asked stupid questions. They just went about their business and politely said 'hello' when passing. I liked that about them, so gave them my excess biscuits, but only after I'd given some to the old man.

The old man had now taken to bringing the bucket of water into the courtyard area in front of my cage. I called it a courtyard for the want of a better term, but it was just the same open-air room that I walked through to get to my cage. I liked the idea of the bucket bath in this area as it offered some privacy, but not much, and it was certainly more comfortable than the area next to the pump. Now he didn't even ask about washing my back every two or three days, because he knew I would stop him and we'd argue. Now he just did it. Bloody hell, I'm glad the boys couldn't see this happening.

I was locked in now and managed a few hours' sleep. Again the activity in my mind kept me awake. Even my nightly training session didn't tire me enough to sleep. There was just too much going on for my poor, fevered brain to switch off.

23.
NIGHTMARE DAY SIXTEEN

Saturday 7 June

I was told on the first day by Manish that my court date was 7 June, but I insisted that was ridiculous and I wouldn't even be here then. Well, here I was and it was 7 June — un-fucking-believable. However, I'd been disappointed before, so I didn't even bother getting dressed; if they called my name it would only take me a minute to put on my trousers. It wasn't as if I needed to jump in the car and drive 45 minutes to town. So, after my morning walk and wash, I relaxed in the cage. Then Gaz called the names for court and I was one of them. I also learnt from Satya that this court appearance was simply to be presented before my Magistrate to confirm I was still in custody and still alive. I quickly put on my good trousers and one of the Rivers T-shirts Sallie had brought me, and wandered over towards the administration gate where Gaz was calling names. The 20 prisoners going to court — including me — were moved into the administration area in preparation for loading onto the prison truck. I wasn't looking forward to the prison truck or the cage at the courthouse, but going to court was going to be something different for the day.

The prison truck reminded me of my neighbour Carl's cattle truck back in Dayboro on the northern side of Brisbane, although Carl's truck seemed in better condition. This was going to be an interesting experience. When all the prisoners were in the administration area, they locked the gate behind us then opened the next gate and, in single file, we walked towards the back of the truck. As I approached the truck I could see a group of police watching me with interest and I braced for what I thought was going to be a beating. I was always surprised that one of the guards or a cop hadn't taken the opportunity to try to smack me around already. As I came close to them and prepared to step onto the truck, a senior police officer pulled me aside and made me stand next to him as the other prisoners climbed onto the truck. When the last prisoner was on board, I made a move to get onto the truck, but the police officer held me back as the gate was closed and he told the truck to go. What the hell was happening now? I was worried. What sort of shit are these pricks going to pull that will legitimise the reason for my imprisonment? I suspected every member of the police of being in cahoots with the SP. Nothing they'd do would surprise me, but I had to be prepared.

Then Umar, the prison clerk, came out and, together with the senior police officer, we walked up the road past the police station to the courthouse. Bloody hell, here I was expecting a beating and now I wandering up the damned road! What is this place? I felt liberated and really enjoyed the walk. It also presented an opportunity to study the outside of the prison in case I needed to do a runner at some point. The walk to the courthouse was about 400 metres and went straight past the police station.

When we got to the court, all the prisoners were locked in a holding cell and I walked towards the cage, but was redirected to the police station and told to sit in a corner. I felt bloody guilty (appropriate for a courthouse) for not being in the courthouse cell, but relieved at the same time, while wondering what their motive was. The police all smiled at me and offered tea, which I accepted. Just like in the prison, the tea came in a very small glass — barely two good mouthfuls. The boy selling the tea was about eight or nine years old and seemed to find it interesting that a white man was in with the police. The senior policeman sat next me and said that they'd all heard of me through the Inspector at the border and all believed the SP was treating me unfairly. They couldn't do much, but thought this hospitality would help. I thanked him for his kindness. He then bought me some biscuits to go with my tea. I didn't have the heart to tell him that I needed to eat another biscuit like I needed an AFL kick in the nuts.

Chapter 23

From my seat in the police station, I could see all the activity going on at the holding cell. It was a strange situation, with relatives and friends trying to deliver goods to their loved ones in the cell. The police would allow it for a while, then start yelling and screaming at the offenders. Women and old men would approach the police and give them money to be allowed to pass goods to a prisoner. One poor guy, who didn't want to pay, continuously defied the police order to back away and was detained and pushed into the small room behind me where he was beaten. It was as if I wasn't even there. The guy started to cry and beg to be released, so they beat him some more. More police arrived and he was dragged away.

Then my time came and I was escorted to the courtroom. On the way, I passed my lawyer, Debu-San.

'Where the hell have you been?'

'I am filing submissions on your behalf.'

'Do you want to tell me about them?'

'Soon.'

He followed me into the administration room where a clerk looked at me, asked me to sign a form that I cleared with my betel-nut-stained-teeth lawyer, and then Debu-San and I found a quiet room for a brief chat. He told me that I looked too good and then showed me a petition for me to be moved to the hospital gaol on the grounds that I was going to die if I remained in the prison. The letter was beautiful and, as I read it, I began to slump and develop all these symptoms — or at least act them out anyway.

Petition from Debu-San
State Verses Paul Jordan (Accused)
Humble petition filed on behalf of the custody accused:-
Most respectfully herewith:-
1. That the petitioner is a foreigner and is inside the jail in connection with this case.
2. That the petitioner has fallen ill seriously and suffering from breathing trouble due to climatic effect and suffocation.

3. That the jail doctor has already examined the petitioner
   but in order to save the life of the petitioner it is essential
   to shift the petitioner to the Government Hospital.

Prayed

It is, therefore, prayed that your honor be kind enough
to direct the petitioner to be shifted to the Government
Hospital in Araria for better treatment.

And for this shall we ever pray.

We also talked about Monday — that was decision day, the day I
was supposed to go to court for my trial. At least then I'd know what my
future held. Frankly, and I know it sounds ridiculous, but I was trying to
prepare myself to do six months in this shit heap. I'd considered escape,
but would have needed a little outside assistance. I knew my friends were
looking at plans to get me out of here, and if I was given more than
six months, then I'd consider escaping, but only if I could do it on my
own. I was concerned that these cops had old rifles and, during an 'aided'
escape, someone might get killed or injured, or one of my friends might
get caught and be stuck in here as well. It just wasn't worth the risk and
it was easier for me to take the severe kick in the arse for being so stupid.

I walked back to prison with the senior policeman. He told me to
contact him if I needed anything. They all said that because I was white
and perceived to be rich and they wanted some money. But the walk
back was nice and I got another good look at the outside of the prison.
The police station next door to the prison was a real bitch. I think I
could have managed all the guards living around the prison, but the cop
shop next door would have been alerted quickly to any disturbance.
My initial plan was probably the right one — going over the back wall
and into the bush area then heading north until I hit the railway tracks
which continued north and ended right on the Nepali border.

Sallie and Martin came to visit. It was nice to see them. They were
surprised to hear that I had been in court today. They brought more
goodies, but I had to tell them not to bring any more. My stash of
possessions was starting to attract too much attention. These people were
prisoners and dirt poor with no possessions and the attraction of my

valuables might have proven too much for them to resist. People were asking for things and I couldn't give to one and not others. I now kept my cage door closed when I was out, but generally spent my days inside.

Again, Ujwal paid the clerk to approve all my goodies without a search. On the way out, Martin and Sallie got to have a look inside the prison yard. This came about because Martin told the loud-talking guard that I should leave for the day and Martin would take my place. Obviously Loud Talker laughed and then showed them inside the yard and I was able to point out my cage. Martin the ex-army officer knew the value of winning hearts and minds and worked hard on the guards. Loud Talker later came to my cell and mentioned that my friend had given him a salute when they first met. Loud Talker was very honoured and felt a bit special. That's what winning hearts and minds is all about, and it costs nothing.

When I walked to the drain for a pee, I walked past the guy who was beaten this morning at the courthouse. He was a little bruised and seemed to be feeling sorry for himself — strange world. I guess he didn't have to sneak things to his friend in gaol any more. In 14 days maybe people will be trying to hand him stuff when he's in the courthouse holding cell.

I spent the rest of the day going though all the stuff Sallie and Ujwal had brought me. They had a restaurant in Nepal make me pancakes with honey. The honey had leaked out of the containers, and the pancakes were a good one inch thick, so I struggled to eat just one pancake, but they were good and it was a nice thought. I gave the others to Sanjay and the old man. Sanjay readily accepted the pancakes but, as usual, the old man insisted that I eat them. He was always worried that I didn't eat enough, but I managed to convince him that I'd already eaten one. At least three times a day he came into my cell and motioned with his fingers to his mouth while saying the word 'kanake' which I took to mean 'food' or 'eat'.

The magazines were great, but I found myself going back to the Sudoku puzzles. They really made me think and took my mind off my situation. And that was pretty much how I spent the remainder of that day.

24.
NIGHTMARE DAYS
SEVENTEEN AND EIGHTEEN

Sunday 8 June

Same shit, different day. Couldn't wait to see Sallie. The visits from her, Martin and Ujwal really made my day and broke it up nicely. I relaxed in my cage, covertly catching up on my text messages to my family. When that was done I hid my cell phone back inside my socks and read. I was lying on my stomach with my head towards the back wall when, a few minutes later, I was surprised by Bala and the Warden.

'Good morning, Paul.'

'Oh, good morning, Bala, you startled me,' I said as I spun around.

'I am sorry Paul, how are you today?'

'I'm pretty good, thanks Bala. What brings you to my lovely home on this fine day?'

'Ha. Once a month my police officers and I make an unannounced search of the prison.'

Oh shit. I had to clench my butt checks as my heart nearly fell out of my arse. 'Really? What sort of things are you searching for?'

'Anything illegal, but mainly cell phones. Paul, I must go, but I will call in on my way out.'

'No problem, see you then.'

This couldn't be happening to me. Now my cage was going to be searched, they would find my phone and I'd lose Bala's support. As soon as Bala and his entourage left, I recovered my phone and slipped it into my underwear right down behind my kit. I looked at the rat holes in the cage and contemplated burying my phone, but thought this would leave some obvious sign and direct them to dig there. I decided to have a look outside for myself. Sure enough, there were bloody cops everywhere, and all looked suspiciously at me; they were probably surprised to see a white man appear from nowhere. I watched the searching as belongings were thrown out of the cells and the prisoners forced to wait outside until the search was complete. When done with one cell, the police all moved to the next and those prisoners were allowed to return and stow their gear. The obvious hole in the searching was that the police weren't searching the prisoners. I decided to keep my cell phone just where it was, but went and sat in the repulsive toilet until I thought the police had been through my cell — I just didn't want to be around in case a cop decided to do a body search. When I left the toilet the police had gone. By the time I returned to my cage, Sanjay was in a flap.

'Sir, the Sub-District Magistrate came to see you, but you not here. Sir, you are very important man if the Sub-District Magistrate is your friend.' Sanjay could barely contain his pleasure and excitement that I was friends with such an important man.

'Okay, Sanjay, thanks mate.'

My cage hadn't been searched and I went to the administration area to see Bala before he left.

The administration area was full of police. Some were wearing black silk bandanas on their heads. I knew Bala was in talking to the Warden so I waited next to Manish's desk while checking out the Rambo wannabes.

'That's a nice bandana mate, are you a Special Forces policeman?'

'No, commando,' replied the cop with some authority and a hint of disgust that a prisoner had asked him a question.

'Wow, commando, you must be good,' I replied and he looked a little further down his nose at me.

You wanker, I thought and had a chuckle. Bala emerged and we spoke briefly before he was escorted away by his police guard and the 'commandos'.

Sallie and Martin arrived shortly after. Martin is discreet and made an excuse after a while to go and take care of something so Sallie and I could have time together. Rajeesh hadn't come today as he wanted the day off. I couldn't say that I blamed him. That drive down and back every day must have been a pain in the arse. Sallie and I talked about my appearance in court tomorrow and I told her that it was likely court would take place without my being there. She disagreed. Anyway, there were three possible outcomes for tomorrow's hearing: 1. all charges would be dropped and I'd be sent out of the country; 2. I'd be sentenced to 20 days including time already served which I could easily do; and 3. we'd go to trial — this would be the worst outcome. Bala and my lawyer believed it would be the second option. I didn't care because I knew I could do another four days on top of the 16 I'd already done.

Bala and my Magistrate (Triparthy) were friends and the only two non-corrupt people in Bihar Province. This could have worked two ways — if Triparthy had been corrupt we might have been able to pay him off by now. Even though Bala and Triparthy were mates, Triparthy would not give anything away to Bala. Bala's support to date had been invaluable. In fact, I'd have been in deep shit without him.

So, after a busy day of searches and visitors, I was left on my own again and spent the last hour of the day, after my old man bucket bath in front of the cage and before lock-up, sitting on the planter box wall with Satya discussing life in general and talking to other prisoners. Satya again asked some young bloke to sing for us. I'm sure the words were nice but, after one song, I thanked him profusely and started a conversation with Satya. Honestly, I'd rather have Tabasco sauce poured in my eyes than listen to another song.

Monday 9 June

I got up early anticipating being released or being told to do four more days. I knew I shouldn't get my hopes up because they'd been dashed repeatedly before, but what could I do? In a place like this all you had were hopes and dreams and today I expected my dreams to be realised. Either way, morale was slightly higher and, as I went through the routine of pouring freezing cold water over me during my morning bucket bath, I prayed, once again, that this would be my last.

Time moved very slowly, the minutes seemed like hours and the hours like days. After an eternity, I looked at my watch to discover it was two minutes after the last time I looked. As I suspected, I wasn't called to go to court and just had to wait it out. By 11.30 I was going crazy. I'd heard nothing and checked my phone every five minutes expecting a message from Sallie to tell me what was happening, but got nothing. I vowed I wouldn't text her because I knew she'd be doing her best and didn't need my interference. But I was dying and, in the end, I just couldn't stand the wait any longer and had to text. Her reply was crippling. 'There are issues,' she wrote, 'be patient and wait.' What fucking issues? I wanted to scream, what now? This couldn't be happening! I just wanted to do a lunatic run at the wall and try to free climb it and then run like the wind. But I knew I'd get caught and would spend years here rather than months.

At 1.00 pm I went to the administration area hoping to see Sallie and the team arriving to see me, because I just couldn't wait any longer. They weren't there so, dejected, I walked away. At the last minute I turned to greet a guard and saw Sallie walk through the main gate.

Sallie and I sat at Manish's desk and she held my hands and told me to concentrate on what she was saying and to be strong. Fuck me, this couldn't be good. I wanted to just pay it all off and die right there. 'Okay,' she began, 'Siddiqui lied, the police report says that you crossed the border with malicious intent to cause harm to India.'

'What? Fuck me!'

'No wait, listen to me. Triparthy [my Magistrate] agrees that you are innocent and even said so in court, but his hands are tied and he has to acknowledge the police report. So he can't turn a five-year maximum term into 20 days on the back of a report like this. Now we go to trial.'

'Fuck me,' I mumbled.

'Listen, the other thing we are now doing, and this came from Triparthy, is to ask the Indian Home Secretary to write a letter authorising your release. Martin is now talking to the Australian High Commissioner who has come in from his day off to get the ball rolling with the Home Secretary. So you will go to court tomorrow and you will plead not guilty and then we'll get you moved to the hospital.'

I was destroyed. I wanted Sallie to go and push things along with Martin, but I also wanted her to stay with me. Eventually she left and I returned to my cage. I just wanted to curl up and slip into a coma until all this was over, so I took half a sleeping pill and slept for the afternoon. I woke at 6.00 pm to the old man nagging me to have my bath. The old man had a worried look on his face as I stumbled into the courtyard suffering from the lingering effects of the sleeping pill. I had a quick wash then returned to my cage. The old man helped me put up my mosquito net and I took another full sleeping pill and settled in for the night. I just wanted to sleep until all this was over.

An hour later, just prior to lock-down, Manish woke me and told me to go to the administration building. I staggered and stumbled into the administration rooms and could feel the resistance of the sleeping pill in my system that needed another seven hours of sleep time. I was directed by Gaz to the Warden's office. Gaz told me to be sick because a medical board was waiting to assess me. 'Thanks, mate,' and I immediately slumped a little further and, with the support of the sleepers, I was in my element and really had my wobbly boot on. When I entered the Warden's office there were two doctors, the prison doctor and Bala waiting for me. I was only wearing shorts, T-shirt and thongs. When they asked what my complaint was, I told them I had terrible headaches and felt as though I was having a heart attack — I just made that up because I had to say something. I also mentioned the horrible fungal infections and ringworm that had recently appeared on my skin. They took my blood pressure, which was a perfect 110 over 70, and my pulse was 60 — bloody hard to fake those. Then they listened to my heart and said everything was normal. 'No,' I said, 'listen again,' which they did with me trying to force the end of the stethoscope into my heart and then moving the end over my heart trying to find a murmur somewhere. Again, they declared my heart was fine. This wasn't going too well. I watched as they wrote and read words like 'suffocation', 'anorexia', 'malnutrition' and 'fungal attacks'. It then occurred to me that this was probably a done deal and, thanks to outside influence, I was getting a report that supported Debu-San's claim about me being on death's door. They dragged out the old scales that I'd stood on when

Chapter 24

I'd first come to prison and had been processed by Gaz and Manish. Then I had weighed 97 kilograms but now weighed 86 kilograms. I'd lost 11 kilograms in 16 days. I knew I'd lost some weight, but didn't think it was that much. Eleven kilograms in 16 days is a bloody good effort — they couldn't even do that on *The Biggest Loser* show. I could have lost more if I'd decided to eat the local food because I was sure that came with a side order of typhoid — that would have been the rapid weight loss program. Those fat people should just spend a few weeks in an Indian prison, drink water and only eat five or six biscuits per day and sleep the rest of the time; easy stuff and better than all those manic work-outs with those two sadistic personal trainers.

They sent me back to the cage. When I left the administration building it was dark outside and the prisoners had been locked in for the night. As I staggered across the yard I wondered whether I had given them enough to be moved to the hospital. I decided a little more wouldn't hurt so, when I walked over the only clean piece of concrete, I went down like a sack of shit. Obviously I had to find a spot where I wasn't going to hurt myself, and a place that was 'relatively' clean, but it was a thing of beauty. As I hit the deck I slapped my hand on the concrete at about the same time as my head hit the cement; although I eased my head slowly to the ground over the last centimetre or so; I didn't want to hurt myself after all. There was instant pandemonium. The prisoners in their cells were watching my late arrival, but when I went down they started yelling and screaming. I silently laughed as I could imagine they were saying stuff like, 'the white boy has gone down,' or 'can someone help that dickhead who fell over,' or 'that was the worst fake fall I've ever seen.'

But there I was and this was how I got to be in this shit hole. Why me? Why is it that I was always the one in the middle of the drama — or the shit, as in this case? Buggered if I knew and I supposed it was all character-building stuff. But, frankly, my character had been built enough and I'd have been happy now to live a quiet life — well, maybe.

Within minutes a prisoner was there to help me up. I didn't know where he had materialised from. He helped me up and I stumbled towards my cage and I think my helper ran away to raise the alarm.

As I walked into the front section of my cage I looked for my helper but, again, I was on my own. I assumed that people would come, so positioned myself on the ground to make it look as though I'd collapsed once more. Again, within minutes people rushed into my cage and all started tripping over my semi-conscious body. I nearly started laughing and could only imagine what my mates would be saying — they would probably start kicking me. The prisoners helped me to my feet and to my mattress. Again, people ran away and I hoped that would be the end of it. It wasn't. Manish and others ran into my cell and asked where it hurt. I moaned that I was very dizzy and had a shocking headache (which I really did) and my heart was racing. 'Okay,' Manish said, 'we'll get some medicine.' Oh shit, what were they going to inject into me; had I gone too far? I'd seen the sick guys lined up at the office. The medic briefly examined each man before giving them all the same injection of something through the same syringe, although he usually changed the needle. I certainly wanted none of that. Manish returned and confirmed that my head ached. 'Yes,' I moaned, so he started rubbing some ointment onto my brow and temple area. About five seconds later I realised it was tiger balm and my head felt like someone was running a blow torch across my temples. Ah, fuck me, that was painful. I hoped they had some ointment for the damn burns this treatment was causing. Then Manish said, 'where else does it hurt, Mr Paul?'

'I'm fine now,' I said, hoping they wouldn't rub any more acid into my body.

'No, you said your heart hurt as well, I remember.' And he started rubbing the napalm balm on my chest. Holy shit it burnt. The pain was something else. They must have got this special tiger balm because I didn't remember it being this bad. I hoped there was a burns unit at this hospital! But, surprisingly, the tiger balm actually worked and my headache miraculously disappeared within minutes — maybe they burnt the nerve endings. All I wanted to do was to slip into a coma and wake up in about three weeks. The sleeping pills were really fighting to be noticed and I struggled to control the urge to sleep, but I couldn't because I had 10 people staring at me and mumbling to one another in Hindi. But then finally they all walked out and I was able to rest.

Chapter 24

Within five minutes Manish was back and he had to wake me.

'Mr Paul, you must come.'

'Oh God, what now?'

'There are people to see you.'

'Okay, let's go.' Now who could this be at this time of night? I wondered. You'd think they would have called first! My house is a mess!

Those sleeping pills were really getting pissed off with me and they fought to keep me asleep as I staggered with Manish to the administration building. Manish stared at me and I could see him wondering whether I was still faking it or whether I was genuinely dying. As I meandered into the Warden's office I saw Bala and the prison doctor. Bala grabbed hold of my arm and led me to a chair.

'Paul, I heard you collapsed, are you all right? What's wrong?'

'Thank you for coming, Bala, it's very kind of you. I'm okay. I just have a terrible headache, I'm dizzy and there is a pain in my heart.'

'I will have you moved to the hospital tomorrow. Can you make it until then?

'I'll be fine Bala. Thanks so much for your kindness.'

'Do you need anything tonight?' he asked, with a concerned look on his face.

Suddenly I thought of the people I missed. I thought of my three children and how much I missed them and wanted to be with them. I thought about my dad and my desperation to make it home before he died. I thought of my brothers and my mother, and I thought of poor Sallie.

'I want to go home now, Bala. This nonsense has gone on for long enough,' I said, barely containing my anger. I wanted to smash something. I wanted to get the angry man at the border and bash him senseless. I really wanted to hurt that low life piece of shit. I made a silent vow; if I'm not at home to see my dad before he dies, I'm going to make the angry man pay, and pay severely.

'Yes I know,' he said, putting his hands on my shoulders. 'We're doing all we can and tomorrow you will go to court and plead not guilty. The right person has given me this advice. So ensure you plead not guilty. If you plead guilty he will have no choice but to convict you and you will get months not days. But the Magistrate won't tell me what the sentence will be so you must plead not guilty. Okay?'

'Thanks Bala, I will because I *am* not guilty.'

'Okay, I will go now,' he said as he stood and shook my hand.

I stumbled my way back to bed realising that the God-awful headache had returned. I pulled my light bulb out, but the guards told me to leave it in. I didn't argue. I just crawled under the mosquito net, pulled my sheet over me and slipped into a coma.

After about four hours of dead sleep, I woke looking directly into the sun. I was confused. The sleeping pills were destroying my ability to think logically. How was the sun in my cage? How did I sleep past Ugly unlocking my cage? No, it wasn't the sun, it couldn't be. Bloody guards were shining a torch in my eyes. I then woke every 30 minutes when the guards entertained themselves by waking me. Maybe this would be my last night in the toilet? They kept talking about moving me to the hospital tomorrow; or was it today now? Yep, today, but who could tell; there was always something thrown in the way, and I was tired of getting my hopes up only to be continuously disappointed.

25.
NIGHTMARE DAY NINETEEN

Tuesday 10 June

I had only been acting, but it had been made easier by the fact that I felt bloody terrible. The headache was a shocker — it would have killed a lesser man. I was covered in spots where the fleas and other insects had feasted on my body. I had bite marks on my feet from the rats. I had ringworm or some other fungal infection growing around my groin. My ear ached and I think something had crawled inside and died. When I used the cotton buds Sallie brought me, the yield was black and messy. I felt very weak after living predominately on biscuits and water for 16 days. I think the only reason I could keep up the sit-ups and push-ups was because I got lighter every day so they became easier.

I decided not to rush the morning and to walk with Satya as it might be my last opportunity. But we didn't walk for long as I was supposed to be dying. The old man prepared my morning bucket bath and then I shaved for the third time in prison. I put on my jeans and black Rivers T-shirt and then packed those items I wanted to keep; everything else I left. Optimistic, I suppose, but all I had was hope.

At 7.30 am my name was called and I crept to the administration building where I was forced to sit. I wondered how getting to court would go today as I wanted to walk, but couldn't because I was supposed to be on death's door. I accepted that I'd just have to go in the cattle truck today with the other guys. I got up to board the truck with everyone else, but was told to sit. When all the prisoners were on the truck, I was escorted to the passenger seat next to the driver. The other prisoners must have bloody hated me for my special treatment and I wondered how much longer they'd accept it. I decided I would refuse any special treatment if the Magistrate sentenced me to a few months in the cage. At court I took my usual seat in the police station and bought chai for all the police from the tea boy. Sallie, Martin and Rajeesh arrived about an hour later, but Sallie was quickly whisked away to do an interview for Indian TV.

At 10.30 am I was called into court and escorted by a policeman to the first real court I'd been to in India. The Magistrate (Triparthy) sat at his bench, the gallery was full and I was told to stand behind a wooden rail at the back of the courtroom. Eventually I heard the Magistrate say my name, my dad's name and then ask me to plead. I remained in my position with my head bowed, leaning on the railing for support. I could sense the whole courtroom looking at me for a response, but I didn't move. It seemed like an eternity and I wondered how long I could keep this up. Finally, Debu-San approached me and touched my arm. He told me to be strong and to plead guilty or not guilty. I looked up and saw everyone looking at me, including Triparthy. I then said, 'I didn't do anything wrong.' That was good enough for Triparthy who nodded to the police to remove me from the courtroom. I was led back to the police station with Sallie and Martin trailing behind.

The police made available our two seats in their court office and again we sat and waited. Sallie could barely contain herself. She said my acting was bloody awful and she had nearly burst out laughing as the whole court had turned to look at me when I hadn't answered.

'You nearly burst out laughing? How do you think it was for me? That silent period was excruciating. I had to use everything I had not to laugh!' Twenty minutes later, a policeman arrived and asked if I was up to walking back to the prison. I said I'd give it a go and off we went. Sallie and Martin were going to visit with Bala, but agreed to visit me later instead.

Back at the prison, I thanked the police officer and returned to my cage. Loud Talker came in and we talked for 15 minutes about life. He seemed to be a smart guy who could do so much more than working in a prison. His brother was a lawyer and his sister a magistrate. During our conversation he quoted Nietzsche, Freud and the Bible — even though he was a Hindu. He told me I'd be going to the hospital today — it had been decided. I thanked him for his help, gave him three clip-on kangaroos for his children, and asked him how long it would be before I was moved. He said a few hours and then said goodbye.

Satya came into my cell to ask how it went in court. I told him that I was being moved to the hospital and that I hoped I wouldn't be back. He told me he expected to be released in a few days. I thanked him for his friendship, kindness and guidance and told him I'd send him a letter when I got my feet back on the ground in Sydney. I then asked if he could translate for me while I spoke to the old man.

The old man was already sitting in my cell with a look of concern on his face — he wasn't sure what was happening. I asked Satya to tell the old man I was being moved to the hospital today and that I probably wouldn't be back. I thanked him for everything he'd done for me and told him that I wouldn't have coped as well as I had without his fatherly kindness. Tears welled in the old man's eyes.

'You have given me hope that I will someday return to my wife and children,' he said. 'I assumed my life was over when they sent me here. Then you came and I knew you were a special man and important too. Then I helped you and I felt very honoured. You have become the son that I desperately miss. I have worried for you so because you have lost weight and you are sick too much,' he continued with tears now flowing down his cheeks as he reached out to place a hand on my cheek. 'I will miss you greatly when you are gone and will not know what to do with myself. These past weeks have gone by quickly because I had you to take care of. May God lead you safely back to your family and bless you forever,' he finished and wiped his tears with his sarong.

I felt bloody awful for the old man and wished I could take him with me. He was such a genuinely good guy and I liked him a lot. I had been paying him, but only with miniscule sums of money every few days and even then he usually spent the money on sweets, and once on warm milk, hoping I'd eat and put on weight.

Satya rose to leave and I walked with him telling him I'd see him before I left. The old man went to leave behind Satya, but I grabbed his arm and gestured for him to come into my cell again. At the court this morning when Sallie had confirmed I'd be going to the hospital I asked her to give me some money so I could give it to the old man. He needed at least 2,000 rupees for his defence in court. I reached into my pocket and pulled out a bundle of rupees. I wanted to cover his court costs as a minimum. I also wanted to ensure he had money so that when he was released he had some money to get all the way back to his village. I also didn't want him to arrive home empty handed so, in total, I gave him 10,000 rupees. That was about $250, which was nothing when I considered what he had done for me. The tears started falling again. He was beside himself. I think it had been a long time since he had seen so much money. He came from a very poor village and 10,000 rupees was equivalent to about six months' pay. If I had $1000 I would have given it to him.

Loud Talker came back to my cell with Manish and said the police were waiting to escort me to the hospital. I grabbed all my gear, but Loud Talker told me to leave my mattress and fan and to only take the things I would need. He said the cell would be locked and all my belongings would be secure for when I came back. I won't be back, I thought, but you can have all this shit anyway.

So, with two plastic bags with clothes, medicines and bottled water, I stumbled towards the administration building. When I got there I looked at the police escort who looked pretty bloody serious. They had their shackles and rope ready and I panicked. I thought about my phone, which was nestled neatly right behind my balls. Amazingly, it never moved, but I was certain they'd search me. They had to. How could I go to a hospital with all this stuff and not be searched? I didn't want them to find the phone because I knew the consequence was 12 months added to my sentence, and it would also look bad for Bala, so I told them I felt sick and had to go to the toilet.

I held my stomach, pushed the door open and went to the squatters. Once inside I pulled my phone apart and removed the sim card and stuck it in my pocket. I then pulled the battery cover off the phone and forced that down the filthy, shit-clogged drain. I stood on the phone a few times to destroy it totally. I then pushed my phone down into the hole as well. But then my phone got stuck and wouldn't budge in or out. It was stuck right there for all to see in the toilet drain. It was under an inch of water and had as much old shit stuck to it as my hand did. Nothing I can do now, I thought, so I left it right there. I wish I really had needed to go because I would have backed one out right on top of it. I did the best I could, washing about five years' worth of shit from my hands. I was disgusted with myself, but thought this was a better option than having the phone found during a search. Now I worried that a prisoner would dig the phone out from the drain and they'd come for me anyway. Fuck me, nothing was easy.

As we walked back through the yard under the gaze of all the prisoners, Satya approached me for a final goodbye. Thankfully he didn't extend his hand to be shaken, but did promise to keep in touch. Back inside the administration building the cops took control of all my possessions and then fitted the shackles. I complained that they were too tight. The police looked at me with an expression that said, 'fuck you, white boy, suffer'. These guys were not the same friendly guys at the courthouse. They were clearly Siddiqui's men. But the Warden intervened and told them to loosen the shackles a little. They weren't built for comfort because they were perfectly round in shape, but unfortunately the wrist is not that shape so they dug in on the sides. Oh well, I was a prisoner after all. The shackles had a rope attached between my hands that was about six feet long. So the cops led me by the rope like a dog on a lead to the open police jeep parked in front of the administration area, but still inside the prison front gate. The cop car was similar to the old jeep that had brought me from the border three weeks back. I got in the back seat and a cop sat either side of me with their rusty old .303 rifles wedged in between their knees. The driver placed my plastic bags behind my seat and we drove to the hospital.

These cops were trying to be the bad guys. I sensed that Siddiqui had given them orders to make life difficult for me. I imagined them driving to some deserted spot where they'd shoot me in the back and then say I tried to escape. The cop sitting to my right just kept staring at me with a look of disgust on his face. I looked back at him a few times and then looked away as he continued to stare. Hang on, I thought, I'm not going to cower to these fools, so I stared back at him with a look that said 'fuck you'. These blokes were going to give me a touch-up for sure, but I wasn't going to give them the satisfaction of beating me mentally. 'Anything wrong, mate?' I said to him while looking straight into his eyes. We seemed to be locked in a staring competition until he eventually looked away. It was strange situation — like a Mexican stand-off. It reminded me of the time I was a security adviser for a gold mine in the Solomon Islands. But that was a completely different sort of stand-off.

26.
PREPARED TO DIE

I finished working in PNG at the end of 1999. In fact the managers decided to give my job to a qualified local. Of course I was pretty pissed off, but these things happen for a reason and, given the adventures that followed, I'm glad it happened. Armed with the Bachelor's Degree that I had just completed after four years as an external student, I found myself looking for a job for the first time in 15 years. That's when reality struck: very few Australian companies were concerned about security and most had no need for a security adviser. It was a good thing for world peace I suppose, but crap when you needed a job.

A few months later I jagged a job as the security manager for a gold mine in the Solomon Islands. You bloody beauty, I thought. This looked like a great opportunity and I couldn't wait to get stuck into the job. As my then wife, Toni, and the kids drove me to the airport I heard a news report on the radio about a sectarian war erupting between the two main tribes in the Solomon Islands. They went on to say that the airport was closed, Honiara was on fire and the Australian Navy was mobilising to evacuate foreigners. Unbelievable. Just my luck. I turned the car around and went home.

A few months later, the Administration Manager from the mining company called and said they wanted to get back to the mine, but the first step was to get back to Honiara and to the office to make preparations and could I go with them? Of course I could; I needed to work and thought that I could still salvage a job out of this. I learnt that I would accompany the Mine Manager and the Administration Manager; the navy had evacuated both during the unrest.

Landing in Honiara was like flying into a set from an old Vietnam movie. There was smoke, buildings were burning and the streets were generally deserted. Men patrolled the streets in Toyota 4 x 4s with machine-guns strapped to the roll bar. It was chaos and I wondered how the city functioned at all. Anyone with money or thought to have money was told very clearly they had to give it to the Malaita Eagles Force (MEF — the group from the island of Malaita that controlled Honiara). Anyone refusing to pay was savagely beaten or murdered.

We stayed at the Mendana Hotel which was located right on the beach. It was actually a nice place and, on the beach side of the hotel, it was easy to forget a war was going on. One night the Administration Manager knocked on my door and showed me a note he'd just been given by reception. The note demanded that $40,000 dollars be paid to the MEF tomorrow at 12.00 noon at the office. The payment was compensation for the police officers who had been killed or injured when the Isotabu Freedom Movement (IFM — the tribe controlling the areas surrounding the mine and most of Guadalcanal) had attacked the mine site. We convened in the Administration Manager's room to discuss the note and our response. We decided that compensation was not warranted and that this was obviously just an attempt to extort money from the largest company on the island.

The next day I sat in the office as the Mine Manager worked on his computer. The office was located at the King Solomon Hotel in an annex that fronted the street. The Administration Manager was chatting to an Australian turned local in the restaurant. I looked up and, through the glass door, saw MEF members walking towards the office. I told the Mine Manager what was coming just as the MEF member pushed the door open and said, 'Well?'

'Well what?' the Mine Manager replied, still typing away on his computer.

'Compensation bilong mi,' replied the MEF guy in Pidgin.

'We won't be paying compensation,' the Manager said as he turned to face the MEF guy.

'YOU PAY! YOU MUST PAY!' The MEF guy was now screaming.

I remained seated watching all this happening, mentally willing the Mine Manager to just go easy.

'You have your answer, so goodbye,' said the Mine Manager as he swung back around towards his computer.

Shit, this isn't good, I thought.

'YOU SMART MOUTH TOO MUCH!' yelled the MEF guy.

'You have your answer, now get out,' said the mine manager with his back still towards the MEF guy. The MEF guy turned, flung the door open and left, but I knew this wasn't the end of it, probably just the beginning. I got up and followed him through the door, telling the Mine Manager to stay and the girl in the office to call her contact in the police. The police contact was a bloke who had been in a senior position prior to the war, but it meant very little now.

As I stood in front of the office I watched the MEF guy run to his Hilux, rip open the passenger door and grab his SLR. Walking back towards me, he chambered a bullet by cocking the weapon. Fucking excellent, I thought, now I earn my money. The MEF guy stopped in front of me, maybe six or seven metres away. He pointed the weapon at my chest and said, 'Get out of the way.'

'No, I can't do that, and you know you don't want to do anything stupid either.'

'Are you the bodyguard?'

'No, I'm here helping them, so we can all get back to work. And that includes getting your people back on the job as well.'

'Mister, get out of my way.'

'You know I can't do that. Why don't you let me buy you a drink at the restaurant and we can discuss this problem?'

'Mister, either move or die.'

I put my hands in front of my body saying, 'This is not something you want to do, mate.'

'Prepare to die, mister,' said the MEF guy as I watched him twist his feet into the dirt in preparation for the impact. I took a half-step back to try to defuse the situation, but the weapon followed and I saw him move the safety catch to fire. He seemed to be mentally willing himself to pull the trigger.

'Hey mate, think about what you're doing. If you cause any problems for me or the boss, the Australian military will be here in force and you will be arrested and put in gaol for a long time. You don't want that and neither do I, so let's discuss this.'

Just then, and right on time because I think my argument meant bugger all to the lunatic, the Administration Manager and the expatriate he was chatting to in the restaurant came around the corner and took in the scene. The expat guy came straight over and touched the MEF guy on the shoulder and whispered something to him. The MEF guy lowered his weapon and glared at me for what seemed like an eternity before returning to his vehicle. At the same time the policeman showed up but, as he had no power, his presence was useless. I returned to the office and saw that the Mine Manager had been peering through the window. He stepped aside and said nothing to me. I called the Australian High Commissioner across the road and got his answering machine. I left a message explaining the situation. It was vital that we had the High Commissioner's support as he also had a team of armed Federal Police providing security to the High Commission staff and now I needed them to help me. The High Commissioner called back about 10 minutes later, which was about the time my pulse descended below 200 beats per minute. He agreed to help and offered four federal agents to assist when required.

The local policeman proved useful after all. He was able to speak to the MEF guys and arrange for a sit-down meeting at the Mendana Hotel that afternoon. We were due to go back to Australia the next day and needed to resolve this nonsense so we could come back in a few weeks and get back to the mine.

The hotel staff were aware of the situation and provided all the support they could. A table was prepared next to the bar in a quiet part of the restaurant. Four federal agents were discreetly positioned throughout the bar just in case the Mine Manager decided to use some of that great diplomacy again. The MEF guys arrived and got straight to the point. They wanted compensation for their efforts in protecting the mine. It was pointed out to them that, in fact, they had run away and this was why the mine had been overrun by the IFM. They would hear none of it and, despite the policeman trying to mediate, things got angry. Eventually, the MEF guys left with the comment, 'if the money isn't paid before you leave tomorrow, we will kill you all if you come back.'

That night, the hotel manager gave me a handful of keys for the empty rooms telling me he didn't want to know where we were staying. I selected three rooms that offered good observation of one another and also easy escape routes. We entered these rooms after last light and didn't use any lights. The next day we left Honiara without any further problems. A month later, we returned to another set of problems, although nothing like that near-death experience in front of the office.

The hospital was only a five-minute drive from the prison and I attracted a lot of stares. I suppose people didn't normally see a white man in shackles in the back of an open police car. At the hospital we parked out the front and then walked to find my new cage. The cops had no idea where I was supposed to be, so they just led me all around the joint. I could see they were getting some enjoyment out of the attention and, by treating me badly, their status grew. It was humiliating being treated this way. I couldn't walk as fast as the cops because I had lost the stamina, and I was supposed to be dying, so they pulled me along as if they were dragging a stubborn dog. Actually, I felt like a slave being dragged to a new plantation. My arms were now extended forward and I periodically stumbled as they yanked me along and forced me to catch up. They led me into one ward that had four beds on either side of the wall with women and kids occupying five of the beds. The cops pointed to a mattress suggesting this was where I'd be staying.

'No,' I said. I'd now had enough of these arrogant pricks. The mattress had old blood, vomit and shit stains on it and there was no way I was lying on that thing. Give me back my mattress at the cage. In fact, the original hessian on the wet cement would have been better than that filthy bloody thing.

'What's the problem, mister?' the senior copper asked.

'The problem is that I am not staying here.'

The cop gave me a 'we'll see about that look' and I thought I was about to get a beating from these four pricks. Fuck it, I thought, do your best, you pricks, I've had enough of all this shit. I took a step back and got ready to defend myself and try to get a couple in with the shackles on when a doctor walked in and asked what the police were doing there. The cops said something in Hindi and the doctor yelled at them, also in Hindi, and I was dragged on another journey around the hospital. They seemed pretty pissed off with the crap they had got from the doctor and seemed intent on taking it out on my wrists by trying to pull the shackles straight through them.

Eventually we arrived at an office building with three guards standing out the front. They had been waiting for us and I was hauled into an office. Inside the office the police left me to the guards who told me to sit on the bed. There were two beds in the room; a bench ran along the length of one wall with a sink at one end and a fridge in the corner. So already it seemed I'd gone from the shithouse to the penthouse. I now had a hospital bed, actually two, which were off the ground, with a mattress that was about 50 millimetres thick — good times.

People paraded past the door to stare at me without shame. It was bizarre that people had no problem coming right up to my face to look at me as if I was an animal in a zoo. I just ignored it now, or sometimes I might say, 'Have you lost something, mate?'

Sallie and Martin arrived to find me sitting on the bed still shackled. Sallie asked the guards to remove the manacles. I rubbed my wrists to get the blood flowing back into the pressured areas. It was bloody strange having Sallie and Martin just wandering around without being searched or having guards supervise everything we did. Sallie and Martin made a list of all the supplies that would make life more comfortable and then told me that Bala's cook would be over later with some food. The guards didn't really know what to make of Sallie and she also drew a lot of attention from the locals. The local women stared at her as the men did me. Sallie and Martin left with their list in hand and began their long journey back to Nepal. As they got into the vehicle, a crowd gathered to see what was going on, so Martin made an impromptu speech which no-one understood and then told everyone to give themselves a clap and they followed his lead with hearty clapping. It was funny — then they were gone.

Chapter 26

I was supposed to be on death's door, but I couldn't live in this old hospital room with potentially unknown bugs and diseases attached to everything, so I started to clean. Everything in the room had a solid layer of dust settled on it that quickly became mud. Everything I thought I'd touch I cleaned with bleach. It took me about an hour and, at the end of that, the place was a little better.

I made my bed using the mattresses from both beds and my mat and sheet from the gaol. A fan was rigged up on the ceiling but had little impact on the horrendous humidity. I sat on my bed and felt grateful that people had helped me to get this room, but I was still a prisoner. I couldn't go anywhere or do anything. I decided to spend the night reading and doing Sudoku. At night I had a bucket bath and found I missed the old man's help and company. I had been with him constantly for 17 days and he had helped me with everything I did. I wished he was here.

Back in my room I discovered they'd rigged the fan with the light bulb. If I turned off the light the fan turned off. So, just like the prison, I had to remove the light bulb and, just like prison, the guards freaked out. There was an urgent knock on the door. I now had the ability to lock the door from the inside which was novel for a prisoner. I unlocked the door and had to show the guards what I'd done. They accepted that I could sleep with the light off. It was a hot night and I missed my little fan, but the thicker mattress meant I slept better than I had for the previous 16 nights.

27.
NIGHTMARE DAYS
TWENTY AND TWENTY-ONE

Wednesday 11 June

I was awake at about 4.00 am and read a little while waiting for the guards to kick on my door at 5.00 am. I had unbolted my side of the door, but the guards had locked the other side as well. But 5.00 am came and went, so I just lay there reading until about 7.00 am when the guards finally opened the door.

I walked to the end of the hallway near the doorway to the bathroom and had a bucket bath with freezing cold water, but it was good to wash the layer of sweat off. It was strange washing without the help of the old man and without the 300-strong audience watching.

Bala sent his cook with some breakfast. He brought some porridge, which wasn't like our porridge and made with oats; it seemed to be made with another type of grain. It was bloody beautiful. He delivered it in a hot plastic container and motioned for me to scrape it onto my plate so he could take the container back to Bala.

Sallie and Martin arrived at about 10.00 am. I'd spent the previous hour looking out my window for their black Pajero. It was hilarious when they arrived. They had so much gear for my room that they looked like they'd been to Biratnagar's version of Ikea. They had two thick foam mattresses, sheets that were really just lengths of white material purchased from a fabric shop, four pillows, towels and food — it was great and really made this ridiculous existence comfortable. Sallie had also bought me a replacement cell phone in Biratnagar. It was a classic phone and almost an antique, but I loved it. All the phone did was make phone calls and send text messages. There was no camera or internet connection and I really liked that. Plus, it was small which made it easy to hide. I was finally able to contact my daughter Sayge, and it was a dream to hear her voice. I'd sent her repeated text messages while in the gaol, but she had never replied. Obviously I thought I'd been forgotten, but it turned out that her mother had stopped paying her ever-increasing phone bills — not a bad idea, but crap timing.

Sallie stayed and helped me put the cell together while Martin went off to wheel and deal. There was still no word on where this supposed letter from the Minister was. Sallie called the High Commission staff in New Delhi and got a little hysterical in her attempt to get them to do something. She told them I wasn't safe anywhere and I was getting sicker. I asked her to go a little easier as I didn't want to be moved back to the gaol. But we had to try everything and anyone we knew. Sallie had left no stone unturned in order to get me released. I found out that the SAS Regiment in Perth was aware of my predicament and Sallie had already spoken to several colleagues who might have had contacts in India. She also had a dozen Australian journalists, entertainers and actors calling their contacts in the government every day. But for me, sitting in a cell at Araria hospital, it seemed as though nothing was happening. I needed pressure to come from all directions. I called a mate who had been my Squadron Commanding Officer a few years back and now held a highly regarded position with the government. He was in a meeting, but I told his secretary that I was in trouble and needed to talk to him as soon as possible. She put me through to the secretary at the meeting location, and my mate walked out of his meeting to talk to me. I thanked him then quickly explained my situation. He took notes, understood and said he'd start making calls the moment he'd finished the meeting.

Martin left at 4.00 pm and there was still no word about the Minister's letter of release. By this time, Martin was talking to the High Commission guys two or three times a day.

Another good thing happened — Sallie was able to stay with me in this room. Bala had given approval for this to happen. What a great guy. But I was worried. This wasn't quite a gaol, but it was still pretty bad.

The other problem was that I couldn't protect her in this place. Frankly, I couldn't really protect myself, let alone her. I introduced Sallie to the bucket bath system. The water was too cold for her. She cried with despair. I felt so bad for her. What woman would do what she had done? What woman would go through what I had put her through? She was amazing.

In the cell we absolutely cooked. It was so damned hot and humid. I set up a mosquito net for Sallie and another for me. This certainly kept the mosquitoes out, but also kept the heat in. Damn, it was hot.

At 9.00 pm the guards frantically knocked and wanted to know about the light. Again, I sorted that out and we tried for sleep in this sauna. At midnight there was a loud thumping on the door followed by yelling for me to open up. When Sallie was ready, I opened the door to be confronted by six or seven men. They were yelling at me, so I thought they were police. Then they tried to take my photo and I heard the word journalist and Patna (the capital of Bihar). I tried to close the door, and one man tried to force his way into the cell. I could see the guard standing there with them and, when I caught his eye, I got no response. I managed to close the door and they eventually left. We were both a little shaken as I tried to work out what the hell had just happened. I knew this would cause problems in the morning.

Thursday 12 June

I woke at around 4.30 am and Sallie woke shortly after. It had cooled slightly so it was nice to lie on the bed. I settled into the very thick mattresses and remembered sleeping on a hessian bag in the prison only a few days ago.

We had a bucket bath at 7.00 am and Sallie called Rajeesh to alert him to the previous night's events and, unbelievably, Rajeesh called Siddiqui (the SP) to lodge a formal complaint. I don't know why he called the enemy, but he did and it caused a few problems. Sallie was also able to speak to Bala to alert him to the incident. Bala was very alarmed and rushed over. In the meantime, I had a visit from the prison clerk, Mr Omar. I mentioned the incident of the previous night and asked Mr Omar to ask the guard why he had let these people in. Mr Omar stood up and approached the now-shitting-himself guard. Mr Omar asked who the people were and why he allowed them entry. Clearly not satisfied with the answer or the speed with which it was delivered, he belted the guard on the head and launched into a tirade of abuse, ridiculing him before letting loose with another belt to the head. He then calmly returned to his seat and told me the people were local criminals and had paid the guard off. He asked that I not report the incident, as the guard was a poor man. I told him it was too late. People already knew.

Twenty minutes later, a policeman arrived and pounded on my door. He told me to get my woman out of the gaol. He said my photo was in the paper from last night and it was causing some problems. This was all clearly a lie as the offenders were not journalists and, even if they had been, they couldn't have delivered the image in time. This confirmed my suspicion that Siddiqui was behind this mess and wanted to cause me more problems. God only knows why this mean prick had it in for me.

Bala came straight over. This guy is the Mayor and the most important guy in town, but the moment Sallie called he dropped everything to help — amazing. Unfortunately, Siddiqui had me on this one, so Bala suggested that Sallie just visit during the day. Sallie was upset, but I was relieved. I didn't like to see her locked up with me; it was heart-breaking. I also couldn't settle with her in my room. I was constantly worried that something would happen to her. So, I was happy to see her return to Biratnagar to the hotel for real food, a proper bed and a nice warm shower.

Back to the issue of getting me out of here — I worried about the paper not being signed and we had heard rumours that it might not be signed. I learnt that the Deputy Head of the Australian Mission was visiting the Joint Secretary's office today to check on the paper. When Martin arrived, I got the sense he was looking for a finish line — he'd had enough. I didn't blame him, we seemed to be getting nowhere and they had had to endure four hours of travel every day — poor bastards — and all because of my stupidity.

Rajeesh was very apologetic about his cock-up this morning and wanted to make amends. I told him it was hotter than hell in my room and could he please find a small fan for me? He returned about 20 minutes later with a massive box about the size of a washing machine, although it looked like a bale of hay stuck inside a plastic box. Apparently it was an evaporative air-conditioner, but all this thing did was to blow very hot, humid air at me at 200 kilometres per hour. It was as if a hurricane had entered the room. I think Rajeesh thought the bigger the unit the bigger the apology! It was a very kind gesture. Rajeesh was a good guy and thought he was doing the right thing.

At 12.00 Martin came in with a grave look on his face. He was preparing me for bad news, but then said the paper had been signed and was with the Bihar government. I could have fucking killed him, but was thrilled that we now seemed to be getting somewhere. Martin and Rajeesh went off to Bala's office to follow up on this good news. On their way out, Rajeesh again apologised for his foolishness. 'Don't worry about that now, mate, just do what you can to find out where this letter is and what we have to do to get it to the local office.'

Sallie and I stayed in the room and then ventured into the hallway for some cool air. The hallway was mildly better than the room. Honestly, the room was like living in the jungles of Vietnam in the middle of summer — hot and humid.

Martin returned with bananas and fruit juice and word that it would only be a few more days. Keep in mind that I'd been hearing this 'few more days' line since day one and it had now been 20 days since my arrest, so the phrase 'a few more days' didn't sit well with me any more. Martin told me that he had a contact in the Australian Embassy in Kathmandu and that, when I was released, they'll have a doctor waiting for me to give me the once over and load me up with injectable antibiotics. He also said they were working on trying to renew my visa for re-entry into Nepal. I got a bit pissed off. First, I didn't actually want a Nepali doctor injecting anything into me. What I had could wait until I got back to Sydney. Second, why the hell was anyone talking about my visa and re-entry? I hadn't been arrested with my passport. There was no exit stamp on my passport so, for all intents and purposes, Nepali Immigration had no record of my leaving Nepal. I asked Martin to let it go and not mention the visa issue to anyone. Martin agreed and that was the end of that. I was certainly grateful though, as Martin's forward planning had been useful on many occasions. Sallie and Martin left at 5.00 pm for the long drive back — poor bastards, I wished I was going with them.

I had a quiet night. I caught up on my writing, I did one Sudoku puzzle, I read some and sat outside with the guards in the cooler evening air for a while. At 6.00 pm I had my bucket bath and, 10 minutes later, started sweating again. By 11.00 pm I entered the free world of sleep.

THE EASY DAY WAS YESTERDAY

28.
LAST DAYS

Friday 13 June

It was too hot to sleep so I was out of bed and stuffing about at around 5.00 am. The juice was refreshing and, when the fridge worked, the juice was cold. Honestly, I had it so good now.

The team arrived at about 10.00 am. Sallie's instincts had been right on the money every time. She started pushing the idea of calling the Bihar Home Secretary, but the others said no, don't push them, they will sign the form in their own time. But she insisted and called anyway. She got straight through to the man himself who was exceptionally polite and assured her that he was aware of the case and would have the documents signed today. There was much excitement and Bala's 2IC said it would only take two hours to process when it arrived in Araria and then I could go free. At 4.30 pm, Martin returned with the news that approval had to come from the courts and that the court was closed for the weekend, so I'd have to wait until Monday for my release. Bugger it, here we go again — there was always something.

Sallie decided she would call the Home Secretary again to see where the letter was and again the others said no, just wait. But, once more, she went with her instincts which again proved to be perfect. The Home Secretary was very polite and said he'd sent the letter 45 minutes ago. The team drove straight to Bala's office. In typical fashion, Bala started kicking arse. The Public Prosecutor started to create some waves until Bala opened up on him with a torrential downpour of abuse until he decided to play the game. There was some concern that I'd have to wait until Triparthy returned from his vacation on Wednesday so he could sign the papers, but Bala kicked some more arse and encouraged the Public Prosecutor to work over the weekend to get the Bihar courts to give Triparthy's replacement permission to sign the papers. So at best I was here until Monday, and worst case until Thursday, but at least I was being released.

The team left late after a huge day and had a hectic drive back to the border before it closed to vehicle traffic at 8.00 pm. I rang Sallie several times and was happy when she finally said they'd made it back to the hotel.

It was a quiet night for me. It rained all night so there was no power or back-up generator. This, of course, meant it was bloody hot all night. The guards must have assumed that this was a great time for someone to escape — they were right — and continually checked that I was still in the room. The meal delivered by Bala's cook was excellent — a small bowl of vegetables in a curry sauce with roti bread on the side. I ate the meal by candlelight, but it was useless trying to read or do Sudoku with a flickering light, so I just lay there in the darkness. I felt as though I was putting on weight at last.

Saturday 14 June

Debu-San (my red-stained-teeth lawyer) came for a visit and was pissed off that he hadn't been included in yesterday's discussions. He was adamant that I needed to wait for Triparthy to return from his holiday before I could be released. I said, 'I don't want to wait until Thursday.'
'I know how you feel,' he said.
'Oh do you?' I replied. 'How much time have you spent in prison?'
'Never,' he replied with a wobble of his head.
'Then, with all due respect, Debu-San, you have no idea how I feel.'
He agreed and we went on to chat about the good things the Magistrate (Triparthy) had done for me. He had told Debu-San that I must plead not guilty, and that if I pleaded guilty he would be left with no choice but to sentence me to months and not days in prison. Triparthy was the one who had told the team to go through the Home Secretary to have the charges dropped. He had also told an open courtroom that he

thought I was innocent. Debu-San said that he'd spoken to three of the four witnesses and they had been briefed on what to say. One witness was the manager of a hotel adjacent to the border, and he was also a former client of Debu-San's, as was his son. Debu-San said the witnesses would support me even though they never saw me at the border. He said the arresting police inspector (Jai Shankar) had made sure that I had compliant witnesses. Finally, Debu-San said his goodbyes and promised to bring his wife next time for a chat. He was a nice guy who was earning great money from his one client.

Sallie, Martin, Ujwal and a former student arrived. It was a waste bringing the former student, but how could we refuse when they had given me so much support during my first 10 days in gaol? Bala sent word that food would arrive at my cell for two and the others were to go to his house for lunch even though he thought he wouldn't be there. What a guy — he probably wouldn't be there, but insisted that the team use his house for lunch and to rest. So Sallie and I ate a nice lunch in my cell and then rested for an hour in the sauna. The other guys returned and hung around for an hour waiting for Bala to get back to his office for a final chat before returning to Nepal. Bala stopped by for a quick chat as he was at the hospital interviewing a doctor for a position. He said he'd be back tomorrow night for a final chat before my release. 'Inshallah,' I said.

As the sun went down, I sat out the front with the guards to enjoy the cooling evening air, but it was still hot and I continuously fanned myself with a cheap fan. A young boy and a girl carrying a baby approached me and said 'hello'. The boy could speak very good English; he was about 14 years old. The girl, his sister, was about 12 and their younger brother was about 18 months. I gave all three some Australian souvenirs Sallie had brought with her and they were thrilled. Apparently their dad was the hospital pathologist and they lived in a house very close to my cell.

I decided to go to bed at around 8.00 pm and read my book for while. At 10.00 pm a doctor knocked on the door. When I answered he told me someone from New Delhi had called to see if I was okay. I was fine, but wish I had acted a little sicker because I didn't want to have to return to the gaol.

Chapter 28

Sunday 15 June

There was a knock on the door at 7.00 am, but I'd been awake reading for hours anyway. The little kids said, 'Congratulations, you will be released.'

'How do you know this?' I asked.

'It is in the newspaper today.'

'Well, let's not get too carried away yet,' I said, but liked the sound of what they were saying.

The guards indicated it was time for a cup of tea, which roughly translated to 'buy us a cup of tea now'. So I gave them the usual 100 rupee note and off the guard went to get tea for the guards and two cups for me. It was a nice way to start the day and I liked the tea. I then had my morning bucket bath and again wondered what the old man was doing. The bucket bath was refreshing as I was covered in a layer of dried sweat from the night of sleeping in the cell next to the hurricane of hot, humid air. The other difference in the hospital was that my shower was in a room so I could close the door and nude up for a good wash.

I decided to sit outside for a while and try to enjoy the day. While I sat there a doctor walked past, looked at me, and said, 'Hey, what are you doing?'

'Bugger all, mate, what are you doing?' I replied with some boredom. I was getting pissed off with the constant staring and enquiries, but he seemed to be a decent bloke and he came over and sat down. I told him my story to which he replied, 'Jesus!'

'Yes,' I said, 'Jesus.'

He then told me that he was a doctor at the hospital, but also had offices at Forbes-Gange. Forbes-Gange was the town next to Araria and on the way to Nepal. He sent a man for more tea, which made me happy, and our conversation continued. He introduced himself as Dr Vijay Chaudry and asked if I would stop by his house for a meal when I was released. I told him my girlfriend would probably want to drive at the speed of light back to Nepal on my release. He then offered his house to Sallie and the team and also offered his car if we should need it. He gave me his contact details and said that, if I needed anything, I should call. Then he was off. What a nice guy.

I received a text from Sallie to say that they weren't coming today, as the vehicle needed repairs. Poor Sallie. I knew she desperately wanted to come and spend the day here, but I was sure the other guys really appreciated the day off.

I spent a lot of time outside today as it was just too hot inside. The kids visited for a while but, all in all, it was a slow, boring day. But it was still so much better than being in the gaol. I really didn't want to go back to that shithouse.

I got a call from Sam, which was good. He sounded well and I was very proud of the way he had handled the situation. He had come second in his bike competition — I was so proud. I hadn't spoken to my little mate, Zac, yet, but had some nice texts from him, which was great for my morale.

Bala came to visit at about 7.00 pm and, as we shared some mango juice, he told me about his girlfriend in Geneva. Apparently Bala had met the lady of his dreams while at university and had fallen desperately in love with her. Unfortunately, she had been offered a job in the Foreign Service while he was offered work with the government, so they were forced to live apart. But for Bala that didn't matter, he still wanted to marry her and then be with her when the time came. To Bala and his girlfriend it didn't matter that it might be 10 years or more — he just knew he only wanted to be with this girl. Unfortunately, his girlfriend's mother had refused permission for them to marry. She thought the marriage wouldn't survive all those years apart and suggested her daughter find someone else. Bala had also received several offers of arranged marriages and the ladies were all from very good and wealthy families. Bala was quite a catch and plenty of families wanted a Sub-District Magistrate for their daughters. But Bala refused all offers and just hoped that one day he could go to Geneva to be with the love of his life.

Bala was very optimistic that I would be released tomorrow. He also thought he should have done more and told Sallie to go to Putna (the capital of Bihar). He believed that, if Sallie had gone to Putna, I would have been released by now. He believed his input had slowed things down.

'Rubbish,' I said, 'I'd be dying in that filthy prison if it wasn't for you, Bala.' Bala and I said our final goodbyes, as he was that confident that I'd be released tomorrow. I wasn't getting too excited at the prospect because I'd been let down so many times before.

Monday 16 June

This was supposed to be the day I got released. I woke early despite wanting to sleep a lot longer. The excitement of being released hadn't surfaced yet as I expected there to be some mundane reason preventing it and ensuring that I would have to stay 'just a few more days'. I had my morning bucket bath, then a lazy glass of tea with the guards and then rested in my room sending text messages to Sallie and the kids. There was a knock on the door and I was bloody surprised when I opened it because my arresting officer, Sub-Inspector Jai Shankar Prakash, was standing there. I hadn't seen him since the day he had delivered me to the gaol, but I had no hard feelings towards him. He had done all that he could to persuade the SP, Siddiqui, to drop the charge. When the SP wouldn't, he had ensured that I was treated well at the prison and also made sure the witnesses for the prosecution were weak.

I shook his hand and we sat in the hallway. I was still concerned about my cell phone, so steered him away from my room. He told me that he had come to organise my escort to New Delhi. He had brought one of his officers with him to escort me on the train. I asked if it was possible for me to be released to the Nepali border. He said that I had to be released into the custody of the Australian High Commission. I let it go at that because I knew Sallie and the team would deal with this when I told them. I asked how I was going to get to New Delhi and was told that we'd take the train. 'First class?' I asked jokingly. 'No,' he said, missing my joke altogether. I had images of this cop and me sitting on top of the train all the way to New Delhi. 'How far is it to New Delhi?' I asked.

'About 14 hours.'

'Bloody hell!'

I then decided I'd try to pay for good seats because that was a long time to be stuffed in with everyone else and I could imagine them all staring at the white man in shackles.

My breakfast arrived just in time, as the conversation with Shankar had died very quickly. Shankar left me to my food and went off to make arrangements. I quickly scribbled a note explaining my conversation with Shankar and gave it to Bala's cook to give to Sallie. As I ate my breakfast it occurred to me that maybe I would be released today. I had received a text from Sallie telling me that I would be, but the question was now where I'd be released. Personally, I hoped I was going to Nepal, but didn't care as long as I was released.

I decided to sit out front today and watch life go by as it was just too hot in the room. There was obviously a specialist clinic on as there were a number of mentally and physically challenged people gathering at the front of building. I'd never seen anything like it. Their tortured limbs bent and pointed in all directions except the right one. Some couldn't walk, so they crawled with their legs dragging behind them. There were others with no arms, some with no legs and others with feet that just didn't work. A pretty young girl came close. She was wearing a beautiful purple and orange sari, but she had no feet and her toes were attached directly to the bottom of her leg. There wasn't a wheelchair in sight, but plenty of lengths of bamboo to help these poor bastards get around. To be born in India to a poor family and with a deformity was a real curse. I looked at some of the useless legs these people were dragging around; had they been in Australia, they would have had these limbs amputated and a usable prosthetic attached. I've seen some terrible things in my life; things that no man should ever have had to see. Rwanda was one; the Iraq War was another.

29.
THE IRAQ WAR 2003

On 8 March 2003, I arrived in Kuwait. It was my first trip to Kuwait, and the Middle East for that matter, and I had no real idea what to expect. So I exited the airport with a heightened level of awareness — I suppose I naively expected everyone to be remotely related to Osama Bin Laden. In situations like this, I trusted no-one. I was supposed to be met by a couple of Brits who worked for the same security company as I did. Apparently they'd been here for a few weeks already, helping CNN prepare to cover the impending war in Iraq. These guys told me a driver would be there as well and the driver's name would be written on a board. As I left the terminal I immediately caught sight of the driver and the Brits approached a few moments later. After the introductions, they said we were going back to the hotel that CNN had taken over.

I checked into the hotel and we hit the buffet for lunch and had a chat about what was going on. One thing was clear, CNN were really chucking some money at this war. They'd taken over the hotel and occupied almost every room. All meals were covered by CNN by way of a buffet, and they'd already purchased two old humvees and two land rovers for those crews embedding with the US military. The Brits told me I'd be going with one of those embedded crews. Bugger; I wish I had been told this prior to leaving Australia because I knew what I needed to survive on operations and had most of the stuff stored at home.

Everyone was preparing as if the war was going to happen so I did the same. I started putting maps together of the whole country and using a highlighter pen to mark the latitude and longitude numbers for rapid identification. I had a medical kit to prepare, a GPS to sort out, two different satellite phones to program, body armour and cold weather gear to prepare. Fortunately, I had gone to a military disposal shop in Hereford the week before and bought a cold weather sleeping bag, a pack for all the gear, a bivvy bag, thermal underwear, cold weather jacket and a good set of walking boots.

That afternoon I met the rest of the crew with whom I would be embedded. There was Walter Rogers, an elderly reporter who had been around for a long time and had a lot of experience. Charlie Miller, the cameraman, was a freelancer and had worked with Walt on a few previous jobs. Charlie also had some previous experience with the British Army. Jeff Barwise, the satellite engineer, was from the south and had that real Bogart twang to his accent. I immediately liked Jeff and his very relaxed nature. This was to be Jeff's first exposure to war.

Jeff showed me the old bucket of shit humvee I'd be driving through this war. She was a real shocker and still had the original army seats and instruments. Jeff had already fitted the satellite dish and communication gear to 'Old Betsy', as we nicknamed her, and had purchased two generators to power everything, so I went shopping to buy those things that would make life more comfortable in the desert during the war.

I bought a small gas burner and three extra disposable butane cylinders, steel drinking mugs for all, cooking pots, extra food, tea, coffee, sugar, drinking chocolate, muesli bars and anything else I could throw into the trolley. Having the ability to make a hot cuppa whenever we had the chance was going to be good for morale, especially first thing in the morning when we would be tired and cold. I went shopping with the CNN logistics guy and a few others. The logistics guy had a pocket full of money and was happy to spend it on whatever we wanted. The local Kuwaiti businesses were making a killing on this war and CNN had a huge budget to throw at the Kuwaiti merchants.

Some of the other guys had plain, military-style uniforms made by the local tailors and, as we collected them, the logistics guy told the tailor to measure me for a set as well. This was great as it meant I could have something made that was more akin to a military style without the camouflage pattern. I liked the idea of lots of big pockets to hold all my life-saving kit, so I jumped at the chance.

A few days later, Walt and Charlie were called forward to their US Army embed unit. Officially, only Charlie and Walt were to be embedded without the hummer or Jeff and me. So off they went and Jeff and I continued to tinker with the car just waiting for the call to move forward. A few hours later we received it. We were told to move to KM 21 on the main highway to Iraq and to be there by 5.00 pm. Jeff and I arrived with plenty of time to spare and waited with a heap of others who were also waiting to be met by their embed units. Like CNN, the other media companies had employed ex-soldiers to drive their cars; there was certainly some testosterone floating around that waiting area.

Some groups were collected after 20 minutes while we waited until 9.00 pm. We followed another humvee through the desert for an hour heading west and eventually arrived at Camp New York. We stopped there for 15 minutes and then drove further into the desert to another camp and arrived at midnight. By now Jeff and I were well and truly buggered and were looking for a rack to get some sleep. Charlie and Walt were there so we grabbed a stretcher each, found some clear space in their tent and fell asleep.

We were up at 6.00 am for shit, shower and shave, followed by a greasy breakfast. Then we waited and waited and waited some more for someone to come for us. Eventually the unit padre came to get us and we followed his humvee further into the desert to the 7th Cavalry location which, according to my GPS, was 25 kilometres from the Iraqi border.

We met the Squadron Commanding Officer (SCO), Terry Ferrel, and I let Walt do his journalist thing and sat in the background waiting for any tactical discussions to begin. The SCO was a big man, maybe 6 feet 3 inches (190 centimetres), and very welcoming to us all. We sat in the operations room getting a brief from the SCO, and I ran my eye over the maps in the ops room looking for any dates that would give me something to work towards, but there was nothing; good for them. The SCO said all would be revealed when it was necessary. We drove to the Apache Company position and set up next to the Company Commander's Abrams tank.

The Company Commander of Apache Company was Captain Lyle. He was a short guy, which was probably good for a tank commander, had blonde hair and seemed like a decent bloke.

That afternoon we practised a ROM (refuelling on the move). Apparently we would be charging into Iraq and, when we were just about to run out of fuel, we would stop, the fuel tankers would catch up and we would just drive through like a petrol station. Sure enough, that's what we did and it worked very well. The Americans are great at mobilising large numbers of people and equipment.

We started to hear word that George W Bush was going to make a speech the next day. The SCO thought we would drive into Iraq at 3.00 am the following morning and drive on for a few hours until Saddam capitulated. He asked where we wanted to position ourselves. 'As far forward as possible,' I answered, without giving the crew the chance to debate the question. The SCO said we couldn't be in front of the forward troop commander's vehicle, but could sit just behind him. Perfect. So that was it. Our position was vehicle number 11 in a convoy of about 400 vehicles.

George W. made his big speech the next day as the crew and half of Apache Troop sat around Walt's radio listening to the BBC. Bush told Saddam that he had 48 hours to capitulate. He told the Iraqi soldiers not to fight, the Iraqi commanders not to fire their weapons of mass destruction (WMDs), and that the US military was bringing help.

Captain Lyle told us that we were moving forward to the attack position the next day, so Jeff and I gave Betsy the once over to ensure we were ready to roll. We checked that the four fuel jerries were full and well secured on the roof and that our water jerries were also full and secured in the back. That afternoon, Apache Troop issued us with 20 individual meals ready to eat (MREs) to keep us going for the first few days of the war.

When we departed for the attack position it was still dark — as it generally is at 4.00 am. We drove for a few hours in the dark and it was a good opportunity to get the night vision goggles (NVGs) on and practise following the tank in front. Only I could see where we were going — the others were driving in complete darkness. At 9.00 am we seemed to arrive in the middle of nowhere when the convoy stopped its armoured vehicles in all-round defence, so I parked Betsy in the middle of A Troop's defensive position about 20 metres from Captain Lyle's Abrams.

Later that day we heard a news report over the short wave radio that the coalition had bombed strategic targets in Baghdad the previous night. The air war had started, so it wouldn't be long before this show would get underway. I was surprised and couldn't believe this was really going to happen. I suppose up until now I was just earning my day's pay and subconsciously thought I'd be back in Kuwait City in a few days.

Captain Lyle started talking about a 16 to18-hour drive to the first objective. It seemed the strategy had changed from simply crossing the border and waiting for capitulation to full-on invasion. This was confirmed when we went to a briefing by the SCO. The SCO told us that the ground war was set to begin on the night of 21 March at midnight — 36 hours away. I was relieved as I wanted to get some rest before the big drive. He continued to describe the battle plan and that the Squadron's first objective was the town of As' Samawah in the southern central region of Iraq. The drive would probably take some 27 hours. Again, I was glad we were leaving in 36 hours so I could try to bank some sleep.

At 1.30 pm, we were back at Betsy heating some MREs and getting a brew on when I heard five patriot missiles launched to the north-east of our position. Immediately the call went around to get into MOP 4 — full NBC suit (a nuclear, biological, chemical protective suit). Something big impacted close to our north. It took the crew and me about three minutes to get completely kitted up, conduct the checks on one another and get inside Betsy. After one hour we stood down. Apparently Saddam had a bit of a go and fired six tactical ballistic missiles (TBM) and the patriots failed to catch one. It landed 10 kilometres to the north of our position.

The result of all this activity was to bring H-hour forward 24 hours. My idea of getting any rest was gone. At 8.30 pm, we decamped our position and moved closer to the border and waited for the crossing point to be cleared. A huge explosion detonated a few kilometres to the south. Saddam had fired another TBM. It seems this speculator bomb had been launched just to see what he could kill on the border. At 1.53 am local time, we crossed into Iraq and, after some initial navigation problems, began the marathon drive to the objective — As' Samawah.

I drove on NVGs until 4.30 am local time, then used the rising sun for light continuing until 8.00 am when we did the first ROM. I was rooted by now; I'd been awake for 29 hours. When we stopped and waited for all vehicles to refuel, I flopped out of the driver's door onto the desert floor to steal a few minutes of shut-eye. After that, we drove and drove and then drove some more. I looked forward to the next ROM. We continued in arrowhead formation across the desert plain. The whole time Charlie was on the bonnet filming the 'wave of steel cross the southern Iraqi plain,' said Walt, commentating from the back seat.

We drove past Bedouin camps with the families looking on in awe as the Abrams and Bradleys flew across the sand doing about 60 kph. I struggled with Betsy trying to stay in one track of Captain Lyle's tank and trying to maintain some speed. The day passed without any sign of the Iraqi army. At night we refuelled and continued the push for As' Samawah.

The drive on NVGs was horrendous. The dust totally enveloped Captain Lyle's Abrams in front making following almost impossible. Continuous driving on NVGs can make you feel nauseous because of the sensory fuck-up with depth perception — like being on a merry-go-round for hours on end. Eventually the driving became too dangerous and, due to the limited threat, we went to white light. By 4.45 am, I had been driving for more than 28 hours and awake for almost 50 hours. I had to sleep a little so, given that we were using white light, I allowed Jeff to drive for two hours and I died in the back seat for 120 minutes of solid sleep.

By first light we had arrived at the preparation area. The Iraqis inside As' Samawah were dropping artillery onto Charlie Company to our east, and the Paladins were retaliating with 155 mm artillery shells. The Kiowa helicopters were firing hellfire missiles at opportunity targets inside the city including the scud missile sites. Tension mounted among the troops as H-hour was continually put back. The whole day was spent on standby. Then word came that the assault was planned for first light.

I rolled out my sleeping bag next to the driver's door and slept for a few hours. The rest of the crew slept in Betsy. They didn't want to sleep on the ground for fear of a mortar attack. I couldn't convince them otherwise, but I needed some rest before all hell broke loose and wasn't going to get that sitting behind the wheel of Betsy.

The next morning I was up at 4.00 am for the dawn attack, which didn't happen. Despite being dog-tired, I was routinely woken through the night by the continuous bombing of As' Samawah. I assumed that the Americans were softening the target for the dawn attack.

Later that day we moved closer to As' Samawah to form up for the attack. The attack was planned for 3.00 pm. I hoped these guys weren't relying on the element of surprise because that was certainly gone, as was the initiative. The Iraqis were working their arses off establishing their defensive positions. Captain Lyle and I had a quiet chat about the forthcoming battle. He told me I could position the vehicle wherever I wanted, but to expect a 'Black Hawk Down' type of firefight. Intelligence reports suggested that the Fedayeen (a specialist unit in the Iraqi army commanded by Uday Hussain, Sadam's oldest son) were recruiting local men to assist in fortifying the town. They had built gun emplacements on most buildings in the city, so the firefight was going to be big. I thought the same, but was confident that the 10 Abrams and Bradleys in front of me, and the Kiowas overhead, would clear a good path through the city so Old Betsy would take limited fire — at least I hoped they would.

As preparation for the assault continued, I heard the dull thud of artillery being fired. I heard six dull thuds and thought the Americans had fired a salvo behind us. Then they impacted. The explosions were deafening as the six shells smashed in about 50 metres from Old Betsy. One man lay screaming on the ground and another was thrown into the back of one of the vehicles. Someone tended the injured while the rest of us scrambled for our vehicles and moved. The Iraqis had us in their sights and their first barrage was on target, so we expected a dozen more rounds to follow in quick succession. The only thing we could do was move and move quickly.

Momentum had been well and truly lost, along with the initiative. Intelligence reported that the Fedayeen were bringing families into their town headquarters. They gave the men an AK47 and instructed them to go and fight the Americans or lose their families who were kept as hostages. We pulled back to a night position about 10 kilometres west into the desert. F16s then proceeded to bomb the shit out of the town all night. The Americans were showing the Iraqis what weapons of mass destruction were all about.

That night I finally got some decent sleep — about five hours — but it was bloody cold. People assume the desert nights are as hot as the days, but the nights were arctic. I wore thermal pants and shirt, my Kuwaiti-made uniform, NBC jacket and pants, arctic jacket, gloves and beanie, I was in my cold weather sleeping bag which was inside my bivvy bag, and I was still cold.

In the morning, after a lazy breakfast of MREs and a hot cup of tea, we moved out on a reconnaissance of a bridge with Apache Troop. This seemed to be just something to keep us occupied for the day while future plans were made for the war. We arrived at the bridge and spoke to the locals who seemed a friendly bunch and happy to see us. All the vehicles were lined up adjacent to a railway track except Captain Lyle's. It was parked on the high ground on the other side of the railway line. Jeff and I were standing in front of Captain Lyle's Abrams chatting when two men stepped out of a hut about 120 metres away. They both carried RPGs and fired them at Captain Lyle's Abrams. Due to their haste in firing, both missiles missed their targets, but the noise of the rockets being fired was enough to ensure that everyone ducked and grabbed a weapon. Captain Lyle's machine-gunner was manning his weapon and immediately opened fire. Jeff and I turned and ran back to Betsy as we watched both men's bodies jump and dance as about 20 rounds lifted them back into the hut. We returned to the firm base with some speed, but it was a quiet drive home. I suppose the crew now realised that this was a war, people were going to die and we were right in the middle of it.

Chapter 29

Back at the base camp we received orders to move, so again, Jeff and I ensured that Betsy was doing okay and we loaded up with MREs, fuel and water. Every time we stopped I pulled out a garbage bag and hung it from the side of Betsy and made sure all our rubbish went into the bag. When it was full, I dug a deep hole and buried the rubbish, ensuring that at least 50 centimetres of sand was loaded on top. The Americans, on the other hand, were absolute pigs. They left rubbish everywhere they went. They just threw it on the ground until the winds carried the rubbish off into the desert. They were also unhygienic. They didn't dig holes to shit. They just shat on the desert floor and the used toilet paper flew across the desert. It was bloody disgusting. I gave my crew a lesson on bush hygiene and how to use the toilet. It always included a shovel and a very deep hole. If the Iraqis wanted to see where the Americans had been, they just had to follow the piles of rubbish.

We finally received orders to push forward to a location north of Najaf. Apparently we were going to secure a series of bridges over the Euphrates River. Captain Lyle gathered us around the front of his Abrams and delivered a set of orders for the move that would be led by his company. We were to be the forward element on the western side of Iraq, heading north. I got settled in to listen to Captain Lyle's orders when, after about five minutes, he asked if there were any questions. I waited and no-one said or asked anything. I couldn't believe it. It was the worst set of orders I'd ever heard. Captain Lyle was a top bloke, but he had spoken for five minutes and told us nothing. He had a map spread out over the front of his tank and most of us only had a view of his back. We were driving about 100 kilometres north into enemy territory where contact with the Iraqis was almost certain and orders lasted five minutes! 'Ah, yes. I have some questions,' I tentatively asked as Captain Lyle looked at me. 'What will the order of march be?'

'As per normal. You guys will follow my Abrams,' replied Captain Lyle. 'Any other questions?'

'Ah, yes. What are the actions on contact?'

'Well, we will return fire.'

Fuck me, I'm getting nowhere with this.

'Any further questions? Right, we're leaving in 30 mikes.'

I decided to have a chat with Captain Lyle once everyone had left. I confirmed with him that, in the event of an ambush, I would use his tank for protection and that I would allow enough room for him to rotate his turret without removing my roof rack so he could return fire. I also told him I'd be travelling without my lights on, as I didn't want to attract fire to the soft-skinned vehicle. Captain Lyle accepted this and I went to get ready for the move, but I still couldn't believe that the whole convoy was moving with lights on. This was just wrong and went against everything I knew.

By 9.00 pm we'd been travelling for about an hour with an average speed of 40 kph. In front I could see the lights of 10 Abrams and Bradleys and behind I could see a line of headlights that seemed to go on forever. Then it started. Charlie thought they were flares. I knew they were tracer rounds. We were being ambushed from the right. The line of tracer seemed to be coming from a machine-gun set on a fixed line as the tanks just drove straight through the fire and the bullets ricocheted off the side of the tanks. I knew we couldn't just drive through the fire because those bullets would easily cut through Old Betsy and all of us inside and then punch through the other side. I accelerated to the left of Captain Lyle's Abrams as bullets smashed into it. All the tanks had now stopped and turned into the ambush and returned fire. The Bradleys opened up with their 20 mm cannons and the tanks used their 50 cal machine-guns. Two of the Abrams fired 120 mm shells from their main guns into the ambush and the explosion on their arrival was deafening. No-one could survive that amount of firepower. The firing stopped and the convoy pushed further north. The crew was now on edge. We had just survived our first ambush — and it wouldn't be our last.

A further 10 kilometres up the road it started again, but this time from the left, although we also took some fire from the right. Captain Lyle swung his turret from side to side engaging targets with his 50 cal machine-gun and main 120 mm gun. I put on my NVGs and could see the ambush on the left about 200 metres away. Incredibly, people were running around with weapons looking for better positions from which to fire. It was strange seeing so much activity in the ambush. RPGs were launched at the tanks, and one landed in front of our vehicle. I watched as three RPGs were fired from the ambush and knew one was aimed at Betsy. I watched it fly straight at the vehicle and grabbed the door handle hoping the blast might throw me free. I cringed slightly as it got closer and waited for the impact, then saw it appear over the right of the car. It must have missed by centimetres. Movement in the ditch about five metres from Betsy caught my eye. This guy seemed to be looking at me as he raised his AK47 and, a millisecond later, his body jumped backwards as it was hit by a five-round burst from the machine-gun of the Bradley behind me. The Americans called in an A10 Warthog, which fired its mini-guns into the ambush. It sounded like the aircraft was letting out a continuous fart as it fired 6,000 rounds per minute and then, for good measure, dropped a 500 lb bomb into the ambush location. That was the end of that and we moved on.

We continued on through very thick palm plantations and I waited for the next attack. This was great ambush country and I spent 90% of my time scanning the plantation on either side with my NVGs looking for indications of an ambush. It was now after midnight, which made the date 25 March, the day I turned 37.

The convoy slowed down, which made us better targets, and eventually we stopped. A patrol of soldiers ran past us and told me the first Abrams had collapsed the bridge we were to use to cross the Euphrates. With the bridge gone we turned around and drove back the way we had come and I couldn't believe we weren't attacked. Retracing your steps is a definite no-no. The engineers loaded the stranded tank with explosives and destroyed it in position. At 1.30 am, on the northern edge of Najaf, we stopped for five hours. I didn't sleep because we seemed to be surrounded by buildings and the Americans were terrible at letting us know what was going on. In fact, when I asked Captain Lyle what the plan was, he seemed not to know either.

After five hours we were told to continue towards the bridges over the Euphrates, but via a different route given that the other was blocked by the destroyed tank. At the same time, a severe dust storm rolled through and I couldn't see more than 20 metres. I wrapped my head in a shamagh (scarf) and put on my goggles in case I needed to exit Betsy. The drive took about 90 minutes, but we hadn't gone very far when the action started. The convoy was getting smashed by small arms fire and rockets from the left and right. I couldn't take cover behind the Abrams because rounds were coming from both directions. The Iraqis couldn't see what they were shooting at because of the dust storm, so they came closer to the road. They thought they couldn't be seen because they couldn't see the convoy. Foolish. The US soldiers could see them very clearly through their thermal imagery. The Iraqis just fired indiscriminately at the noises. Every vehicle had bullet impact marks except Betsy — bloody lucky. Poor old Betsy's soft skin wouldn't have coped with striking bullets. There were rounds landing all around our vehicle and, during a break in the fire, the crew from the tank behind came to see if we had a casualty, and to look at the bullet holes in Betsy — thankfully there weren't any. Apparently they saw a guy through their thermal imagery firing directly at old Betsy. Must have been a crap shot.

We continued on through the pea-soup dust as the firing intensified. The Iraqis were really laying down some heavy fire from both sides of the road. By now the team had their ballistic helmets on and I suggested they turn and face the doors. The rationale was that the bullet-proof vests had ballistic plates in the front and rear, but if they got hit on the side, the bullets could easily penetrate the Kevlar. So facing the door meant penetrating bullets would, hopefully, hit the ballistic plates.

Through the dust, I realised I was driving around a roundabout, when I saw a white mini-van parked on one of the entry roads to the roundabout. The side door of the van was flung open, and three Iraqis leapt out and started firing at Captain Lyle's Abrams in front of us. Captain Lyle swung his turret around and his gunner let them have it with about five rounds each. Idiots! Why would they attack a tank with AK47S? And why did they shoot the tank and not Old Betsy? We were just as close. Mind you, I'm glad they decided to shoot the tank. They mustn't have seen Old Betsy, but I decided then that I really had to find a weapon to protect myself and the team — this was getting out of control.

We finally arrived at the bridge to find three Iraqis on the ground next to a Multiple Launch Rocket System (MLRS). They were taken away by the intelligence guys for a chat while the rest of us had a good look at the MLRS and, more importantly, what they had in the back of the truck. They had so much ammo in there and I wasn't sure why they hadn't sent some down range at the approaching Americans. Maybe they hadn't realised we were there. Maybe they just hadn't wanted to die. I later learnt that the Kiowa helicopters had thrown a hellfire missile at these guys (which would explain the bits and pieces of human remains scattered about the place) and I suppose this had prompted them to lay down their arms. In the back of the truck I also spotted three AK47s and about 10 magazines and made a mental note to come back and borrow one of them later.

The next day we continued to be hammered by the dust storm. The crew and I were pretty knackered as the dust, combined with sporadic attacks on the perimeter, kept us all up most of the night. That morning the intelligence guys reported a number of T72 tanks and BMPs (Soviet-style armoured personnel carriers) heading towards our location from the north. I moved Old Betsy to a safer location behind a building and faced her south in case we had to do a runner. A group of B52 bombers dropped twenty-six 2000 lb bombs along the road to the north and on top of the supposed attack. The explosions were horrendous and felt like an earthquake measuring 9 on the Richter scale. That was the end of the attack. We later learnt that what the spy planes thought were T72 tanks and BMPs were actually hundreds of camels walking on the road!

I remembered those AK47s in the back of the abandoned truck and decided to borrow one and a handful of mags. I wrapped it in my jacket and found a quiet old shed and pulled the weapon apart and cleaned it. I wanted to ensure that, if I pointed the thing, it was going to work. It seemed to be in good condition and sounded better with a light oil on the internal working parts. I put a magazine on the weapon, cocked it and, with the safety catch on, placed it next to my driver's seat. It was certainly a comfortable feeling having the extra protection. It was about this time that the other soldiers started asking why I didn't have a weapon and offered to find one for me if I thought I needed one.

Later that afternoon, Captain Lyle yelled out across the position, 'Hey, SAS, have you seen an AK47? We seem to be missing one.' People laughed.

'No,' I replied, 'but I have one if you want to buy it.'

So that was it; everyone now knew that I had a weapon. Then some soldiers decided to do me a favour by giving me extra AK47 magazines. By the time I'd received 20, I had to say, 'That's enough, thanks.'

The next day, with my newly acquired weapon wedged beside my seat, we pulled 40 kilometres back down ambush alley to a rest position to sleep and reload. The rear guys had set up a shower facility and kitchens. The showers were as hot as hell and I had a good sweat going by the time I got out. The food was processed, but a nice change from the MREs.

Finally, I was able to get a full six hours' sleep and it was nice lying on the desert floor watching hundreds of rockets flying overhead and onto the next town. We spent two days in that location, managed to have a boiling hot shower every day, and ate two meals a day in the field kitchen. We also resupplied our food, water and fuel. On the second afternoon we got orders to move early the next morning to Karbala to act as a blocking force.

Charlie became confused with timings the next morning and had us all up two hours before necessary. We had time to pack all our kit away and have a cuppa. Walt needed at least an hour to stow his kit. At 4.00 am we were following Captain Lyle in his Abrams. All the other Abrams and Bradleys had been loaded onto semi-trailers for part of the travel to Karbala. It was a cold morning and, after a few minutes of driving, we stopped to allow another brigade to pass.

By mid-morning we were two-thirds of the way to Karbala when we stopped and they unloaded the Abrams and Bradleys and drove to a position about 10 kilometres south of Karbala and 100 kilometres south of Baghdad. Captain Lyle told me they were expecting trouble that night, possibly in retaliation for the 300 Close Air Support (CAS) missions planned for Karbala. Then it started — and didn't stop. The noise was unbelievable and relentless. Fuck me, I'd hate to be on the end of that barrage. Karbala must have been getting totally smashed. The

Iraqis returned some artillery which landed about two kilometres away. They were positioning their artillery pieces in schools and hospitals making it difficult for the coalition to retaliate.

I spent my time digging a huge garbage pit; big enough to bury our rubbish and for the four of us to take cover if the Iraqis got a bit more accurate with their artillery. I explained this concept to the crew and told them to jump straight in if the artillery got too close.

The next day we held fast and listened to the hundreds of shells pouring into Karbala in front of the infantry assault. I could just imagine the troops getting stuck into some serious fighting at reasonably close quarters.

At 'O dark hundred' the next morning, Charlie had me up telling me he saw a desert dog wander around Old Betsy and he was concerned it would come close. I rolled out of my warm sleeping bag, had a close look at the 'dog' with my NVGs and saw tumble weed rolling around.

That afternoon we attended another ordinary orders group and were told we were moving to act as a blocking force as the 1st Brigade moved through to secure the final bridge to Baghdad. We were told to be ready to leave at 4.00 am.

The next morning Charlie struck again and had us up at 2.30 am telling me that we had 40 minutes to be ready. We sat around until 6.00 am, but at least we had time for a hot brew on that cold morning.

We finally got moving and drove fast over formerly ploughed fields. It was bloody tough going on Old Betsy and we struggled to keep up with Captain Lyle. After about two hours the column of armoured vehicles fanned out into extended line and I sensed they were moving into attack formation. In the distance I could see a white and orange sedan and people piling into the vehicle. I later learnt that this was an Iraqi taxi. The taxi withdrew, Captain Lyle's Abrams had its main gun trained on the withdrawing taxi and I was certain he was going to fire. He didn't. Apache Troop continued to the abandoned position that included a number of old Soviet-style anti-aircraft guns. Captain Lyle directed his tank to drive over the top of one of the guns. But the tank didn't roll directly over the top and slightly missed one of the barrels which slammed down on top of the tank behind Captain Lyle's turret and head.

Instinctively, Captain Lyle dropped into his tank and, a millisecond later, the gun fired. The tank rolled to a halt and I was certain Captain Lyle was dead inside the Abrams. I pulled up next to the Abrams and climbed on top of the tank expecting to see carnage inside. Instead, I saw Captain Lyle bleeding from his face where his helmet had been ripped off his head by the 20 mm shell. His gunner was calling over the radio for a medic while I applied direct pressure to his face. It was a foolish thing for Captain Lyle to do and he nearly paid the ultimate price.

We pushed on for a few more kilometres and then stopped for the night and to refuel. The crew and I managed to get our heads down by about 11.00 pm, but the next morning I woke to a savage attack on our position. Hundreds of bullets were being fired and I rolled out of my sleeping bag and grabbed the AK47. I then realised the fucking Americans were all test-firing their weapons and there was no contact. Bastards — I nearly had a heart attack. I wandered over to Captain Lyle's tank, got his attention as he directed his gunner on the 50 cal, and motioned with my AK47 that I was going to fire as well. He gave me the nod, so I fired 10 bullets on semi-automatic and two 5-round bursts on full auto.

We received word to drive to our blocking position south-west of Baghdad. In single file, we wove our way through the back roads in the southern districts of Baghdad, then started to enter built-up areas. Women and kids ran from houses waving white flags and cheering the arrival of the Americans. We eventually found ourselves on a major freeway heading north towards the western suburbs of Baghdad. Five of the armoured vehicles in front crashed through the barriers and drove on the other three lanes heading south and Captain Lyle's Abrams and five vehicles remained on the three lanes heading north — I stayed behind Captain Lyle.

The convoy travelled at a reasonable speed — perhaps 70 kph — and, looking in the mirror, I could see vehicles on both sides of the roads as far as my eyes could see. Any wonder the Iraqis were waving white flags; what fool would take this lot on? It seemed like the finale to this war was going to be a fizzer. Then the first crack rang out, and then another, and then it was on.

Chapter 29

The houses on each side of the freeway — maybe 200 metres away — seemed to erupt. People were running to their verandahs and firing wildly at the convoy. RPG rockets filled the gaps in the air where there were no bullets. There were hundreds of people firing at the convoy and everyone in the convoy was firing back. The noise was unbelievable. Machine-guns on the Abrams seemed to fire continuously and only stopped when the main 120 mm gun was ready to fire. In between the racket I could hear the Bradleys firing their 20 mm cannons into houses, vehicles and people. Captain Lyle was directing his machine-gunner to targets and firing his M4 at separate targets. Bullets and rockets were being fired from both sides of the freeway so there was nowhere to hide Old Betsy from the impact. I tensed, waiting for bullets to start hitting Old Betsy. The guys had their helmets on and seemed to slide down in their seats.

The closer we got to Baghdad, the more intense the fire became — if that was possible. Charlie was trying to film without compromising our position by filming a road sign or significant feature, while Jeff and Walt looked for anyone specifically targeting Old Betsy. But the noise was just too loud and, most of the time, I couldn't hear Walt's concerns and Jeff would have to yell in my ear. Unbelievably, things got more intense and violent. F14s started firing missiles into specific strongholds and, when they'd dropped their payload, the mortars and artillery started smashing dangerously close. Those artillery guys were really working overtime as the explosions on each side of the road were continuous. For us, it was just a matter of hanging on and not getting too close to Captain Lyle's Abrams, as it was taking a lot of hits and we hadn't taken any at that time.

Every 200 to 300 metres, Captain Lyle's tank stopped and his turret rotated towards a target; the barrel was raised to the correct elevation and then, BOOM! The sound was deafening and the over-pressure immediate; I was continually forced to pop my ears.

Finally we arrived at the overpass near the Abu Ghraib prison and the troop positioned in all-round defence. I found a dip between the freeways that offered some dead ground protection for Old Betsy and the crew. The firing continued so we remained in the centre of the road for the night. The only problem was that three armoured personnel carriers (APCs) decided to park next to us and it wasn't until well after dark that I discovered the hard way that these were mortar APCs and they fired missions all night.

By morning the firing had become sporadic and we decided to drive east to the forward edge of the troop's position along the road to Baghdad. The carnage along the road was shocking. Dead bodies littered the roads everywhere. Some lay next to burnt-out Iraqi tanks, others next to civilian vehicles and others just lay where they had been shot. When we got to the forward edge we saw the results of the battle that had occurred a few hours earlier. The troop had destroyed six Iraqi tanks and close air support had destroyed three. More bodies littered the area. These soldiers seemed to have died horrible deaths. Bits and pieces of bodies were strewn all over.

Jeff and I went to have a look at the destroyed Iraqi tanks and BMP. Jeff took some photos and we returned to Betsy to continue work. Then Jeff said, 'Hey that guy moved.' I turned and saw one of the many 'supposedly dead' Iraqis sit up. We both had just been looking at the guy. I ran back to him while Jeff ran to the nearest US vehicle to report the matter. The guy put up his hands, surrendering — he had no weapon. He was an officer in the Special Republican Guard. He had terrible wounds to his right leg and great chunks of his butt were gone. He looked bloody frightened and seemed to think we were going to kill him. I grabbed his extended hand and made sure he was aware I was there to help. He cried and started kissing my hands. 'Oh mate, don't do that,' I muttered in disgust, making a mental note to scrub my hands when this was done.

Charlie and I gave him some water and he threw it up and went unconscious for a while. I checked his wounds, plugged the craters where he was bleeding and decided to give him an IV. A young soldier arrived with the IV gear, but didn't know how to use it, so I put the IV line in. The man was very dehydrated and had lost a lot of blood, so finding a vein was hard work — almost impossible, in fact. I tried the usual spots for a vein: behind his thumb on his wrist and the inside of the elbow, but there was nothing — he was flat. The tourniquet had been tight above his bicep for a few minutes now and I saw a thin, faint blue line on his bicep and decided to have one last go. The cannula went in smoothly, but I got no flashback of blood to confirm that I was in the vein. I assumed this was because he was so low on blood, but I was pretty sure I was in the view and confirmed this when I hooked on the fluid and it ran through. I opened the line up so the fluid entered his veins as fast as possible. I contemplated putting another line in his neck when the medic APC arrived with a doctor on board. The doc took over and they stretchered the Iraqi officer into the APC and departed. As I watched the APC leave, I wondered if the Iraqis would treat an Aussie or Yank casualty so well. I decided it didn't matter; we had done the right thing.

Walter really got some mileage out of that incident on CNN, and he said some nice things about me, so I was grateful. All the while I was treating the Iraqi, Walt was talking to Anderson Cooper in Atlanta and, a couple of times during the event, Walt referred to me as Anderson. No dramas. At the end of the day it was a good morale boost for the crew as we'd been surrounded by death and destruction for too long and it was nice to do something good. Later, when Jeff and I talked over the incident, I laughed as I said, 'You would have shat yourself if the guy sat up while you were taking a photo of his supposed dead body.' 'Yer damned right,' replied Jeff in his southern drawl.

We made our way back to the headquarters location where the SCO had set up his tactical operations command (TOC). After a brew, I wandered over to the TOC and saw the Iraqi major on a stretcher next to the medic APC. Apparently they couldn't push him back to the rear and better medical care as the roads weren't yet secure, so he was stuck with us. I crouched down next to him and he again grabbed my hands and let rip with a mouthful of Iraqi. I had no idea what he was saying, so just nodded and smiled. He was probably asking why I hadn't just let him die in peace instead of forcing him to go through all this agony. The doctor told me he wasn't sure whether he would survive as he had a sizable chunk of metal stuck in the back of his leg and, every time he moved, he'd open an artery and blood would piss out of him. I patted his hand and said goodbye, but he pulled me back and reached into his pocket and pulled out his beret. He looked long and hard at it and then handed it to me. Of course I said 'no'. I knew how precious a beret could be, but he insisted, so I took it with many thanks. I still have it and it sits next to my SASR beret. Both are very special for different reasons.

Over the next few days, things slowed down quite a bit and people started to wonder when all this was going to end. But the nights were interesting. The constant stream of jets flying over Baghdad left a trail of criss-crossing smoke very high in the sky. Their presence meant Baghdad was still copping a pounding and wasn't yet secured. Actually, the nightly performance was a nice distraction as sleep was hard to find. I seemed to wake every 45 minutes or so to have a look around. I didn't trust these guys to provide a secure perimeter and worried that someone might sneak into our position with a blade.

Later in the day, as I sat in the SCO's Bradley talking shit, I heard that the city was surrounded — nothing could get in and nothing could get out. The 2nd Brigade was poised to sweep through the south-west corner of the city. Now we were getting serious. Maybe this thing would be over soon.

The next day, the SCO told me the 2nd Brigade had launched the attack on the south-west corner of the city and had met only light resistance. Apparently they were just testing the waters and the final assault through the city was imminent.

Captain Lyle told me he was going to Abu Ghraib prison later in the day to conduct a recon with a view to using the prison as a divisional headquarters. Frankly, I was beyond bored as nothing was happening, so I accepted his invitation to tag along. I piled into the back of his Troop Sergeant's Bradley for the rough ride out to the prison.

When we arrived at the front gates they were closed and chained shut, but they were no match for an Abrams tank that just drove straight at the gates until they smashed open. It occurred to me that I was probably the first civilian to enter the gates of the now infamous Abu Ghraib prison. The prison was bloody interesting and sad at the same time. I found the Warden's office and out the front two poor bastards had been buried up to their shoulders in the front lawn and had been stoned to death. The looks of agony on the faces of these poor bastards formed the basis of future nightmares. I entered the Warden's office, which was palatial. There was marble everywhere and where there wasn't marble, there was something gold-plated, and where there wasn't gold-plating, there was a photo or painting of Saddam. Saddam was everywhere. I realised that there was a photo or painting of Saddam on every wall in this prison. I continued to explore the prison, but it never left the back of my mind that the place could be booby trapped, so I only entered buildings after I saw a soldier walk out. Cowardly maybe, but the soldiers were looting everything, so I guessed they would have tripped any booby traps for me.

The gruesome scenes continued. I found the gallows — a sight that sent a cold shiver up my spine. The room was a place of fear, desperation and death. It was clear the Iraqis had executed as many prisoners as they could before their hasty retreat as the bodies were all piled on top of one another in a pit below the gallows. The cells were miserable little rooms and all the walls seemed to be covered in blood or shit. Talk about being terrified into going straight.

The next night, as I prepared to bed down, I heard Walt on his satellite phone; he was obviously talking to CNN Atlanta. Walt seemed agitated when he came over to my army stretcher.

'Hey Paul, Atlanta wants us to go to Baghdad as soon as we can. Apparently there are pictures all over the news of the US Army pulling down statues of Saddam.'

'Right, well we can't go tonight. Let's go over to the TOC and have a chat with the SCO,' I replied, as I dragged my arse out of my sleeping bag. I sort of felt bad that I was about to tell the SCO we were leaving. He was a great guy and one of the best commanders I'd worked with. He treated us far better than he really had to.

The SCO reported skirmishes along the road to Baghdad, but said it was up to us to decide when we dis-embedded. I suggested we meet again at first light and decide what we'd do. That agreed, we all hit the sack.

Just before the sun's first rays made their appearance, I was out of bed and had my gear packed away. As the crew slept, I wandered over to the TOC to see how secure the road to Baghdad was. The lads on duty said nothing had been reported through the night, so all was quiet. They also said they could alert the other units along the road of our expected arrival. I felt pretty good about all this and, knowing how important it was to get the crew to Baghdad to start reporting, I thought the risk level acceptable, so decided to make that recommendation to the crew. When I got back to Old Betsy, Walt and the guys were up and packing their kit away. I told Walt I thought we should go for it and outlined the reasons for my decision. He agreed and went to say his goodbyes to the SCO, Captain Lyle and the troops. Jeff, Charlie and I loaded all the gear on board and then I drove Old Betsy over to the fuel truck for one last top-up. The SCO and Captain Lyle were there, so it was nice to say a final goodbye to these two solid soldiers. They had been very generous to us and, while we were leaving to do other things, they probably had a few more months in this place. They explained that, under the rules of embedding, to dis-embed meant you could not come back. They told us to disregard this and come back if we ran into trouble.

The road to Baghdad was lonely. There were no other vehicles on the road except burnt-out tanks and vehicles and, of course, the charred remains of some poor souls on the road. We all had eyes like dinner plates as we scanned both sides of the road for trouble. This was the first time in four weeks that we had travelled without a protection detail of 400 armoured vehicles and we all felt quite naked.

We'd heard about the deserting Iraqi soldiers and the roads were littered with evidence of this. There were soldiers' uniforms and AK47s everywhere, and I'd never seen so many boots. They were all over the place.

We forged ahead down the lonely road and eventually came across an American checkpoint. The soldiers told us to park the car and report to the Operations Officer (OPSO). The OPSO told us it was too dangerous to continue and that we should wait with them. We asked what the problem was. The OPSO said that parts of the city were still being fought over. I told him that we were going to the Palestine Hotel which seemed to be in the cleared area of the city. Eventually he agreed — he didn't have the authority to detain us — but urged us to stay with him a little longer. Walt and I decided to keep going.

Chapter 29

At 11.00 am we arrived at the Palestine Hotel — the first CNN crew in Baghdad. Walt was thrilled and the crew went straight to work broadcasting live from the footpath in front of the hotel. I went to the hotel to secure rooms for the crew and find something cold for everyone to drink.

An hour later, another crew drove in and, by the end of the day, the media circus was in full swing. There were journalists, cameras and satellite trucks covering every spare piece of ground. When we first arrived in Baghdad, I had my own room in the hotel. By the end of the day, I was sharing my room with five other security guys. I didn't mind; I'd spent the last weeks sharing the desert with 1,000 men. But what did piss me off was the lack of hot water. In fact, the water was arctic and I was screaming for a decent wash.

My stay in Baghdad was short and the crew and I separated quite soon after arrival. Jeff was flat out building satellites and generators and whatever else was needed to make CNN look good. Jeff was the coolest person I've ever been with under fire and probably one of the hardest working lads I've worked with. He never stopped and never complained. Three days later, Walt, Charlie and I said goodbye to Jeff and drove back to Kuwait.

It took us 21 days to get to Baghdad driving north and eight hours to drive back heading south. I was relieved to cross the border into Kuwait late in the afternoon and even more relieved to arrive back at the CNN hotel. All the CNN personnel were waiting for us and cheered as we drove up. It was a nice touch. They also threw a party that night for us, but all I wanted to do was to soak in a bath and drink a cold beer. In fact, I drank three beers and topped up the bath with hot water three times. Two days later, I flew home to Australia.

30.
FREEDOM BECKONS

Sallie and the team spent a few hours getting the police to accept that my release to the Australian High Commission also meant I could be released to Rajeesh, who was the Australian High Commission representative. So now that was sorted, and I was no longer taking the death train to New Delhi.

It was 1.00 pm and there was still no word of movement for me. I sat waiting in the heat, constantly glancing at the main entry to the hospital for the car, but it didn't come. All this stuffing around because I crossed into India by a few metres —extraordinary, unbelievable. What a dickhead I was.

Martin mentioned further conversations with the Australian Embassy in Kathmandu. Apparently, once we crossed the border, I could drive four hours to another town and get a new visa, or apply when I got to Kathmandu. But if I went to Kathmandu, the Immigration Office might blacklist me for future entry into Nepal. Damn, why were we still doing this? My visa was current and my passport indicated that I hadn't actually left the country, so I wanted to leave it alone. 'Leave it be,' I said, 'I'll go to Kathmandu and take my chances.'

It was now 4.00 pm and I learnt that the Chief Justice Magistrate who had replaced Triparthy had decided to take two days off. We had spent time and money getting permission for his replacement to sign my release and now he had gone too. Of course this would happen to me. Now we had to get permission for the other guy to sign my release. Having secured this, the Magistrate decided he didn't want to sign today — he'd do it tomorrow. Martin and Sallie went off. Sallie stormed into the District Magistrate's office and let rip. He was in the middle of a meeting and was damned surprised when Sallie stormed in and opened up. The other people in the room also contributed to the discussion and the District Magistrate called the interim Magistrate and told him to sign the thing, but he still refused to sign my release, citing a technicality. Sallie was furious and couldn't go with Bala and Martin to see the Interim Magistrate. Bala and Martin went in with both barrels blazing — particularly Bala. As it turned out, the technicality was that the court closed at 3.30 pm and he had been presented with the release order at 3.45. Following threats from both Bala and Martin, the Interim Magistrate agreed to sign my release during the first 15 minutes of court tomorrow.

So I was here for another night. I knew something would go wrong and I was glad I hadn't got my hopes up. The team left very late tonight and Bala had to call the immigration guys at the border to ask them to stay until the team arrived otherwise they'd be stuck at the border all night. The immigration guys at the border felt suitably embarrassed about the whole situation and agreed to do whatever was needed to help.

Bala sent over a nice letter with my dinner. He referred to the Interim Magistrate as a sadistic man who was out for himself. Bala was a great guy and one of many who had made this nightmare tolerable.

The kids came by for a visit as I sat out the front. I asked if they were allowed to go to the shops on their own. 'Of course,' said the eldest. I had a craving for chocolate, so I asked the kids to go to the shop and buy me some. Twenty minutes later, they returned with a handful of chocolate and the exact change. I told them to keep the change, but they refused.

'We have our own money, thank you,' they said. Then I told them it was a gift from one friend to another. Then they accepted the money. I put the chocolates in the fridge, then went back outside. It was a nice night and I wanted to stay up as late as I could. I had a good feeling about tomorrow.

Tuesday 17 June

The guards knocked on the door at 6.30 am and asked if I wanted chai. This translated to 'we want chai so get off your arse and give us some money to go and buy some and then we're going to keep your change without even offering to give it to you.' I had them trained (as they had me) and they knew to buy me two glasses, as one just wasn't enough. In fact, if I'd bought the equivalent of the jug of tea I normally drink in the morning, I'd have 12 glasses of their stuff. Their chai is really tasty. It's sweet, milky and scented with cloves.

I thought about my kids again. I thought about them a lot. They were great people and I wished I had been a better father to them. I missed them like crazy and couldn't wait to hug them all. When I first arrived in gaol I couldn't think about the kids without getting teary. Now I could handle it because I was getting out, but I loved them more than ever — they provided the meaning in my life and I was so proud of who they were.

By 7.00 am the waiting had begun. It wouldn't be like yesterday when I gazed at the main gate all day waiting for the team or the police to arrive, but they hadn't. However, Bala had been at the hospital yesterday with a heap of police. I had panicked and had been certain they were here to charge me with some other offence. Then I heard that a doctor had murdered a nurse on Sunday afternoon. Apparently he had drugged her then cut her throat — poor woman, but I'm glad the reception wasn't for me. Later, Bala mentioned that the police had charged a doctor with murder. He said the doctor was from Forbes-Gange. I told him I had met a doctor the day before from Forbes-Gange. 'He was a nice guy, we had a long chat and some chai,' I said. 'This is a different doctor, Paul. This man is a murderer,' Bala told me. I walked into my cell and found the piece of paper with the doctor's name on it and returned to Bala, who was seated outside my room. 'The name of the doctor I met was V.J. Chaudry.'

Bala looked stunned. 'This is the man. He must have left you and gone to his office and murdered his nurse. This is unbelievable.'

Apparently, the doctor had been having an affair with the nurse and had wanted to break it off. Instead of doing the usual thing and telling her it was over, he decided to kill her.

'Paul, this man is now in your prison — but not in your cell.'

What a crazy world. Yesterday I was having a cup of chai with a nice doctor and today that same doctor is in gaol for murder.

Then I heard that all the poor people were waiting to see Bala under a tree in front of his office. The queue had become longer because he was focusing on my problems. Part of the tree had collapsed and fallen on a woman and her baby, killing them both. We all felt terrible. If we hadn't been here and Bala hadn't been such a great guy, that lady and her baby would still be alive. And then I felt drawn back to that arsehole Siddiqui and the angry man at the border. If it hadn't been for that sadistic, corrupt arsehole I wouldn't be here and Bala could have focused on the real community issues. What recourse could there be in a country like India where a scam goes wrong so the chief cop decides to throw everything at you? It was clear to the Magistrate and prosecutor that this was a joke, but Indian law doesn't accept the excuse that the law was broken by mistake — you either broke the law or you didn't. But if the SP had been a decent cop he would have told the local cops to have a chat with me and send me back across the border. Instead, he decided to waste all these resources, money and people's time that should have gone into making the community safer. Not to mention the money my company has spent, the stress, the risk to my health, the stress on Sallie and my family, it went on and on, all because of one fat, sadistic cop.

So I waited. Sallie arrived to hang out with me and wait. Martin and Rajeesh were with my lawyer trying to get the release signed. I introduced Sallie to the kids and Sallie immediately took to the little girl. The girl couldn't speak English, but enjoyed the attention from Sallie. Two police cars arrived, bringing my arresting officer, Sub-Inspector Shankar. He told me I would soon have to go back to the gaol to be released. Then he came back to me and told me that the paperwork was being completed at the hospital. Martin and Rajeesh arrived and confirmed that the release order had been signed.

I went to my room to pack the items I wanted to take with me and separate those that could stay behind. I called in the four guards and gave them 100 rupees each — they were very happy. They'd made a lot of money out of me over the past week. One guard had a shocking pair of shoes on his feet. They were falling apart at the sides and I didn't know how they stayed on his feet. I gave him my hiking boots. I just didn't want to take them back home. These shoes had walked over some God-awful, disgusting ground. I was certain they had diseases on them that hadn't been discovered and that bleach wouldn't kill.

The decision was then made that I could be released from Bala's house, so we all got into the car and drove there. Martin dropped us off then went to pay my lawyer, Debu-San. The bill came to US$180 for exclusive service for 24 days — he had charged me double. Sallie and I were on our own until Bala's cook arrived with lunch. He was a great cook, but really pushy and got pissed off if all the food wasn't eaten. I obliged with gusto.

I walked out onto the front lawn to ask Shankar how much longer it would be. He was on the phone and Bala's cook was there as well. Bala's cook had a terrified look on his face. I started to panic and tried to read what was going on. Shankar told me I had to go to the prison to sign my release and I agreed. Sallie came out as I was walking off with Shankar and demanded to know what was going on. When she heard, she said, 'No, absolutely not!' Shankar knew by the look on Sallie's face that he shouldn't push the issue so said we could stay here and he would bring the Warden over. Actually, I wanted to go to the prison to see all my friends and to say thanks, but it wasn't to be.

Bala returned with some more police and there was further discussion. Finally, at 2.00 pm, the Warden and clerk came to Bala's house to say goodbye. I thanked them both for being so kind to me while I was in gaol. They could have made life pretty bad for me, but in general I was treated slightly better than the other prisoners and I was grateful. I shook Bala's hand and didn't know what to say. I couldn't thank him enough for what he'd done for me and words couldn't express my gratitude. Then we got in the car and started our two-hour drive back to the Nepali border with Shankar and his team escorting us.

Martin drove the car to ensure there were no unforeseen stops and did a great job dodging the erratic traffic and keeping us alive. The usual driver sat in the passenger seat in a constant state of panic and doing all he could to drive the car from the passenger seat with Martin getting more and more pissed off with him. Sallie and I sat in the back seat and listened to the Australian music CD the driver had brought. It was a bumpy road and, while the team had made this journey twice every day for the past two weeks, it was my first time in this direction.

I felt overwhelmed to be released, but was holding back my joy until I actually crossed the border. I was also bloody drained and still felt quite weak as we approached the border control point. Ujwal came to our vehicle as we pulled up just beyond the immigration office — the same immigration office where I had originally been questioned 24 days ago. Ujwal collected Martin's and Sallie's passports and, along with Shankar, went to the immigration office to have their passports stamped and to have my paperwork finalised. That took about 10 minutes and I sat in the locked vehicle examining the border. I couldn't see any obvious indications that this was a border but, as I looked more closely, I could see that damned boom gate raised behind a big tree. There's no way I could have seen that in the bloody rickshaw, even if I had been looking for it. No excuse though — it was my fault; I should have known where I was.

Sallie and Martin returned with Shankar and the immigration officer who had sat quietly on day one when the mad man fucked me over. I wanted to get out of the car and slam my fist into the little fat prick's head, but Sallie told me he'd been very nice and was extremely apologetic for what had happened. So, after shaking hands with Shankar, I shook hands with the little fat prick. Everyone got back into the vehicle and we drove over the border.

Sallie looked at me and I realised I was free and thanked the team for their efforts. I was free because of Sallie, Martin, Ujwal, Rajeesh, Bala and all my friends in the media and IFJ. I sent a text message to my children, mother and friends informing them that I was now across the border and free. I received a flood of replies. We drove the short distance to the Nepali police compound so we could thank the Nepali Superintendent of Police for all his efforts. We only stayed for 15 minutes and then pushed on to the hotel where Sallie and Martin had stayed, and where I'd stayed and run the course before being arrested.

THE EASY DAY WAS YESTERDAY

The hotel staff greeted me as I hobbled through the front door. They'd known what was going on and hadn't seen me since the police brought me back here 24 days ago. My luggage was still here and Sallie had repacked it all for me. Ujwal arrived and told me all my former students had come yesterday as a welcoming party, but they didn't believe I'd be released today, so decided not to come. Just quietly, I was relieved. I just wanted to get on the plane and start making my way back home. Ujwal was only able to secure two extra tickets for today's flight, so Martin and Rajeesh got the flight the next day before both flying to New Delhi. Martin needed to go to the Australian High Commission to wind things up there and pass on our gratitude.

I carried my bag down the stairs and then to the car and was exhausted by the slight exercise — and strained my back in the process. We said our goodbyes to Rajeesh and Martin and again I thanked them both for their amazing efforts. We loaded up and headed to the airport. The flight to Kathmandu was only an hour, but I was still in a surreal world. One minute I was a prisoner and the next I was on a plane flying home. I wondered how people responded after being inside for years — I was only inside for 24 days, not even a month, and I felt like kissing the ground or doing some cartwheels. I remember a similar sense of relief and weariness when I came back from a month in Aceh following the Asian Tsunami, the tidal wave of death and destruction that ended the lives of thousands of people in 2005.

31.
ASIAN TSUNAMI

On 26 December 2005, as I was recovering from too much Christmas food and alcohol, I wandered into my bedroom where the TV was still on from my morning ritual of watching the news before dragging my arse out of bed. A news flash was on the screen talking about a massive earthquake off the coast of Aceh that had generated tidal waves throughout the region. The news anchor was reporting 10,000 dead in several countries. I walked back to the verandah and told my guests, who were left over from Christmas, that tidal waves had killed a heap of people in Asia.

Later in the day I contacted Rob, my cameraman mate at Channel 7, guessing that he would be on his way to Aceh. He said he was at Sydney airport with a young female journalist named Jess. I gave him some ideas on what Aceh was like and the issues he might face when he arrived. I had worked in Aceh a few years previously, so had a pretty good idea what they would face.

The next day the family and I decided to go to the beach for the day. We went to our favorite spot — Mooloolaba on the Sunshine Coast. It was a good day, but in the background, Sallie began contacting the Australian media offering assistance. I got a call from the News Director at Channel 9 who said he wanted me to go, and that was effectively the end of my day with the family. Sam was playing chess with a guy on the picnic table and I went from one phone call to another. The poor kids and Toni once again were put in the background while I pulled this job together. The family, as always, was supportive and understanding. I went to the chemist and bought anti-bacterial soap, face masks, insect repellent and an assortment of other products I thought I might need.

That evening, 27 December, I departed Brisbane for Aceh. Apparently, two Channel 9 crews had flown out the day before and would be there when I arrived. I flew via Singapore then to Medan in southern Sumatra. I was in Medan by 8.00 am and was due to depart for Banda Aceh at 12.00. When I walked into the departure lounge, every plane had been delayed and four other planes were due to go to Banda Aceh before mine.

Medan airport was a nightmare. Aircraft from relief agencies blocked the runway and parking areas, which meant that planes could only land after other planes had departed and made room on the tarmac. I bumped into Rob and Jess at Medan where they'd been delayed for 12 hours. My plane departure time was continuously postponed. I started calling all my contacts in Medan looking for a driver because I thought driving to Banda Aceh might be quicker than waiting for a plane that might not actually leave. If I had a vehicle I could buy food, water, assorted camping equipment, fuel and a small generator and transport it all to Banda Aceh. But there were no cars to be had; all available drivers were already in Banda Aceh. Fortunately, at 10.30 pm, my plane began to board. I said my goodbyes to Rob and Jess and said I'd see them there at some stage.

I arrived in Banda Aceh at midnight with some trepidation. When I had worked in Aceh with Exxonmobil, Banda Aceh was a no-go city and to go there meant certain kidnapping. But that wasn't the case this time. The place was deserted; we even had to unload our luggage from the plane ourselves. When I had found my pack, I wandered across the tarmac and out the front of the airport and smelt that horrible, yet familiar smell of death. It was putrid and the air was thick with that gag-inducing rotting, human flesh smell. There is no other smell like that of a dead body and certainly nothing like that of thousands of dead bodies.

The whole place was in darkness; there were no city lights or any other lights for that matter, and I wondered what the hell I was going to do and where the Channel 9 guys were. In front of the airport there were a handful of old crappy cars with the drivers standing in a small group chatting. Instinctively I found myself creeping up next to them to listen to what they were talking about. Obviously they were talking in Acehnese rather than Bahasa Indonesia, so I had no idea what was being said. I said 'hello' to the group and they all jumped then started hassling me for my business. These guys were trying to make a few bucks as pretend taxi drivers. One of them said he knew where my friends were staying. 'How do you know who my friends are?' I asked with some concern. This was clearly a scam to get me into his car where I'd be whisked away to some jungle camp and locked in a bamboo cage. 'All the people are staying at the same place. I can take you for 10 dollars.'

'Okay, let's go.' I had no real options here and I knew the general direction of town from the airport so would know if we were heading for the jungle.

The driver was very good and gave me a run-down on events over the previous two days, pointing out the beginnings of mass graves on the roadside. It was obvious when we drove close to a mass grave as the concentration of rotting bodies not yet covered generated a smell that became more powerful as we got closer and weaker as we moved away.

The driver pulled up outside the Governor's compound which was called Pondopo. He said everyone was using Pondopo as a work space and the odd satellite truck gave some weight to his story. I gave him his 10 dollars and thanked him as I walked into the compound. It was now 1.00 am, and only a few people were moving around, but I could see plenty of white faces sleeping in the buildings and on the lawn in front of the main building.

Bugger it. I was tired, so I decided to find a spare section of grass and try to get a few hours' sleep. I rolled out my sleeping bag, lay it on my sleeping mat and used my pack as a pillow. I was just slipping off to sleep when someone grabbed the world and gave it a fucking good shake. I sat up immediately as people ran from all the buildings screaming. But the shaking stopped as quickly as it had started and people slowly went back to their beds. Fuck me, that was big; now I knew what an aftershock felt like.

In the morning I found the Channel 9 guys. They were set up in one of the buildings and, like me, had just gone through their first night. They had been in the group running out of the building the previous night when the earth shook but, unlike the locals, they weren't screaming. I packed all my kit away and loaded my day pack with the items I thought I'd need during the day: binoculars, satellite phone, cell phone, water, snack bars, umbrella, super glue, rope, trauma kit, digital camera, face mask, Vicks Vaporub, gloves, hat, sunscreen, mosquito repellent, GPS and hand-held radios. The guys had already secured a vehicle and driver so we headed out looking for news and didn't have to go far.

Close to Pondopo was a river that ran through the middle of Banda Aceh. All the boats moored in the river had been smashed together up against the bridge and reduced to a tenth of their previous size. It was a bizarre sight, but illustrated the power of the water and the size of the tsunami when it hit. The smell was constant, but stronger when we got closer to a dead person — most of the dead could be smelt but not seen, because they were under collapsed houses or drowned inside garages.

A tip truck drove past us with a couple of local lads sitting high on top of a pile of bodies. There were stiffened limbs hanging over the sides of the truck and I wondered how they managed to keep the load on board, there were so many. We followed the truck on the road towards the airport to a mass grave. It was clear that other trucks had dumped their loads here already because the massive pit was nearly full. We estimated there to be about 300 bodies in the grave already and the truck we followed still hadn't dumped its load. It was hard to tell how deep the pit was; there could have been another hundred or so bodies in the bottom of the pit. Honestly, there are no words to describe how bloody awful, cruel, devastating and sad this sight was. Babies, children, women and men dumped like garbage into a mass pit, all intertwined into grotesque positions. It was something you should never see, but we couldn't tear our eyes away and all stood in silence for a moment. I knew then that this would be big for the crews and part of my plan had to include the safety of their minds and emotions.

The crew put on their face masks with some Vicks rubbed on the outside of the mask to try to block the horrible smell. I didn't bother with the mask, but continued to breathe through my nose; the smell was bad, but I didn't want to taste it.

When the crew had all they needed, we headed back to Pondopo so they could file their stories back to Sydney. This gave me the chance to look over Pondopo and the living arrangements we had; it wasn't good. I had heard stories of stealing as expensive equipment was laid out everywhere with no security controlling who walked into the sleeping and storage areas. I'd also just been told by the News Director in Sydney that another crew from the *Today* show and one from *A Current Affair* were on their way. That would put our numbers at around 17 including a local interpreter and me. I had to find something better; something that I could secure and something more comfortable just for us.

Rob and Jess from Channel 7 had finally arrived and both looked pretty dishevelled. They'd had a horror trip to Aceh starting three days previously, and poor Jess had been forced to leave most of her gear in Medan, so didn't have a change of clothes. Rob and I were, and still are, good mates and have travelled to some real shit holes together, but on this job I was working for his opposition, which was another reason we had to get away from Pondopo and each other. Nine wanted to win the ratings for this one and were throwing a lot at it. My job was to help them win the ratings war, but more importantly to keep them safe, just as I'd done for 7 when working for them.

At this point, we had two crews with three people in each crew, a local interpreter, two drivers and two vehicles over which I needed to gain some control. I needed to be sure the drivers would always be available when required and didn't just disappear whenever they felt the need. So, while the crews were hunched over laptops cutting their stories, I grabbed the interpreter and we went to have a chat with the drivers. I told them they needed to be on location at 7.00 am every morning unless told otherwise; one of them needed to stay on location through the night so we always had a vehicle to respond to immediate news or emergencies. They had to keep their vehicles full of fuel and this had to be done before or after work and not with the crew in the vehicle. They had to ensure they had a spare tyre and tyre-changing kit in the car; they were not to drink alcohol at any time and they had to check the vehicle fluid levels every morning. Finally, I told them I would be checking their vehicles whenever I felt like it and if anything was not right, I would deduct money from their pay; but if they worked well, I'd give them a bonus. They seemed happy with this direction.

As I walked with the interpreter back to the temporary workspace, I asked him for two things: find three more vehicles and drivers, and start looking for a house for us to rent for a month or so. He agreed to do this, but I sensed he was pissed off that I was now directing traffic and giving him instructions when he felt he was working for the crew and not me. So I softened the blow by telling him the crew would be rapt if he found a nice house for them to live in.

The daily tremors continued and life became more difficult at Pondopo. The crew were eating canned food and drinking bottled water, which was okay for a disaster zone, but the reality was that fresh food was available in the makeshift markets springing up around town. Our problem was that we had no way of preparing it.

The interpreter took me to a few different houses he'd found and they were fine, but not big enough for 17 of us. By New Year's Eve I was getting frustrated at the lack of progress in the house-hunting department when a middle-aged, fat guy on a motor scooter approached me at the entry to Pondopo and asked if I was looking for a house. I really couldn't be bothered driving out to look at another shack. I took the fat man to the interpreter so I was clear what he was saying. He said he had a big three-bedroom house with two bathrooms and a kitchen and lots of space for the cars.

'Okay, let's go and look,' I said to the interpreter. I turned to the fat man and said, 'Saya hunya mulihat lihat saja.' (I am just looking.)

'Tidak masala,' he replied. (No problems.)

The house was close to Pondopo and on the road to the airport — in fact the location was great. The only thing the fat man forgot to tell me was that construction of the house wasn't actually completed. The place had no doors or windows and had an Acehnese family living there. But it was certainly big enough and the best we'd seen, and the family seemed friendly enough. Over a cup of tea, we discussed the arrangements. We were going to move in the next day (New Year's Day), the fat man would put temporary covers over the doors and windows, he'd buy a truck-load of mosquito coils, the family would move into the back room, the ladies would cook breakfast and dinner for all of us and the husband would keep an eye on all our gear. In turn, we'd pay rent and pay for all the food for everyone in the house. We shook hands and the deal was done; I hoped the crews would be happy with this — it was a bloody big call.

That night was probably the quietest New Year's Eve I've ever had. I had one shot of rum with the crew and Rob and Jess and was in my sleeping bag by 10.00 pm.

The next day, I picked up the *A Current Affair* crew from the airport. They dropped their gear at the house and I introduced them to the family and the fat man. They looked really unsure of the house as they dropped their gear into one of the front rooms and then headed straight out on a story. At times like that you start wondering whether you've made the right choice.

I went with them on this story because I wanted to orientate them to their new surroundings. Banda Aceh was actually a small town and easy to navigate around and, as each new crew came in, I gave them the same orientation tour around town. The guys were wandering the streets of Banda Aceh absorbing all the destruction when I walked over to a bloke in his twenties. He was in front of a shopfront that seemed flooded, but not collapsed. He was slowly moving furniture out of the garage next to the shopfront. I had a look and it was clear a lot of water and mud had pushed through the whole building and forced all the furniture up against the back wall. I couldn't see how the building could possibly have stayed upright. The bloke invited me to sit in one of the chairs and, in my poor Bahasa, I struck up a conversation with him. He pulled out a packet of 2-minute noodles and started eating them dry, insisting that I take a few as well. I felt like a shit for taking food from a bloke who was probably eating his last bit of food, but he insisted and it really did reinforce for me the kind-hearted nature of the Acehnese people. I asked him about his shop and his family when he stopped and pointed to his family. It was only then, when I focused my eyes into the dark corner of the garage, that I could see the mud-covered small bodies of his two children and his wife. They were jammed into the corner, but I could see his wife's arms wrapped around the two kids. Damn. This poor bastard was one of thousands who had lost it all and then had to dig them out and potentially watch them being unceremoniously thrown into a pit with hundreds of others. There was nothing to say to the bloke. Words would have seemed false and, really, what can you say at a time like that? He had tears in his eyes, so I just put my hand on his shoulder, gave him a squeeze and a pat, then left him to his work and his grief.

The first night in the house was a shocker. One of the kids screamed all fucking night. The crews all looked like shit the next day and were clearly not overly thrilled at my selection of accommodation. But things slowly improved and, the next evening, the ladies had prepared a great meal of nasi goreng with eggs and we had plenty of cold soft drink and water. The kids got used to the idea of having all the white men in the house as well and, at night, the guys would have a rum and coke and sit around and chat with one of the kids on their laps or playing at their feet. This was really good therapy for the guys — really grounding stuff — and got them away from the carnage outside the house.

The old woman in the house was a strict Muslim. She was never seen without her head scarf and never smiled at the crews. But she eventually came around as well and the lads started giving her a hug each day when they came back to the house. At first I thought she was going to have a heart attack and I waited for the fat man to run and talk to the local Imam, but she got used to the idea and I started to notice her hanging around at the end of the day waiting for all the lads to arrive back so she could get that hug.

The Australian Army had already arrived and had taken over the local hospital. As usual, they did a great job and, as luck would have it, I knew a handful of the senior members, including the RSM and CO. The Australian Defence Force had a navy supply vessel located off the coast of Banda Aceh and decided to start using a landing craft to deliver equipment and supplies to the mainland. Channel 9 wanted to cover the first landing and, by now, had imported a portable satellite dish complete with two operators from Singapore. These guys had set up the satellite dish on the river bank adjacent to the proposed landing craft position. The narrow, single-lane road on the river bank was in very poor condition and there were a few bodies on the road and on the side of the road to dodge. One body was in a black plastic bag, but the hand was exposed and the crabs had eaten away the flesh exposing the skeletal hand. This body was only 30 metres or so from the dish.

While we were ready, the navy wasn't, and the landing operation was postponed until the following day. I visited the two satellite operators at about 4.00 pm to ensure they were secure. They'd set up a two-man tent next to the dish where they housed all the techy stuff that went with the dish. I told them they'd be spending the night with the dish as we weren't filming until the next day. I'd been in Aceh for more than two weeks by now and had grown used to the smell of rotting human flesh and wasn't concerned about the multiple bodies everywhere. These guys had been in Aceh for two days and, when I told them they were sleeping there for the night, they went white and stole some quick glances at the body close by with the exposed, bony hand.

'Ahhhh, no, ahhhhh, we are not,' one of them replied.

I nearly said, why not? Then I realised the problem — too many pulse-less bedfellows.

Fuck it, I thought. I'll go back to the house, grab a few things, have a quick feed and then come back to relieve them. A quiet night out under stars would be nice.

'Okay, I'll be back in an hour to relieve you and I'll stay with the kit through the night.'

The relief that washed over them made them look as if they had just received a stay of execution.

An hour later, I was back and they'd gone. By 9.00 pm it was dark and I was covered in mosquito repellent and lying on my sleeping back in front of the tent. Fortunately, we had a nice onshore breeze that reduced the humidity and ensured the stench from my roommates was blown the other way. I slipped into that point where you are not fully asleep, but not quite awake. It's that point when your brain runs wild to the point of hallucination. I dreamt that the skeleton hand from my mate up the road had broken from the body and had crawled towards me and was now crawling around me, but I knew I was dreaming, so couldn't shake myself awake. But then I could hear the hand. The phalanges were scraping the rocks around my body as the hand moved in short bursts. The sound got louder until it was becoming all too real and I sat up abruptly. I dug my maglite torch from my pocket and shone it around looking for the hand and saw about 20 mid-sized mud crabs walking around me. They looked as if they were positioning themselves for a frontal assault on their evening meal — me. When I stood up, they all scurried around and I could hear a series of 'plops' as they all dropped back into the water. Sleeping was going to be a challenge with the crabs wanting to eat me and the hand wanting to choke me.

The *A Current Affair* crew had to leave for a few days to cover a story in Jakarta. When they returned to the house, it was like Christmas. They brought a load of presents for the kids and ladies and something to drink for the men. The kids thought it was wonderful and the ladies prepared an extra special feast for that night. The crew spent the night playing with the kids and their new toys while others had the kids listening to music through headphones. It was fun and good therapy.

By the final week, we had all slipped into a daily routine. For me, it was a case or speaking to each crew to determine their plans for the day and then allocating vehicles, drivers and interpreters in accordance with my assessment of the risk involved in each task. In other words, the crew covering a story or going to an area that carried the most risk got the best resources, and I went with that crew. At the end of the day, I inspected the vehicles and gave the drivers their pay and money to fill the fuel tanks. Every few days I paid the fat man for food and rent and he sent the ladies off to the market. Secretly, we also gave the ladies extra money for their pockets, because we weren't sure the fat man was giving them any. Every morning at 2.00 am the crew from the *Today* show had to go to wherever the satellite dish was set up so they could report in time for 6.00 am in Sydney. I was able to convince one of the drivers to leave his vehicle for me and I drove them there, waited with them, and then drove back for another hour of sleep.

After almost a month on the ground, and after the huge benefit organised in Australia in which all the crews were involved, we all left Aceh. I was absolutely rooted. In fact, I didn't know how stuffed I was until I got on the plane out of Singapore and was asleep before the plane left the terminal and only woke when the wheels touched down in Brisbane.

Aceh left a huge mark on my soul. The Acehnese people were great and I loved the location, but I was glad to leave all that misery behind, and felt guilty for doing so. It was easy to report on their misery and horrendous loss, and it was easy to leave, but these people had poured their hearts out to us, they had invited us into their lives at an incredibly emotional time and then we had left them behind with nothing but that terrible loss.

32.
HOME

We arrived at Kathmandu and Sallie took control of the luggage. She refused to allow me to lift another thing. The Australian Consul General and a member of his staff were there to meet us and drive us to the hotel. They were very kind and concerned. Not only was I slow to move because I was tired, but my back was giving me hell, so I walked very slowly and with a stoop. Fuck me, I was embarrassed — I felt like I was a 100-year-old loser and I just wanted people to forget this ever happened and get on with their lives. I said I didn't need a doctor, but just needed some rest. Ujwal had booked us into a magnificent hotel and we all sat in the lobby while our room was being prepared and took the opportunity to discuss the visa issue. They said they had a contact in the immigration office who could help with the visa renewal, but again it could complicate things if I wanted to return to Nepal. They examined my passport and common sense prevailed. We agreed to run the gauntlet tomorrow and believed that the immigration officer would be none the wiser. The Consul guys left, but agreed to return the next day to take us to the airport and see us through immigration.

Sallie and I went to our room — and what a room it was. I suppose anything was better than the shit hole I'd been living in. The room was huge — a massive lounge, the biggest bed I've ever seen, a beautiful bathroom and a very long and deep bath. All of this was in the one big room with a view over the traditional gardens and pool. It was all quite surreal and like one of those dreams in prison. Sallie ran me a nice hot and deep bath while she cleared some e-mails. I'd been having cold water bucket baths for 24 days, so when I got into the hot water it hurt my skin, but it hurt so good. Sallie brought me a beer and I took a tentative sip and only managed to get through half the can. After a shower to wash my hair, Sallie and I pored over the room service menu and decided on the salad, club sandwich and a bottle of Moet.

Relaxing on the lounge in our dressing gowns, we picked at the food, but struggled to get through it and had to force down more than one glass of champagne each. But it was great just sitting and enjoying freedom, and I knew Sallie felt relieved after a long and successful job. But I couldn't relax. I kept looking at my watch and imagining Ugly Guard coming to lock the door for the night — and I wondered what the old man was doing.

The next day we wandered through the streets of Kathmandu and bought some gifts for Sallie's parents who had been looking after her girls while she was away. I also went to a drug store and bought antibiotics for an ear infection I could feel getting worse and some painkillers for my back. The Australian Consulate guys arrived and drove us to the airport with Ujwal following with all the training gear. The Consul General agreed to remain at a discreet distance as we passed through immigration and would only approach if there was a problem. Fortunately, all went well, although the airline initially had a problem with Sallie's passport. This was cleared up, we were away and waiting for our plane home. Following a brief stop in Bangkok, where I was left to rest in the business class lounge while Sallie did some more shopping, we arrived in Sydney just in time for Sallie's daughter's birthday. It was Thursday already. I'd been out of gaol for two days and still wondered what the old man was doing. Was Satya still taking his evening walk? Who was the loud-talking guard yelling at? I had my watch set on prison time, so I always knew what the prisoners were doing.

I was exhausted, but we had so much to do. I really needed to get these medical problems sorted and Sallie had made an appointment for me to see her doctor. She was excellent and gave me a complete once-over. She also prescribed different antibiotics for my ear and something for my skin infections. She asked me if I had been interfered with.

'Pardon?'

'Were you interfered with?' she said, continuing to look down at her pad. 'You know, sexually interfered with,' she said, after realising I either had no idea what she was talking about or was stunned.

'Ah, no; nothing like that!'

She gave me a handful of antibiotics for the ear infection and to fix up any issues that hadn't appeared at that time.

On Friday afternoon I had an appointment with a psychiatrist. Again, Sallie organised this and I was grateful. I'm not the sort of bloke to pour out my feelings to a shrink, but Colin was a mate whom I'd known for a few years and an exceptional counsellor. I was glad to have the opportunity to vent and clear some of my thoughts. Colin had been great during my short stay in gaol, passing on frequent tips through Sallie to help me cope. He suggested going away for a holiday for a while and doing nothing but relaxing. I told him of my need to use sleeping pills to sleep. Colin thought that was okay and that sleeping was good recovery time, so I continued with the pills at night. He also suggested that I stop wearing a watch so I could stop myself looking at Indian time. Colin told me not to drive as some people have flashbacks and, if you happen to be driving at the time, you could get in trouble. It was all good advice except the last point, as I wouldn't have any choice but to drive.

That night, we all went over to a friend's house for a welcome-back party. Dierdre was also our company accountant and had organised catering and plenty to drink. It was a nice gesture by Dierdre and Andrew to open up their house like that. I was absolutely knackered, but really wanted to say thanks to everyone. It was a great night and I met people I didn't previously know who had gone out of their way to help. I am extraordinarily lucky to have such great friends and family, and to be born an Aussie with a government that cares. But again, I was well and truly fucked and just needed to lie down and do, and think about nothing for a long time.

The next day, I said goodbye to Sallie and the girls and flew back to Brisbane. My car was still parked in the long-term car park at the international terminal and I was surprised that it still started — I thought the battery would be flat — and it cost me $350 in parking fees. I drove straight to Trevor's house where Sam was staying and together we went home. He had been great during this whole drama and had always kept things in perspective. When I got home I gave Zac a big hug, but Sayge was a little remote, so I let her be. Then it was back to my normal life. I planned to take some time off and go skiing with the boys for a week but, after three days, I had a crisis with a client in Baghdad and spent too much time on the phone trying to sort that out. Normality, with all its pitfalls, had returned.

If you enjoyed this book, you may also be interested in…

'Geordie Doran is a legend to all soldiers of the Special Air Service . . .' CHRIS RYAN

GEORDIE

SAS FIGHTING HERO

GEORDIE DORAN WITH MIKE MORGAN

WHO DARES WINS

Geordie Doran ranks as one of the most remarkable fighting soldiers of the twentieth century. From humble origins, Geordie embarked upon an extraordinary career of fighting adventure which included active service in the Infantry, the Parachute Regiment and the SAS.

9780752460536; £8.99

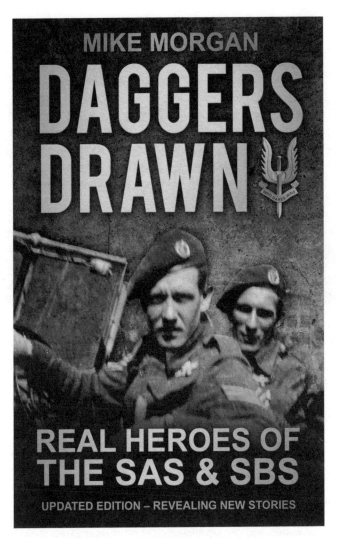

MIKE MORGAN

DAGGERS DRAWN

REAL HEROES OF THE SAS & SBS

UPDATED EDITION – REVEALING NEW STORIES

Thirty vivid stories, including some new and previously unpublished,
supported by an updated selection of rare archive and action photographs,
explore the larger-than-life escapades of the Special Air Service in the
Second World War.

9780752466064; £8.99

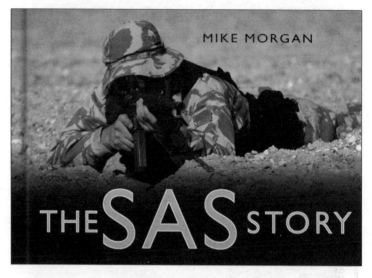

MIKE MORGAN

THE SAS STORY

Mike Morgan tells the story of the SAS, from its beginnings in the Second World War, through its involvement in the 'bush wars' of the 50s and 60s, and the more secretive military operations of the Cold War era, through to the Gulf Wars of more recent years. He also looks at what it takes to be an SAS soldier, their selection and training, their weapons and equipment, and their links to the Special Forces of other nations.

9780750948401; £8.99

Visit our website and discover thousands of other History Press books.

www.thehistorypress.co.uk